ISBN 978-1-332-91450-0
PIBN 10437424

PRINCIPIA LATINA.—Part I.

A

FIRST LATIN COURSE.

COMPREHENDING

GRAMMAR, DELECTUS, AND EXERCISE-BOOK,

WITH VOCABULARIES.

For the Use of the Lower Forms in Public and Private Schools.

BY WILLIAM SMITH, D.C.L., LL.D.,

EDITOR OF THE CLASSICAL AND LATIN DICTIONARIES.

SEVENTEENTH EDITION, THOROUGHLY REVISED,

*WITH THE ACCIDENCE ARRANGED AS IN THE PUBLIC
SCHOOL LATIN PRIMER.*

LONDON:

JOHN MURRAY, ALBEMARLE STREET.

1874.

LONDON:
PRINTED BY WILLIAM CLOWES AND SONS,
STAMFORD STREET AND CHARING CROSS

PREFACE.

THE following work is the first of a short series which the writer has undertaken with the view of facilitating the study of the Latin language. It is the result of many years' practical teaching, and seeks to combine the advantages of the older and more modern methods of instruction. While boys are sometimes compelled to commit to memory all the grammatical forms and syntactical rules without having their knowledge tested by any practical application in the construction of sentences, so that they frequently forget the former part of the Grammar by the time they have finished the latter, they are in other cases burdened by a large number of explanations and cautions, and by complicated rules for the formation of cases and other inflectional forms. The latter error is almost as grave as the former in the case of young boys, as they are thus taught analytically what ought to be first learned synthetically.

The main object of this work is to enable a beginner to fix the Declensions and Conjugations thoroughly in his memory, to learn their usage by constructing simple sentences as soon as he commences the study of the language, and to accumulate gradually a stock of useful words. It is divided into two parts:—

I. The first part contains the Grammatical forms, with exercises upon all the inflections, in which the simple rules of syntax are introduced, as they are required for the formation of sentences.

II. The second part contains an explanation of some of

the more important idioms of the language, such as the construction of the Accusative Case and the Infinitive Mood, of the Ablative Absolute, of the Gerund and Gerundive, &c., exemplified by Exercises upon each construction. The Vocabularies to both parts are printed at the end of the second, and Alphabetical Indices of the Latin and English words in the Vocabularies are appended to them.

The work thus contains Grammar, Delectus, and Exercise-book, with Vocabularies, and consequently presents in one book all that the pupil will require for some time in his study of the language. It is confidently believed that a boy who has gone carefully through the work will have acquired a sound knowledge of the chief grammatical forms, and of the most important syntactical rules, and will thus be prepared to enter upon the systematic study of a larger Grammar with advantage and profit,

PREFACE TO THE NEW EDITION.

This edition has been thoroughly revised, and various improvements have been introduced. At the urgent request of numerous teachers, the Cases and Tenses have been arranged in the body of the work, according to the plan of the Public School Latin Primer, and not printed in an appendix, as in former editions. The rules for the Pronunciation of Latin have been drawn up by the Rev. Dr. Abbott, Head Master of the City of London School. In the revision of the present edition the writer desires to express his obligations for much valuable assistance to Mr. T. D. Hall, the joint-author with him of the 'Student's Latin Grammar,' and of the 'English-Latin Dictionary.'

W. S.

CONTENTS.

PART I.
GRAMMATICAL FORMS.

PART II.

SOME SYNTACTICAL RULES.

PART I.

GRAMMATICAL FORMS.

I.—THE ALPHABET. PARTS OF SPEECH.

1. *Alphabet.*—The Latin Alphabet consists of 25 letters, the same as the English without *W*.

A, B, C, D, E, F, G, H, I, J, K, L, M, N, O, P,
a, b, c, d, e, f, g, h, i, j, k, l, m, n, o, p,

Q, R, S, T, U, V, X, Y, Z.
q, r, s, t, u, v, x, y, z.

The letters are divided into Vowels and Consonants.

The Vowels are *a, e, i, o, u, y*. The remaining letters are Consonants.

The Diphthongs are *ae, oe, au*, which are in common use, and *eu, ei, ui*, which occur in only a few words.

The diphthongs *ae, oe*, are pronounced as *ē*.

A Long Syllable has the mark (ˉ) over the vowel. A Short Syllable has the mark (˘) over the vowel.

2. *Parts of Speech.*—There are eight parts of speech in the Latin language.

1. Substantive, or Noun.	5. Adverb.
2. Adjective.	6. Preposition.
3. Pronoun.	7. Conjunction.
4. Verb.	8. Interjection.

There is no article in the Latin language : hence the Latin **mensă** means not only *table*, but also *a table* and *the table.*

PR. L. I.   B

II.—PRONUNCIATION.

The letters in Latin were probably pronounced as follows :—

VOWELS AND DIPHTHONGS.

Latin	ā	=	English	*a* in father.
,,	ă	=	,,	*first a* in away, or *a* in villa.
	ē	=		*ai* in pain.
	ae	=		*ai* in pain.
	oe	=		*ai* in pain.
	ĕ	=		*e* in men.
	ī	=		*i* in machine.
	ĭ	=		*i* in pity.
	ō	=		*o* in glory.
	ŏ	=		*o* in top.
	ū	=		*u* in rule.
	ŭ	=		*u* in full.
	au	=		*ow* in power.
	eu	=		Latin ĕ followed quickly by Latin ŭ (differs little from present pronunciation).
	ei	=		Latin ĕ followed quickly by Latin ĭ (differs little from *ai* in plain).

CONSONANTS.

Latin	c, ch	=	English	*k*.
,,	g	=	,,	*g* in get.
	s	=	,,	*s* in sin.
,,	t (ratio)	=	,,	*t* in cat, not *sh*, as in nation.
,	j	=		*y* in yard.
,	v	=		*v*.
,,	z, ph, th	=	,,	*z, ph, th*.

Latin *s* between two vowels = (sometimes) English *s* in rose, *e.g.* 'rosa'

III.—SUBSTANTIVES OR NOUNS.

Nouns are declined by *Number* and *Case*.

There are two Numbers: *Singular* and *Plural*.

There are six cases: *Nominative, Vocative, Accusative, Genitive, Dative, Ablative.*

There are three Genders: *Masculine, Feminine,* and *Neuter.*

Nouns which may be either Masculine or Feminine are called *Common.*

There are five Declensions, distinguished by the endings of the Genitive Case.

	I.	II.	III.	IV.	V.
Gen. Sing.	ae	ĭ	ĭs	ûs	ĕī
Gen. Plur.	A-rum	Ō-rum	-um Ĭ-um	Ŭ-um	Ē-rum

The *Stem* is that part of the word which remains after the changeable endings are taken away.

The *Stems* of Nouns can be ascertained by taking away the terminations *um* or *rum* of the Genitive Plural. Hence the final letter of the Stem is in—

I.	II.	III.	IV.	V.
A	O	consonant or I	U	E

IV.—THE FIRST OR A DECLENSION.

The Nominative Singular of Nouns of the First Declension ends in ă.

	Sing.			Plur.	
Nom.	Mens-ă (*fem.*)	*a table*	Mens-ae,	*tables*
Voc.	Mens-ă,	*O table*	Mens-ae,	*O tables*
Acc.	Mens-am,	*a table*	Mens-ăs,	*tables*
Gen.	Mens-ae	*of a table*	Mens-ārum,	*of tables*
Dat.	Mens-ae	*to or for a table*	Mens-īs,	*to or for tables*
Abl.	Mens-ă,	*by, with, or from a table.*	Mens-īs,	*by, with, or from tables.*

NOTE.—Fīlĭă, *a daughter;* dĕă, *a goddess;* ĕquă, *a mare;* ăsĭnă' *a she-ass;* and a few others, make the Dative and Ablative Plural in ābŭs: filiābŭs, deābŭs, ĕquābŭs, ăsĭnābŭs, etc.

GENDER.—All Nouns of the First Declension are Feminine, unless they designate males: as naută, *a sailor.*

RULE 1.—The Nominative Case denotes the SUBJECT. A Verb agrees with its Nominative case in number and person: as, pŭellă currĭt, *the girl runs;* pŭellae currunt, *the girls run.*

RULE 2.—The Accusative Case denotes the OBJECT. Transitive verbs govern an Accusative case: as, ăquĭlă ălās hăbĕt, *the eagle has wings.* NOTE.—In Latin the verb is put last and the Accusative case before it.

Singular, 3 pers.	Plural, 3 pers.
Currĭt, (*he, she, it*) *runs.*	**Currunt**, (*they*) *run.*
Hăbĕt, (*he, she, it*) *has.*	**Hăbent**, (*they*) *have.*

EXERCISE I.

1. Filia currit. 2. Filiae currunt. 3. Regina coronam habet. 4. Puella coronam habet. 5. Filia pecuniam habet. 6. Femina pecuniam habet. 7. Roma portas habet. 8. Coloniae portas habent. 9. Puellae rosas habent. 10. Feminae rosas habent. 11. Columbae alas habent. 12. Insulae oras habent.

1. The woman runs. 2. The women run. 3. The dove has wings. 4. The eagles have wings. 5. The colony has gates. 6. The island has coasts. 7. The girls have money. 8. The women have money. 9. The colony has women. 10. The island has colonies. 11. The woman has a crown. 12. The islands have roses.

RULE 3.—When two Nouns in Latin are connected by the verb "To be," they are put in the same case: as, Brĭtannĭă est insŭlă, *Britain is an island.* Use the Nominative case after the verb "To be."

RULE 4.—The latter of two Nouns is put in the Genitive case when the one is dependent upon the other: as, Brĭtannĭă est insŭlă Eurōpae, *Britain is an island of Europe.*

Est, (*he*) *is.*   **Sunt,** (*they*) *are.*

EXERCISE II.

1. Sicilia est insula. 2. Sicilia est insula Europae. 3. Roma est regina Italiae. 4. Incolae Italiae sunt poetae. 5. Incolae insularum sunt nautae. 6. Incolae Britanniae sunt agricolae. 7. Insula est patria nautarum. 8. Graecia est patria poetarum. 9. Amicitia est gloria vitae. 10. Inimicitia incolarum est causa pugnae.

1. Britain is the queen of islands. 2. Britain is the native-land of sailors. 3. Italy is the native-land of poets. 4. The inhabitants of Britain are sailors. 5. The inhabitants of Sicily are sailors. 6. The inhabitants of Gaul are husbandmen. 7. Britain is the native-land of glory. 8. Friendship is the crown of life. 9. The battle is the cause of glory. 10. The enmity of the sailors is the cause of the battle.

V.—THE SECOND OR O DECLENSION.

The Nominative Singular of Masculine Nouns of the Second Declension ends in ŭs and ĕr, and of Neuter Nouns in um.

A. *Masculine.*

1.

	Sing.			Plur.	
Nom.	Dŏmĭn-ŭs,	a lord	Dŏmĭn-ī,	lords
Voc.	Dŏmĭn-ĕ,	O lord	Dŏmĭn-ī,	O lords
Acc.	Dŏmĭn-um,	a lord	Dŏmĭn-ōs,	lords
Gen.	Dŏmĭn-ī,	of a lord	Dŏmĭn-ōrum,	of lords
Dat.	Dŏmĭn-ō,	to or for a lord	Dŏmĭn-īs	to or for lords
Abl.	Dŏmĭn-ō,	by, with, or from a lord.	Dŏmĭn-īs	by, with, or from lords.

2.

Nom.	Măgistĕr,	a master	Măgistr-ī,	masters
Voc.	Măgistĕr,	O master	Măgistr-ī,	O masters
Acc.	Măgistr-um,	a master	Măgistr-ōs,	masters
Gen.	Măgistr-ī,	of a master	Măgistr-ōrum,	of masters
Dat.	Măgistr-ō,	to or for a master	Măgistr-īs,	to or for masters
Abl.	Măgistr-ō,	by, with, or from a master.	Măgistr-īs,	by, with, or from masters.

3.

Nom.	Pŭĕr,	a boy	Pŭĕr-ī,	boys
Voc.	Pŭĕr,	O boy	Pŭĕr-ī,	O boys
Acc.	Pŭĕr-um,	a boy	Pŭĕr-ōs,	boys
Gen.	Pŭĕr-ī,	of a boy	Pŭĕr-ōrum,	of boys
Dat.	Pŭĕr-ō,	to or for a boy	Pŭĕr-īs,	to or for boys
Abl.	Pŭĕr-ō,	by, with, or from a boy.	Pŭĕr-īs,	by, with, or from boys.

NOTE.—Proper Names in ĭus make ī in the Vocative, as, Mercŭrĭus, *Mercury, Voc.* Mercŭrī. Also the Vocative Singular of fīlĭus, *a son,* is fīlī, and of gĕnĭus, *a guardian deity,* is gĕnī.

There is one Noun of the Second Declension ending in ĭr, namely, vĭr, *a man* (as distinguished from *a woman*). It is declined like pŭĕr:

4.

	Sing.			Plur.	
Nom.	Vĭr,	a man	Vĭr-ī,	men
Voc.	Vĭr,	O man	Vĭr-ī,	O men
Acc.	Vĭr-um,	a man	Vĭr-ōs,	men
Gen.	Vĭr-ī,	of a man	Vĭr-ōrum,	of men
Dat.	Vĭr-ō,	to or for a man	Vĭr-īs,	to or for men
Abl.	Vĭr-o,	by, with, or from a man.	Vĭr-īs,	by, with, or from men.

B. *Neuter.*

Sing.		Plur.	
N.V.A.	**Regn-um,** *a kingdom,* or *O kingdom*	**Regn-ă,**	*kingdoms,* or *O kingdoms*
Gen.	**Regn-ī,** *of a kingdom*	**Regn-ōrum,**	*of kingdoms*
Dat.	**Regn-ō,** *to* or *for a kingdom*	**Regn-īs,**	*to* or *for kingdoms*
Abl.	**Regn-ō,** *by, with,* or *from a kingdom.*	**Regn-īs,**	*by, with,* or *from kingdoms.*

GENDER.—Most Nouns in **ŭs** are Masculine, but names of trees are Feminine; as, mālŭs, *an apple-tree.*

Three Nouns of the Second Declension ending in **ŭs** are Neuter: virŭs, *poison;* vulgŭs, *the multitude;* pĕlăgŭs, *the (open) sea.* They are used only in the Singular. (*N.B.* Vulgus is sometimes Masculine.)

EXERCISE III.

Masculine Nouns in **ŭs.**

1. Filius currit. 2. Servi currunt. 3. Dominus servos habet.
4. Filius domini servos habet. 5. Dominus servos et equos habet.
6. Filii dominorum equos et tauros habent. 7. Avus servos et equos habet. 8. Filius amici hortum habet. 9. Filii inimicorum gladios habent. 10. Rhodanus est fluvius Galliae. 11. Rhodanus et Rhenus sunt fluvii Galliae. 12. Hortus rosas habet.

1. The slave runs. 2. The sons run. 3. The grandfather has a slave. 4. The son of the grandfather has slaves. 5. The sons of the grandfather have slaves. 6. The sons of the lords are sailors.
7. The sons of the slaves are husbandmen. 8. The lord has slaves and horses. 9. The Rhone and the Rhine are rivers of Europe.
10. The friends of the grandfather are poets. 11. The enemies of the lord have swords. 12. The rivers of the island have banks.

RULE 5.—The Dative Case indicates the person who gains or receives anything: as, Măgistĕr cŏlumbam pŭĕrō dăt, *the master gives a dove to the boy.*

Dăt, (*he, she, it*) *gives.*   Dant, (*they*) *give.*

EXERCISE IV.

Masculine Nouns in **ĕr.**

1. Puer librum habet. 2. Magister librum puero dat. 3. Filius libros habet. 4. Dominus servos et ministros habet. 5. Dominus agrum ministro dat. 6. Socer agros et ministros habet. 7. Socer agrum genero dat. 8. Magistri libros pueris dant. 9. Gener servum puero dat. 10. Puer librum ministro dat.

1. The boys have books. 2. The lord gives a field to the boys.
3. The fathers-in-law and the sons-in-law have fields. 4. The father-in-law gives servants to the son-in-law. 5. The friends

have books. 6. The enemies have servants and fields. 7. The masters give gardens to the boys. 8. The master gives doves to the boys. 9. The grandfather gives fields to the master 10. The fathers-in-law give fields and bulls to the sons-in-law.

EXERCISE V.

Neuter Nouns.

1. Amici sunt donum coeli. 2. Amicitia est donum Dei. 3. Dona avi sunt praemia diligentiae. 4. Aurum et argentum sunt metalla. 5. Magister argentum puero dat. 6. Discipuli sunt gaudium magistrorum. 7. Bellum est causa morborum. 8. Oppidum muros et portas habet. 9. Templa sunt gloria Graeciae. 10. Romani gladios et scuta habent.

1. Friends are the gift of God. 2. The boys and girls are the joy of the grandfather. 3. The grandfather gives gold and silver to the boys. 4. Greece and Sicily have temples. 5. The temples of Greece have gifts. 6. The father-in-law gives gold and silver to the temples. 7. The metals are the cause of war. 8. The queen has lands and towns. 9. The queen gives rewards to the inhabitants. 10. The lord gives shields and swords to the servants.

VI.—ADJECTIVES OF THE FIRST AND SECOND DECLENSIONS.

Adjectives in ŭs, ă, um, or ĕr, (ĕ)rӑ, (ĕ)rum, are declined in the Masculine and Neuter like Nouns of the Second Declension, and in the Feminine like Nouns of the First Declension: as bŏnŭs, bŏnӑ, bŏnum, *good;* nĭgĕr, nĭgrӑ, nigrum, *black;* tĕnĕr, tĕnĕrӑ, tĕnĕrum, *tender.*

1.

	Sing.			Plur.		
	M.	F.	N.	M.	F.	N.
Nom.	Bŏn-ŭs	bŏn-ă	bŏn-um	Bŏn-ī	bŏn-ae	bŏn-ă
Acc.	Bŏn-ĕ	bŏn-ă	bŏn-um	Bŏn-ī	bŏn-ae	bŏn-ă
Voc.	Bŏn-um	bŏn-am	bŏn-um	Bŏn-ōs	bŏn-ās	bŏn-ă
Gen.	Bŏn-ī	bŏn-ae	bŏn-ī	Bŏn-ōrum	bŏn-ārum	bŏn-ōrum
Dat.	Bŏn-ō	bŏn-ae	bŏn-ō	Bŏn-īs	bŏn-īs	bŏn-īs
Abl.	Bŏn-ō	bŏn-ă	bŏn-ō	Bŏn-īs	bŏn-īs	bŏn-īs

2.

	M.	F.	N.	M.	F.	N.
N.V.	Nĭgĕr	nigr-ă	nigr-um	Nigr-ī	nigr-ae	nigr-ă
Acc.	Nigr-um	nigr-am	nigr-um	Nigr-ōs	nigr-ās	nigr-ă
Gen.	Nigr-ī	nigr-ae	nigr-ī	Nigr-ōrum	nigr-ārum	nigr-ōrum
Dat.	Nigr-ō	nigr-ae	nigr-ō	Nigr-īs	nigr-īs	nigr-īs
Abl.	Nigr-ō	nigr-ă	nigr-ō	Nigr-īs	nigr-īs	nigr-īs

3.

	Sing.			Plur.		
	M.	F.	N.	M.	F.	N.
N.V.	Tĕnĕr	tĕnĕr-ă	tĕnĕr-um	Tĕnĕr-ĭ	tĕnĕr-ae	tĕnĕr-ă
Acc.	Tĕnĕr-um	tĕnĕr-am	tĕnĕr-um	Tĕnĕr-ōs	tĕnĕr-ās	tĕnĕr-ă
Gen.	Tĕnĕr-ĭ	tĕnĕr-ae	tĕnĕr-ĭ	Tĕnĕr-ōrum	tĕnĕr-ārum	tĕnĕr-ōrum
Dat.	Tĕnĕr-ō	tĕnĕr-ae	tĕnĕr-ō	Tĕnĕr-ĭs	tĕnĕr-ĭs	tĕnĕr-ĭs
Abl.	Tĕnĕr-ō	tĕnĕr-ă	tĕnĕr-ō	Tĕnĕr-ĭs	tĕnĕr-ĭs	tĕnĕr-ĭs

4.

FEMININE ADJECTIVE DECLINED ALONG WITH FEMININE NOUN.

Sing.

N.V.	Parvă mensă,	a small table, or O small table
Acc.	Parvam mensam,	a small table
Gen.	Parvae mensae,	of a small table
Dat.	Parvae mensae,	to or for a small table
Abl.	Parvă mensă,	by, with, or from a small table

Plur

N.V.	Parvae mensae,	small tables, or O small tables
Acc.	Parvās mensās,	small tables
Gen.	Parvārum mensārum,	of small tables
Dat.	Parvīs mensīs,	to or for small tables
Abl.	Parvīs mensīs,	by, with, or from small tables.

5.

MASCULINE ADJECTIVES DECLINED ALONG WITH MASCULINE NOUNS, BOTH OF SECOND DECLENSION.

(A.)

Sing.

Nom.	Bŏnŭs dŏmĭnŭs,	a good lord
Voc.	Bŏnĕ dŏmĭnĕ,	O good lord
Acc.	Bŏnum dŏmĭnum,	a good lord
Gen.	Bŏnĭ dŏmĭnĭ,	of a good lord
Dat.	Bŏnō dŏmĭnō,	to or for a good lord
Abl.	Bŏnō dŏmĭnō,	by, with, or from a good lord.

Plur.

N.V.	Bŏnĭ dŏmĭnī,	good lords, or O good lords
Acc.	Bŏnōs dŏmĭnōs,	good lords
Gen.	Bŏnōrum dŏmĭnōrum,	of good lords
Dat.	Bŏnīs dŏmĭnīs,	to or for good lords
Abl.	Bŏnīs dŏmĭnīs,	by, with, or from good lords.

(B.)

Sing.

Nom.	Bŏnŭs pŭĕr,	a good boy
Voc.	Bŏnĕ pŭĕr,	O good boy
Acc.	Bŏnum pŭĕrum,	a good boy
Gen.	Bŏnĭ pŭĕrĭ,	of a good boy
Dat.	Bŏnō pŭĕrō,	to or for a good boy
Abl.	Bŏnō pŭĕrō,	by, with, or from a good boy.

Plur.

N.V.	Bŏnī pŭĕrī,	good boys, or O good boys
Acc.	Bŏnōs pŭĕrōs,	good boys
Gen.	Bŏnōrum pŭĕrōrum,	of good boys
Dat.	Bŏnīs pŭĕrīs,	to or for good boys
Abl.	Bŏnīs pŭĕrīs,	by, with, or from good boys.

6.

NEUTER ADJECTIVE DECLINED ALONG WITH NEUTER NOUN,
BOTH OF SECOND DECLENSION.

(A.)

Sing.

N.V.A.	Magnum regnum,	a great kingdom, or O great kingdom
Gen.	Magnī regnī,	of a great kingdom
Dat.	Magnō regnō,	to or for a great kingdom
Abl.	Magnō regnō,	by, with, or from a great kingdom.

Plur.

N.V.A.	Magnă regnă,	great kingdoms, or O great kingdoms
Gen.	Magnōrum regnōrum,	of great kingdoms
Dat.	Magnīs regnīs,	to or for great kingdoms
Abl.	Magnīs regnīs,	by, with, or from great kingdoms.

(B.)

Sing. only.

N.V.A.	Magnum pĕlăgus,	the great sea
Gen.	Magnī pĕlăgī,	of the great sea
Dat.	Magnō pĕlăgō,	to or for the great sea
Abl.	Magnō pĕlăgō,	by, with, or from the great sea.

7.

MASCULINE ADJECTIVE OF SECOND DECLENSION DECLINED WITH
MASCULINE NOUN OF FIRST DECLENSION.

Sing.

Nom.	Clārŭs naută,	a famous sailor
Voc.	Clārĕ naută,	O famous sailor
Acc.	Clārum nautam,	a famous sailor
Gen.	Clārī nautae,	of a famous sailor
Dat.	Clārō nautae,	to or for a famous sailor
Abl.	Clārō naută,	by, with, or from a famous sailor.

Plur.

N.V.	Clārī nautae,	famous sailors, or O famous sailors
Acc.	Clārōs nautăs,	famous sailors
Gen.	Clārōrum nautārum,	of famous sailors
Dat.	Clārīs nautīs,	to or for famous sailors
Abl.	Clārīs nautīs,	by, with, or from famous sailors.

RULE 6.—Adjectives agree with their Nouns in gender, number, and case.

Note that the Adjective in Latin is sometimes placed after the Noun.

EXERCISE VI.

A.—1. Servus est timidus. 2. Columba est timida. 3. Gaudium est magnum. 4. Servi sunt mali. 5. Insulae sunt magnae. 6. Oppida sunt parva. 7. Muri sunt alti. 8. Puellae sunt bonae. 9. Horti sunt lati. 10. Alae sunt albae.

1. The sword is long. 2. The island is long. 3. The shields are long. 4. The slaves are timid. 5. The doves are timid. 6. The towns are great. 7. The temples are small. 8. The shields are wide. 9. The kingdom is great. 10. The friends are good.

B.—1. Columba albas alas habet. 2. Multae columbae albas alas habent. 3. Graecia multa templa habet. 4. Splendida templa sunt gloria Graeciae. 5. Bellicosa regina multas terras habet. 6. Oppidum magnum multas portas habet. 7. Magister librum bono puero dat. 8. Avus praemium bonae puellae dat. 9. Pericula nautarum sunt magna. 10. Dominus acutos gladios habet.

1. The queen has many islands. 2. The queen gives swords to the inhabitants. 3. Gaul has many towns. 4. The temples are great and splendid. 5. The daughters of the women are good. 6. The son of the warlike queen has a sharp sword. 7. The high banks have many roses. 8. The Rhone is a great and broad river. 9. The roses of the high banks are white. 10. The Rhine is a rapid river.

C.—1. Puer est aeger. 2. Puella est aegra. 3. Aurum templi est sacrum. 4. Regina est pulchra. 5. Filiae sunt tenerae. 6. Filii sunt miseri. 7. Morbus molestus est tenero filio. 8. Exemplum servi noxium puero est. 9. Praemia diligentiae sunt grata discipulis. 10. Magnus est numerus puerorum.

1. The pupils of the master are sick. 2. The master gives a book to the sick boy. 3. The black slaves are troublesome to the lord. 4. Great is the number of black slaves. 5. The splendid gifts of the temple are sacred. 6. Great is the diligence of the beautiful girl. 7. The diligence of the girl is pleasing to the grandfather. 8. The example of the slaves is injurious to the pupils. 9. The disease is troublesome to the wretched girl. 10. The master gives rewards to the beautiful girl.

VII.—The Third or Consonant and I Declension.

The Nominative Singular of Nouns of the Third Declension ends in various letters. Their stems end in some consonant or i.

A. *Masculine and Feminine Nouns.*

I. Stems ending in a Consonant.

1. Nouns the stems of which end in the labial (lip) letters *p, b, m.*

	Sing.	1.	Plur.	
N.V.	Trăb-s(f.), a beam, or O beam		Trăb-ĕs,	beams, or ,O beams
Acc.	Trăb-em, a beam		Trăb-ĕs,	beams
Gen.	Trăb-ĭs, of a beam		Trăb-um,	of beams
Dat.	Trăb-I, to or for a beam		Trăb-ĭbŭs,	to or for beams
Abl.	Trăb-ĕ, by, with, or from a beam.		Trăb-ĭbŭs,	by, with, or from beams.

2.

N.V.	Princep-s (c.), a chief, or O		Princĭp-ĕs,	chiefs, or O chiefs
Acc.	Princĭp-em, a chief [chief		Princĭp-ĕs,	chiefs
Gen.	Princĭp-ĭs, of a chief		Princĭp-um,	of chiefs
Dat.	Princĭp-I, to or for a chief		Princĭp-ĭbŭs,	to or for chiefs
Abl.	Princĭp-ĕ, by, with, or from a chief.		Princĭp-ĭbŭs,	by, with, or from chiefs.

3.

N.V.	Hiĕm-s (f.), winter, or O		Hiĕm-ĕs,	winters, or O winters
Acc.	Hiĕm-em, winter [winter		Hiĕm-ĕs,	winters
Gen.	Hiĕm-ĭs, of winter		Hiĕm-um,	of winters
Dat.	Hiĕm-I, to or for winter		Hiĕm-ĭbŭs,	to or for winters
Abl.	Hiĕm-ĕ, by, with, or from winter.		Hiĕm-ĭbŭs,	by, with, or from winters.

2. Nouns the stems of which end in the guttural (throat) letters, *c, g.* Note.—In the Nominative and Vocative Singular *cs, gs* are contracted into *x.*

	Sing.	1.	Plur.	
N.V.	Dux (c.), a leader, or O leader		Dŭc-ĕs,	leaders, or O leaders
Acc.	Dŭc-em, a leader		Dŭc-ĕs,	leaders
Gen.	Dŭc-ĭs, of a leader		Dŭc-um,	of leaders
Dat.	Dŭc-I, to or for a leader		Dŭc-ĭbŭs,	to or for leaders
Abl.	Dŭc-ĕ, by, with, or from a leader.		Dŭc-ĭbŭs,	by, with, or from leaders.

	Sing.		Plur.	
N.V.	Lex (f.),	a law, or O law	Lĕg-ĕs,	laws, or O laws
Acc.	Lĕg-em,	a law	Lĕg-ĕs,	laws
Gen.	Lĕg-ĭs,	of a law	Lĕg-um,	of laws
Dat.	Lĕg-ī,	to or for a law	Lĕg-ĭbŭs,	to or for law:
Abl.	Lĕg-ĕ,	by, with, or from a law.	Lĕg-ĭbŭs,	by, with, or from laws.

3.

	Sing.		Plur.	
N.V.	Jūdex (c.)	a judge, or O judge	Jūdĭc-ĕs,	judges, or O judges
Acc.	Jūdĭc-em,	a judge	Jūdĭc-ĕs,	judges
Gen.	Jūdĭc-ĭs,	of a judge	Jūdĭc-um,	of judges
Dat.	Jūdĭc-ī,	to or for a judge	Jūdĭc-ĭbŭs,	to or for judges
Abl.	Jūdĭc-ĕ,	by, with, or from a judge	Jūdĭc-ĭbŭs,	by, with, or from judges.

Ĕrăt, (he, she, it) was   Ĕrant, (they) were.

Exercise VII.

1. Trabes sunt longae. 2. Romulus Romanorum rex erat. 3. Pax regi jucunda erat. 4. Judices erant justi. 5. Duces erant benigni. 6. Leges Romanorum severae erant. 7. Reges arces firmas habent. 8. Arx urbis est firma. 9. Hiems agricolis molesta erat. 10. Oppida regis firma erant.

1. The beams were long. 2. Rome is a city of Italy. 3. The leader of the Romans was warlike. 4. Peace was pleasant to the leaders. 5. The king gives the city to the leader. 6. The judges were kind and just. 7. The king gives a book to the severe judge. 8. The disease is troublesome to the king. 9. The example is injurious to the judges. 10. The sons of the judges are severe.

3. Nouns the stems of which end in the dental (teeth) letters *t, d*.

	Sing.		Plur.	
N.V.	Aetā-s (f.),	an age, or O age	Aetāt-ĕs,	ages, or O ages
Acc.	Aetāt-em,	an age	Aetāt-ĕs,	ages
Gen.	Aetāt-ĭs,	of an age	Aetāt-um,	of ages
Dat.	Aetāt-ī,	to or for an age	Aetāt-ĭbŭs,	to or for ages
Abl.	Aetāt-ĕ,	by, with, or from an age.	Aetāt-ĭbŭs,	by, with, or from ages.

2.

	Sing.		Plur.	
N.V.	Lăpĭs (m.),	a stone, or O stone	Lăpĭd-ĕs,	stones, or O stones
Acc.	Lăpĭd-em,	a stone	Lăpĭd-ĕs,	stones
Gen.	Lăpĭd-ĭs,	of a stone	Lăpĭd-um,	of stones
Dat.	Lăpĭd-ī,	to or for a stone	Lăpĭd-ĭbŭs,	to or for stones
Abl.	Lăpĭd-ĕ,	by, with, or from a stone.	Lăpĭd-ĭbŭs,	by, with, or from stones.

3.

	Sing.		Plur.	
N.V.	**Mīlĕ-s** (*c.*),	*a soldier,* or *O*	**Mīlĭtĕ-s,**	*soldiers,* or *O soldiers*
Acc.	**Mīlĭt-em,**	*a soldier* [*soldier*	**Mīlĭtĕ-s,**	*soldiers*
Gen.	**Mīlĭt-ĭs,**	*of a soldier*	**Mīlĭt-um,**	*of soldiers*
Dat.	**Mīlĭt-ī,**	*to* or *for a soldier*	**Mīlĭt-ĭbŭs,**	*to* or *for soldiers*
Abl.	**Mīlĭt-ĕ,**	*by, with,* or *from a soldier.*	**Mīlĭt-ĭbŭs,**	*by, with,* or *from soldiers.*

Rule 7.—The Ablative case indicates—(1) The instrument or means by which something is done · as, dŏmĭnŭs hastā servum occīdĭt, *the lord kills the slave with a spear.*

(2) The time when something is done or takes place : as, noctēs hĭĕmĕ longae sunt, *the nights are long in winter.*

Occīdĭt, (*he, she, it*) *kills.*   **Occīdunt,** (*they*) *kill.*

Exercise VIII.

1. Miles gladio obsidem occidit. 2. Miles lapide comitem occidit. 3. Pedites custodes gladiis occidunt. 4. Tempestates auctumno magnae sunt. 5. Equites et pedites timidi erant. 6. Custodes auri erant timidi. 7. Mors est lex naturae. 8. Civitas Romanorum clara erat. 9. Voluntas judicis justa est. 10. Milites judices hastis occidunt.

1. Tempests in the winter are great. 2. A tempest in the summer is troublesome. 3. A long night in the winter is pleasant. 4. The inhabitants kill the soldiers with stones. 5. The hostages kill the foot-soldiers with spears. 6. The wish of the companion is just. 7. The horse-soldiers and foot-soldiers have swords. 8. The guardian of the silver was timid. 9. The boy has many stones. 10. The king has many soldiers and companions.

4. Nouns the stems of which end in the liquids *l*, *r*, and the sibilant *s*.

1.

	Sing.		Plur.	
N.V.	**Consŭl** (*m.*),	*a consul,* or *O*	**Consŭl-ēs,**	*consuls,* or *O consuls*
Acc.	**Consŭl-em,**	*a consul* [*consul*	**Consŭl-ēs,**	*consuls*
Gen.	**Consŭl-ĭs,**	*of a consul*	**Consŭl-um,**	*of consuls*
Dat.	**Consŭl-ī,**	*to* or *for a consul*	**Consŭl-ĭbŭs,**	*to* or *for consuls*
Abl.	**Consŭl-ĕ,**	*by, with,* or *from a consul.*	**Consŭl-ĭbŭs,**	*by, with,* or *from consuls.*

2.

	Sing.		Plur.	
N.V.	**Clāmŏr** (*m.*),	*a shout,* or *O*	**Clāmŏr-ēs,**	*shouts,* or *O shouts*
Acc.	**Clāmŏr-em,**	*a shout* [*shout*	**Clāmŏr-ēs,**	*shouts*
Gen.	**Clāmŏr-ĭs,**	*of a shout*	**Clāmŏr-um,**	*of shouts*
Dat.	**Clāmŏr-ī,**	*to* or *for a shout*	**Clāmŏr-ĭbŭs,**	*to* or *for shouts*
Abl.	**Clāmŏr-ĕ**	*by, with,* or *from a shout.*	**Clāmŏr-ĭbŭs,**	*by, with,* or *from shouts.*

	Sing.	**3.**	Plur.	
N.V. **Ansĕr** (*m.*),	*a goose,* or *O goose*	**Ansĕr-ĕs,**	*geese,* or *O geese*
Acc. **Ansĕr-em,**	*a goose*	**Ansĕr-ĕs,**	*geese*
Gen. **Ansĕr-ĭs,**	*of a goose*	**Ansĕr-um,**	*of geese*
Dat. **Ansĕr-ĭ,**	*to* or *for a goose*	**Ansĕr-ĭbŭs,**	*to* or *for geese*
Abl. **Ansĕr-ĕ,**	*by,* *with,* or *from a goose.*	**Ansĕr-ĭbŭs,**	*by, with,* or *from geese.*

4.

N.V. **Pătĕr,**	*a father,* or *O father*	**Patr-ĕs,**	*fathers,* or *O fathers*
Acc. **Patr-em,**	*a father*	**Patr-ĕs,**	*fathers*
Gen. **Patr-ĭs,**	*of a father*	**Patr-um,**	*of fathers*
Dat. **Patr-ĭ,**	*to* or *for a father*	**Patr-ĭbŭs,**	*to* or *for fathers*
Abl. **Patr-ĕ,**	*by, with,* or *from a father.*	**Patr-ĭbŭs,**	*by, with,* or *from fathers.*

5.

N.V. **Flŏs** (*m.*),	*a flower,* or *O flower*	**Flŏr-ĕs,**	*flowers,* or *O flowers*
Acc. **Flŏr-em,**	*a flower*	**Flŏr-ĕs,**	*flowers*
Gen. **Flŏr-ĭs,**	*of a flower*	**Flŏr-um,**	*of flowers*
Dat. **Flŏr-ĭ,**	*to* or *for a flower*	**Flŏr-ĭbŭs,**	*to* or *for flowers*
Abl. **Flŏr-ĕ,**	*by, with,* or *from a flower.*	**Flŏr-ĭbŭs,**	*by, with,* or *from flowers.*

EXERCISE IX.

1. Puer patrem et matrem habet. 2. Puellae fratres et sorores habent. 3. Odores florum sunt varii. 4. Color floris est jucundus. 5. Labor aestate molestus est. 6. Calor solis molestus est. 7. Tota urbs est praeda victoris. 8. Aggeres et fossae sunt munimenta castrorum. 9. Clamor militum molestus est.

1. The father of the judge is just. 2. The mother of the soldier is sick. 3. The hostage has a brother and a sister. 4. The colours of the flowers are various. 5. The brother gives a flower to (his) sister. 6. The shout of the soldiers was great. 7. The heat of the sun is great. 8. The heat is troublesome in the summer. 9. The mounds of the camp are high. 10. The cities are the booty of the soldiers.

5. Nouns the stems of which end in *ōn* or *ŏn* (*ĭn*).

	Sing.	**1.**	Plur.	
N.V. **Lĕo** (*m.*),	*a lion,* or *O lion*	**Lĕŏn-ĕs,**	*lions,* or *O lions*
Acc. **Lĕŏn-em,**	*a lion*	**Lĕŏn-ĕs,**	*lions*
Gen. **Lĕŏn-ĭs,**	*of a lion*	**Lĕŏn-um,**	*of lions*
Dat. **Lĕŏn-ĭ,**	*to* or *for a lion*	**Lĕŏn-ĭbŭs,**	*to* or *for lions*
Abl. **Lĕŏn-ĕ,**	*by, with,* or *from a lion.*	**Lĕŏn-ĭbŭs,**	*by, with,* or *from lions.*

2.

N.V. **Virgo,**	*a maiden,* or *O maiden*	**Virgĭn-ĕs,**	*maidens,* or *O maidens*
Acc. **Virgĭn-em,**	*a maiden*	**Virgĭn-ĕs,**	*maidens*
Gen. **Virgĭn-ĭs,**	*of a maiden*	**Virgĭn-um,**	*of maidens*
Dat. **Virgĭn-ĭ,**	*to* or *for a maiden*	**Virgĭn-ĭbŭs,**	*to* or *for maidens*
Abl. **Virgĭn-ĕ,**	*by, with,* or *from a maiden.*	**Virgĭn-ĭbŭs,**	*by, with,* or *from maidens.*

Exercise X.

1. Leones sunt validi. 2. Virgo est timida. 3. Calor molestus est multis hominibus. 4. Consuetudo altera natura est. 5. Sermo oratoris est doctus. 6. Pavones agricolae sunt pulchri. 7. Mors hominibus certa est. 8. Multitudo morborum est infinita. 9. Juno erat dea Romanorum. 10. Vita hominibus grata est.

1. The lion is strong. 2. The maidens are timid. 3. The multitude of men is infinite. 4. The soldier kills the lion with a sword. 5. The father gives a peacock to the maiden. 6. The heat is troublesome. 7. The heat in autumn is injurious to men. 8. The discourses of the orators were learned. 9. Juno and Minerva were goddesses of the Romans. 10. The peacock was sacred to Juno.

II. Stems ending in I.

1.

	Sing.		Plur.
N.V.	Host-is (c.),	an enemy, or O	Host-ēs, enemies, or O enemies
Acc.	Host-em,	an enemy [enemy	Host-ēs, enemies
Gen.	Host-is,	of an enemy	Host-ium, of enemies
Dat.	Host-i,	to or for an enemy	Host-ibus, to or for enemies
Abl.	Host-ĕ,	by, with, or from an enemy.	Host-ibus, by, with, or from enemies.

Some stems in *i* have the Nominative in *e* and are thus declined :—

2.

N.V.	Nŭb-ēs (f),	a cloud, or O	Nŭb-ēs, clouds, or O clouds
Acc.	Nŭb-em,	a cloud [cloud	Nŭb-ēs, clouds
Gen.	Nŭb-is,	of a cloud	Nŭb-ium, of clouds
Dat.	Nŭb-i,	to or for a cloud	Nŭb-ibus, to or for clouds
Abl.	Nŭb-ĕ,	by, with, or from a cloud.	Nŭb-ibus, by, with, or from clouds.

Exercise XI.

1. Cives agros et hortos habent. 2. Rex civibus praemia dat. 3. Nubes atrae sunt causa tempestatum. 4. Rupes sunt durae. 5. Urbs turres altas habet. 6. Clades hostium magna erat. 7. Classis Romana duces peritos habet. 8. Valles hostibus notae erant. 9. Graecia valles angustas habet. 10. Virgo pulchram vestem habet.

1. The citizens were timid. 2. The valleys are known to the citizens. 3. The mother gives a garment to the maiden. 4. The citizens kill the enemies with swords. 5. The rocks are known to the citizens. 6. The valleys of Greece are narrow. 7. The Roman fleet has a skilful leader. 8. The maidens have beautiful garments. 9. The slaughter of the soldiers was great. 10. The leaders of the enemies were skilful.

B. *Neuter Nouns.*

I. Stems ending in a Consonant.

Substantives the stems of which end in *n, r, s, t.*

1.

	Sing.			Plur.	
N.V.A.	Nŏmĕn,	a name, or O	Nŏmĭn-ă,	names, or O names
Gen.	Nŏmĭn-ĭs	of a name [name	Nŏmĭn-um,	of names
Dat.	Nŏmĭn-ī,	to or for a name	Nŏmĭn-ĭbŭs,	to or for names
Abl.	Nŏmĭn-ĕ,	by, with, or from a name.	Nŏmĭn-ĭbŭs,	by, with, or from names.

2.

N.V.A.	Fulgŭr,	lightning, or O lightning	Fulgŭr-ă,	lightnings, or O lightnings
Gen.	Fulgŭr-ĭs,	of lightning	Fulgŭr-um,	of lightnings
Dat.	Fulgŭr-ī,	to or for lightning	Fulgŭr-ĭbŭs,	to or for lightnings
Abl.	Fulgŭr-ĕ,	by, with, or from lightning.	Fulgŭr-ĭbŭs,	by, with, or from lightnings.

3.

N.V.A.	Crūs,	a leg, or O leg	Crūr-ă,	legs, or O legs
Gen.	Crūr-ĭs,	of a leg	Crūr-um,	of legs
Dat.	Crūr-ī,	to or for a leg	Crūr-ĭbŭs,	to or for legs
Abl.	Crūr-ĕ,	by, with, or from a leg.	Crūr-ĭbŭs,	by, with, or from legs.

4.

N.V.A.	ŏpŭs,	a work, or O work	ŏpĕr-ă,	works, or O works
Gen.	ŏpĕr-ĭs,	of a work	ŏpĕr-um,	of works
Dat.	ŏpĕr-ī,	to or for a work	ŏpĕr-ĭbŭs,	to or for works
Abl.	ŏpĕr-ĕ,	by, with, or from a work.	ŏpĕr-ĭbŭs,	by, with, or from works.

5.

N.V.A.	Corpŭs,	a body, or O body	Corpŏr-ă,	bodies, or O bodies
Gen.	Corpŏr-ĭs,	of a body	Corpŏr-um,	of bodies
Dat.	Corpŏr-ī,	to or for a body	Corpŏr-ĭbŭs,	to or for bodies
Abl.	Corpŏr-ĕ	by, with, or from a body.	Corpŏr-ĭbŭs,	by, with, or from bodies.

6.

N.V.A.	Căpŭt,	a head, or O head	Căpĭt-ă,	heads, or O heads
Gen.	Căpĭt-ĭs,	of a head	Căpĭt-um,	of heads
Dat.	Căpĭt-ī,	to or for a head	Căpĭt-ĭbŭs,	to or for heads
Abl.	Căpĭt-ĕ,	by, with, or from a head.	Căpĭt-ĭbŭs,	by, with, or from heads.

II. Stems ending in I.

The Nominative in *ĕ, ăl, ăr.*

1.

	Sing.			Plur.	
N.V.A.	Măr-ĕ,	the sea, or O sea	Măr-ĭă,	seas, or O seas
Gen.	Măr-ĭs,	of the sea	Măr-ĭum,	of seas
Dat.	Măr-ī,	to or for the sea	Măr-ĭbŭs,	to or for seas
Abl.	Măr-ī,	by, with, or from the sea.	Măr-ĭbŭs,	by, with, or from seas.

	Sing.	**2.**	Plur.
N.V.A.	**Ănĭmăl,** *an animal, or O animal*	**Ănĭmăl-Iă,**	*animals, or O animals*
Gen.	**Ănĭmăl-Is,** *of an animal*	**Ănĭmăl-Ium,**	*of animals*
Dat.	**Ănĭmăl-I,** *to or for an animal*	**Ănĭmăl-Ibŭs,**	*to or for animals*
Abl.	**Ănĭmăl-I,** *by, with, or from an animal.*	**Ănĭmăl-Ibŭs,**	*by, with, or from animals.*

3.

N.V.A.	**Calcăr,** *a spur, or O spur*	**Calcăr-Iă,**	*spurs, or O spurs*
Gen.	**Calcărĭs,** *of a spur*	**Calcăr-Ium,**	*of spurs*
Dat.	**Calcărī,** *to or for a spur*	**Calcăr-Ibŭs,**	*to or for spurs*
Abl.	**Calcărī,** *by, with, or from a spur.*	**Calcăr-Ibŭs,**	*by, with, or from spurs.*

Exercise XII.

A. 1. Nomen Carthaginis clarum erat. 2. Litora erant angusta. 3. Elephanti magna capita et parva crura habent. 4. Balaenae parva ora habent. 5. Fulgur est rapidum. 6. Opus est durum et molestum. 7. Ira causa multorum scelerum est. 8. Juno antiquis temporibus erat dea. 9. Sidera nautis grata sunt. 10. Frigus hieme est molestum.

1. The name of Cicero is renowned. 2. The works of Cicero are renowned. 3. Elephants have a strong body. 4. The legs of elephants are small. 5. The mouths of whales are small. 6. Elephants have great heads and small eyes. 7. The crimes are known to the judge. 8. The cold is troublesome to the maiden. 9. The time of the year is pleasant. 10. The shore is wide.

B.—1. Maria sunt domicilia piscium. 2. Calcaria sunt decus equitis. 3. Litora maris sunt magna. 4. Nautae retia habent. 5. Vectigalia sunt magna. 6. Gramen animalibus gratum erat. 7. Calcaria equitis sunt nova. 8. Maria sunt profunda. 9. Genera animalium sunt varia. 10. Equites aurea calcaria habent.

1. The sea is deep. 2. The shores of the seas are high. 3. The deep sea is the abode of fishes. 4. The nets of the sailors are golden. 5. The king gives golden nets to the sailors. 6. The spurs of the horse-soldier are golden. 7. The king gives a golden spur to the horse-soldier. 8. The animal is strong. 9. Many animals are strong. 10. The tax is troublesome.

Nouns of Third Declension, and Adjectives of First and Second Declensions, declined together.

1. Magnus Dux,—*a great leader.*

	Sing.	Plur.
Nom.	**Magnŭs dux**	**Magnī dŭcēs**
Voc.	**Magnĕ dux**	**Magnī dŭcēs**
Acc.	**Magnum dŭcem**	**Magnōs dŭcēs**
Gen.	**Magnī dŭcĭs**	**Magnōram dŭcum**
Dat.	**Magnō dŭcī**	**Magnĭs dŭcĭbŭs**
Abl.	**Magnō dŭcĕ**	**Magnĭs dŭcĭbŭs**

2. Bŏnă Mătĕr,—*a good mother.*

	Sing.	Plur.
N.V.	Bŏnă mătĕr	Bŏnae mătrēs
Acc.	Bŏnam mătrem	Bŏnās mătrēs
Gen.	Bŏnae mătrĭs	Bŏnārum mātrum
Dat.	Bŏnae mātrī	Bŏnĭs mătrĭbŭs
Abl.	Bŏnă mătrĕ	Bŏnĭs mătrĭbŭs

3. Răpĭdum Flŭmĕn,—*a rapid river.*

	Sing.	Plur.
N.V.A.	Răpĭdum flŭmĕn	Răpĭdă flŭmĭnă
Gen.	Răpĭdī flŭmĭnĭs	Răpĭdōrum flŭmĭnum
Dat.	Răpĭdō flŭmĭnī	Răpĭdĭs flŭmĭnĭbŭs
Abl.	Răpĭdō flŭmĭnĕ	Răpĭdĭs flŭmĭnĭbŭs

VIII.—ADJECTIVES OF THE THIRD DECLENSION.

I. ADJECTIVES OF THREE TERMINATIONS end in ĕr, rĭs, rĕ, and are declined like Nouns of the Third Declension. They have three terminations in the Nominative and Vocative Singular only : as, ācĕr, ācrĭs, ācrĕ, *sharp.*

	Sing.			Plur.	
	M.	F.	N.	M. and F.	N.
N.V.	Acĕr	ācrĭs	ācrĕ	Acrēs	ācrĭă
Acc.	Acrem	ācrĕ	ācrĕ	Acrēs	ācrĭă
Gen.	Acrĭs	(of all genders)		Acrĭum	(of all genders)
Dat.	Acrī	(of all genders)		Acrĭbŭs	(of all genders)
Abl.	Acrī	(of all genders)		Acrĭbŭs	(of all genders)

II. ADJECTIVES OF TWO TERMINATIONS are declined like Nouns of the Third Declension. They have two terminations in the Nominative, Vocative, and Accusative Singular only. They include—

    1. Adjectives ending in Ĭs : as, tristĭs (*masc.* and *fem.*), tristĕ (*neut.*), *sad.*

    2. Comparatives, ending in ĭŏr, ĭŭs : as, mĕlĭŏr (*masc.* and *fem.*), mĕlĭŭs (*neut.*), *better.*

1.

	Sing.		Plur.	
	M. and F.	N.	M. and F.	N.
N.V.	Trist-ĭs	trist-ĕ	Trist-ēs	trist-Ĭă
Acc.	Trist-em	trist-ĕ	Trist-ēs	trist-Ĭă
Gen.	Trist-ĭs	(of all genders)	Trist-Ĭum	(of all genders)
Dat.	Trist-I	(of all genders)	Trist-Ĭbŭs	(of all genders)
Abl.	Trist-I	(of all genders)	Trist-Ĭbŭs	(of all genders)

2.

	Sing.		Plur.	
	M. and F.	N.	M. and F.	N.
N.V.	Mĕlĭŏr	mĕlĭŭs	Mĕlĭŏr-ēs	mĕlĭŏr-a
Acc.	Mĕlĭŏr-em	mĕlĭŭs	Mĕlĭŏr-ēs	mĕlĭŏră
Gen.	Mĕlĭŏr-ĭs	(of all genders)	Mĕlĭŏr-um	(of all genders)
Dat.	Mĕlĭŏr-I	(of all genders)	Mĕlĭŏr-Ĭbŭs	(of all genders)
Abl.	Mĕlĭŏr-ĕ or I	(of all genders)	Mĕlĭŏr-Ĭbŭs	(of all genders)

III. ADJECTIVES OF ONE TERMINATION are of various endings and declined like Nouns of the Third Declension: as, fēlix, *fortunate*; prūdens, *prudent*.

1.

Sing.			Plur.	
M. and F.		N.	M. and F.	N.
N.V. Fēlix			Fēlĭc-ēs	fēlĭc-Iă
Acc. Fēlĭc-em,		fēlix	Fēlĭc-ēs	fēlĭc-Iă
Gen. Fēlĭc-Is	(of all genders)		Fēlĭc-Ium	(of all genders)
Dat. Fēlĭc-I	(of all genders)		Fēlĭc-Ibŭs	(of all genders)
Abl. Fēlĭc-I *or* ĕ	(of all genders)		Fēlĭc-Ibŭs	(of all genders)

2.

N.V. Prūdens		.	Prūdent-ēs	prūdent-Iă
Acc. Prūdent-em		prūdens	Prūdent-ēs	prūdent-Iă
Gen. Prūdent-Is	(of all genders)		Prūdent-Ium	(of all genders)
Dat. Prūdent-I	(of all genders)		Prūdent-Ibŭs	(of all genders)
Abl. Prūdent-I *or* ĕ	(of all genders)		Prūdent-Ibŭs	(of all genders)

ADJECTIVES OF THE THIRD DECLENSION, DECLINED WITH NOUNS OF THE FIRST, SECOND, AND THIRD DECLENSIONS.

1. Cĕlĕrĭs Săgittă,—*a swift arrow.*

Sing.	Plur.
N.V. Cĕlĕrĭs săgittă	Cĕlĕrēs săgittae
Acc. Cĕlĕrem săgittam	Cĕlĕrēs săgittas
Gen. Cĕlĕrĭs săgittae	Cĕlĕrum săgittārum
Dat. Cĕlĕrĭ săgittae	Cĕlĕrĭbŭs săgittĭs
Abl. Cĕlĕrĭ săgittă	Cĕlĕrĭbŭs săgittĭs

2. Tristĕ Proelium,—*a sad battle.*

N.A.V. Tristĕ proelium	Tristiă proeliă
Gen. Tristĭs proeliī	Tristĭum proeliōrum
Dat. Tristĭ proeliō	Tristĭbŭs proeliĭs
Abl. Tristĭ proeliō	Tristĭbŭs proeliĭs

3. Fēlix Hŏmo,—*a happy man.*

N.V. Fēlix hŏmo	Fēlĭcēs hŏmĭnēs
Acc. Fēlĭcem hŏmĭnem	Fēlĭcēs hŏmĭnēs
Gen. Fēlĭcĭs hŏmĭnĭs	Fēlĭcĭum hŏmĭnum
Dat. Fēlĭcĭ hŏmĭnĭ	Fēlĭcĭbŭs hŏmĭnĭbŭs
Abl. Fēlĭcĭ *or* ĕ hŏmĭnĕ	Fēlĭcĭbŭs hŏmĭnĭbŭs

EXERCISE XIII.

A.—1. Ira furor brevis est. 2. Ira militum erat acris. 3. Via est facilis. 4. Omne initium est difficile. 5. Leges hominibus utiles sunt. 6. Vulnus militis est leve. 7. Carmen est dulce. 8. Naves hostium sunt celeres. 9. Tempus humanae vitae breve est. 10. Rex cives fideles habet.

1. The soldiers have sharp arms. 2. The arrow is swift. 3. Labour is easy in the winter. 4. Labour is difficult in the summer. 5. Arms are useful to soldiers. 6. The soldiers have short swords. 7. The beginning of the song is difficult. 8. The songs are easy. 9. The wounds of the soldier are light. 10. The arrows are sharp and swift.

B.—1. Consilium ducis audax est. 2. Consilia ducis Romani audacia sunt. 3. Tempus praesens felix est. 4. Regnum Persarum erat potens. 5. Animalia rapacia sunt velocia. 6. Vetus vinum est bonum. 7. Rex ingentem numerum militum habet. 8. Leges Romanorum erant praestantes. 9. Praemia equitum ingentia erant. 10. Agricolae vinum vetus habent.

1. The plans of the leader were prudent. 2. Elephants are prudent animals. 3. The booty of the Romans was immense. 4. The beginning was fortunate. 5. The Romans have excellent laws. 6. The king gives immense rewards to the soldiers. 7. Lions are rapacious animals. 8. The father gives old wine to the boy. 9. The present times are fortunate. 10. The Romans are powerful.

IX.—THE FOURTH OR **U** DECLENSION.

. The Nominative Singular of Masculine and Feminine Nouns of the Fourth Declension ends in **ŭs**, and of Neuter Nouns in **u.**

1.

	Sing.		Plur.
N.V.	**Grăd-ŭs** (m.), a step, or O step	**Grăd-ŭs,**	steps, or O steps
Acc.	**Grăd-um,** a step	**Grăd-ŭs,**	steps
Gen.	**Grăd-ŭs,** of a step	**Grăd-ŭum,**	of steps
Dat.	**Grăd-ŭī,** to or for a step	**Grăd-ĭbŭs,**	to or for steps
Abl.	**Grăd-ŭ,** by, with, or from a step.	**Grăd-ĭbŭs,**	by, with, or from steps.

2.

N.V.A.	**Gĕn-u**(n.), a knee, or O knee	**Gĕn-ŭă,**	knees, or O knees
Gen.	**Gĕn-ŭs,** of a knee	**Gĕn-ŭum,**	of knees
Dat.	**Gĕn-ŭ,** to or for a knee	**Gĕn-ĭbŭs,**	to or for knees
Abl.	**Gĕn-ŭ,** by, with, or from a knee.	**Gĕn-ĭbŭs,**	by, with, or from knees.

Note.—Some Nouns of the Fourth Declension make the Dative and Ablative plural in -ŭbŭs: as, ăcŭbŭs, arcŭbŭs, portŭbŭs, vĕrŭbŭs, with a few others. Also, the Dative Singular ŭī is sometimes contracted into ŭ: as, grădŭī, grădŭ.

EXERCISE XIV.

A.—1. Quercus sunt altae. 2. Manus hominibus utiles sunt. 3. Visus et auditus sunt utiles hominibus. 4. Acus est acuta. 5. Portus est tutus. 6. Cursus militis erat celer. 7. Arcus Scytharum leves erant. 8. Arcus coelestis varios colores habet. 9. Fructus ficūs erat dulcis. 10. Caput est sedes omnium sensuum.

1. The oak is useful to man. 2. The city has beautiful harbours. 3. The Scythians have arrows and bows. 4. The needles are sharp. 5. The girl has a sharp needle. 6. The harbours of the city are safe. 7. The number of the harbours is great. 8. Hearing and seeing are useful (pl.) to animals. 9. The fruit of fig-trees is sweet. 10. The soldier kills the lion with (his) hand.

B.—1. Cornua tauri acuta sunt. 2. Magister cornu puero dat. 3. Genua hominibus utilia sunt. 4. Magistratus· sunt legum ministri. 5. Exercitus arma magnifica habet. 6. Duces exercitūs audaces erant. 7. Rex equitatum peditatumque* habet. 8. Voluptas sensibus grata est. 9. Oculi sunt instrumenta visūs. 10. Aures sunt instrumenta auditūs.

1. The knees of elephants are hard. 2. The horns of the stag are hard. 3. The king gives a beautiful horn to the soldier. 4. The magistrates are the guardians of the laws. 5. The leader of the cavalry is bold. 6. Greece has many harbours. 7. Every animal has senses. 8. Eyes and ears are the instruments of the senses. 9. Sharp needles are useful to women. 10. The leaders of the infantry are powerful.

* Quĕ, *and* (placed after the word which it unites to the preceding).

X.—The Fifth or E Declension.

The Nominative Singular of Nouns of the Fifth Declension ends in ēs.

	Sing.		Plur.
N.V.	Dĭ-ĕs, *a day,* or *O day*	Dĭ-ĕs,	*days,* or *O days*
Acc.	Dĭ-em, *a day*	Dĭ-ĕs,	*days*
Gen.	Dĭ-ēī, *of a day* .	Dĭ-ērum,	*of days*
Dat.	Dĭ-ēī, *to* or *for a day*	Dĭ-ēbŭs,	*to* or *for days*
Abl.	Dĭ-ē, *by, with,* or *from a day.*	Dĭ-ēbŭs,	*by, with,* or *from days.*

NOTE.—In Nouns like rēs, where ēs is preceded by a Consonant, the e becomes short in Gen. and Dat. Singular: as, rĕī, spĕī.

GENDER.—All Nouns of the Fifth Declension are Feminine except dĭēs, which is either Masculine or Feminine in the Singular, and always Masculine in the Plural; and mĕrīdĭēs, *midday,* which is always Masculine.

RULE 8.—When the Ablative Case indicates the place *where,* it is used with the Preposition ĭn, *in :* as, hostēs ĭn plānĭtĭē ĕrant, *the enemies were in the plain.* See Rule 7, p. 13.

Exercise XV.

1. Dies sunt sereni. 2. Numerus dierum serenorum parvus est. 3. Deus est dominus omnium rerum. 4. Dux magnam victoriae spem habet. 5. Fides servorum rara erat. 6. Exercitus in magna planitie erat. 7. In acie multi pedites erant. 8. Fortuna est domina rerum humanarum. 9. Facies filii pulchra erat. 10. Magna est pueri segnities.

1. The number of days is infinite. 2. God is the creator of all things. 3. Many things are hurtful to man. 4. The mother gives many things to the girl. 5. In the line-of-battle were many horse-soldiers. 6. The cavalry was in the plain. 7. The reward was the beginning of hope. 8. The leaders have great hope of victory. 9. The fidelity of sons was rare. 10. The slothfulness of the girl is troublesome to the mother.

XI.—SOME IRREGULAR NOUNS.

The following words are thus declined :—

Dĕŭs, *God*. (2 Decl.)			Dŏmŭs, *f. a house*. (2 and 4 Decl.)	
	Sing.	Plur.	Sing.	Plur.
N.V.	Dĕŭs	Dĕĭ, Dĭĭ, *or* Dī	Dŏmŭs	Dŏmŭs
Acc.	Dĕum	Dĕŏs	Dŏmum	Dŏmŏs (*rarely* dŏmŭs)
Gen.	Dĕĭ	Dĕŏrum, *or* Deûm	Dŏmŭs	Dŏmŭum, *or* dŏmōrum
Dat.	Dĕŏ	Dĕĭs, Dĭĭs, *or* Dīs	Dŏmŭĭ	Dŏmĭbŭs
Abl.	Dĕŏ	Dĕĭs, Dĭĭs, *or* Dīs	Dŏmŏ	Dŏmĭbŭs

N.B. The form *dŏmĭ* is used only in the sense of *at home*.

Bōs, *an ox or cow*. (3 Decl.)			Sĕnex, *an old man*. (3 Decl.)	
	Sing.	Plur.	Sing.	Plur.
N.V.	Bōs	Bŏvēs	Sĕnex	Sĕnēs
Acc.	Bŏvem	Bŏvēs	Sĕnem	Sĕnēs
Gen.	Bŏvĭs	Bŏvum, *or* bŏum	Sĕnĭs	Sĕnum
Dat.	Bŏvī	Bōbŭs, *or* būbŭs	Sĕnī	Sĕnĭbŭs
Abl.	Bŏvĕ	Bōbŭs, *or* būbŭs.	Sĕnĕ	Sĕnĭbŭs

Vīs, *f. strength*. (3 Decl.).			Jūpĭtĕr (=Jŏv-pĭtĕr, *i. e.* pătĕr), (3 Decl.) *the god*.	
	Sing.	·Plur.	Sing.	
Nom.	Vĭs	Vīrēs	Jūpĭtĕr	
Acc.	Vim	Vīrēs	Jŏvem	
Gen.	wanting	Vīrĭum	Jŏvĭs	
Dat.	wanting	Vīrĭbŭs	Jŏvī	
Abl.	Vī	Vīrĭbŭs	Jŏvĕ	

Jusjūrandum, *n. an oath* (properly two words, Jus, 3 Decl. and jūrandum, 2 Decl.).		Respublĭca, *f. a commonwealth, a republic* (properly two words, Res, 5 Decl. and publĭca, 1 Decl.).	
	Sing.		Sing.
N.V.A.	Jusjūrandum	*N.V.*	Respublĭca
Gen.	Jūrisjūrandī	*Acc.*	Rempublĭcam
Dat.	Jūrĭjūrandŏ	*Gen.*	Rĕĭpublĭcae
Abl.	Jūrĕjūrandŏ	*Dat.*	Rĕĭpublĭcae
		Abl.	Rĕpublĭca

EXERCISE XVI.

A.—1. Di sunt immortales. 2. Jupiter et Neptunus sunt dii Romanorum. 3. Quercus Jovi sacrae erant. 4. Domus urbis sunt pulchrae. 5. Divitiae magnae in domo patris sunt. 6. Divitiae ingentes in domibus incolarum sunt. 7. Canes domuum custodes sunt. 8. Homines in domibus sunt, bestiae in silvis. 9. Dis sacrum est monumentum. 10. Vis fluminis ingens est.

1. Men are mortal, the gods immortal. 2. The oak is sacred to Jupiter. 3. Thunderbolts are the arms of Jupiter. 4. Many

trees are sacred to the gods. 5. The number of the gods is immense. 6. The number of the houses is immense. 7. (There) were immense riches in the houses of the citizens. 8. The monuments are sacred to the gods. 9. Jupiter has many temples in Italy. 10. Oxen have great strength (pl.).

B.—1. Senex est debilis et aeger. 2. Funera senum et juvenum sunt multa. 3. Nomen Ciceronis senibus notum est. 4. Boves magnas vires habent. 5. Magna est vis conscientiae. 6. Civis jusjurandum judici dat.* 7. In republica Romana sunt multi servi. 8. Respublica Romanorum potens erat. 9. Cornua bovis dura sunt. 10. Boves et equi in agro sunt.

1. The strength (pl.) of oxen is immense. 2. The king gives many oxen to the soldiers. 3. The old-men are feeble and sick. 4. The old-man gives gold and silver to the young-man. 5. The house of the old-man is full of riches. 6. Gold and silver are in the houses of the citizens. 7. In the Roman commonwealth were many brave citizens. 8. The friends of the commonwealth were few. 9. The grass is pleasing to the oxen. 10. The fields are sacred to Jupiter.

* Jusjurandum dat, in English, *takes the oath.*

XII.—Some Irregular Adjectives.

The following words have in the Genitive Sing. **īŭs** (rarely **ĭŭs**) and in the Dative **I** :—

ūnŭs, ă, um,	*one, alone.*
sōlŭs, ă, um,	*alone.*
tōtŭs, ă, um,	*whole.*
ullŭs, ă, um,	*any.*
nullŭs, ă, um,	*no, none.*
ūtĕr, utră, utrum,	*which of two.*
neutĕr, neutră, neutrum,	*neither.*

altĕr, altĕră, altĕrum, *one of two ;* altĕr . . . . altĕr, *the one . the other.*

ălīŭs, ălĭă, ălĭŭd, *one of any number ;* ălĭŭs . . . . ălĭŭs, *one . . . . another ;* in pl. *some, others.*

For example

	Sing.			Plur.		
	M.	**F.**	**N.**	**M.**	**F.**	**N.**
Nom.	Ŭn-ŭs	ŭn-ă	ŭn-um	Ŭn-ī	ŭn-ae	ŭn-ă
Acc.	Ŭn-um	ŭn-am	ŭn-um	Ŭn-ōs	ŭn-ăs	ŭn-ă
Gen.	Ŭn-īŭs	(of all genders)		Ŭn-ōrum	ŭn-ărum	ŭn-ōrum
Dat.	Ŭn-ī	(of all genders)		Ŭn-īs	(of all genders)	
Abl.	Ŭn-ō	ŭn-ă	ŭn-ō	Ŭn-īs	(of all genders)	

The Genitive Singular of altĕr is *altĕrīŭs*, and of ălĭŭs is *ălīŭs.*

Exercise XVII.

1. Virtus sola dat veram voluptatem. 2. Cives Ciceroni uni dant honorem. 3. Utri dat (*does he give*) laudem? Neutri. 4. Alii

sunt docti, alii indocti. 5. Alīus (*gen.*) vires, alīus (*gen.*) divitiae sunt magnae. 6. Alter est Graecus, alter Romanus. 7. Tota vita hominis memorabilis erat. 8. Alteri (*dat.*) laudem, alteri (*dat.*) culpam dant. 9. Ciceroni dat totam laudem. 10. Neutra civitas habet laudem ullam.

1. He gives the whole booty to the soldiers. 2. Cicero alone was pleasing to the citizens. 3. He was troublesome to neither. 4. To which-of-the-two does he give the praise? 5. Neither of the men has any abode. 6. Virtue alone gives true honours. 7. Life is troublesome to no good man. 8. Rome alone was head of (all) cities. 9. He was unfriendly to neither. 10. The one was pleasing to the citizens, the other was troublesome.

XIII.—COMPARISON OF ADJECTIVES.

Adjectives have three Degrees of Comparison : Positive, Comparative, and Superlative : as,

Positive.	Comparative.	Superlative.
Altŭs, *high.*	**Altiŏr,** *higher.*	**Altissĭmŭs,** { *highest, most high, or very high.*

The Comparative is formed by adding *iŏr* and the Superlative by adding *issĭmus* to the Positive, after taking away the termination of the Genitive Singular : as,

Posit.			Comp.	Sup.
Nom.	Gen.			
Altŭs,	**Alt-i,**	*high,*	**Alt-ior,**	**Alt-issĭmŭs,**
Lĕvĭs,	**Lĕv-is,**	*light,*	**Lĕv-ior,**	**Lĕv-issĭmŭs,**
Fēlix,	**Fēlĭc-is,**	*fortunate,*	**Fēlĭc-ior,**	**Fēlĭc-issĭmŭs,**
Prūdens,	**Prūdent-is,**	*prudent,*	**Prūdent-ior,**	**Prūdent-issĭmus.**

The Comparative is declined on p. 18 (mĕl-ior).

The Superlative is declined like bŏnus, bŏna, bŏnum.

EXCEPTIONS.

I. Adjectives ending in *er* form the Superlative in *rĭmus* : as,

Posit.			Comp.	Sup.
Nom.	Gen.			
pulcher,	pulchr-ī,	*beautiful,*	pulchr-ior,	pulcher-rĭmus.
līber,	lībĕr-ī,	*free,*	lībĕr-ior,	līber-rĭmus.
ācer,	acr-ĭs,	*sharp,*	ācr-ior,	ācer-rĭmus.
cĕler,	cĕlĕr-ĭs,	*swift,*	cĕlĕr-ior,	cĕler-rĭmus.

Also vĕtŭs (*Gen.* vĕtĕr-is), *old,* has a Superlative, vĕter-rĭmus,

II. The following six Adjectives ending in *ĭlis* form their Superlative in *ĭimus :* as,

Posit.		Comp.	Sup.
făcĭlis,	*easy,*	făcĭl-ior,	făcĭl-lĭmus.
diffĭcĭlis,	*difficult,*	diffĭcĭl-ior,	diffĭcĭl-lĭmus.
sĭmĭlis,	*like,*	sĭmĭl-ior,	sĭmĭl-lĭmus.
dissĭmĭlis,	*unlike,*	dissĭmĭl-ior,	dissĭmĭl-lĭmus.
grăcĭlis,	*thin,*	grăcĭl-ior,	grăcĭl-lĭmus.
hŭmĭlis,	*low,*	hŭmĭl-ior,	hŭmĭl-lĭmus.

IRREGULAR COMPARISON.

Posit.		Comp.	Sup.
bŏnus,	*good,*	mĕlior,	optĭmus.
mălus,	*bad,*	pējor,	pessĭmus.
magnus,	*great,*	mājor,	maxĭmus.
parvus,	*small,*	mĭnor,	mĭnĭmus.
multus,	*much,*	plūs (*neuter*),	plūrĭmus.
nēquam (*not declined*),	*worthless,*	nēquior,	nēquissĭmus.
dīves,	*rich,*	dītior,	dītissĭmus.
sĕnex,	*old,*	sĕnior [nātū *mājŏr*],	[maxĭmus *nātū*].
jŭvĕnis,	*young,*	jūnior [nātū *mĭnŏr*],	[mĭnĭmus *nātū*].
sŭpĕrus,	*upper,*	sŭpĕrior,	suprēmus, summus.
infĕrus,	*lower,*	infĕrior,	infĭmus, īmus.
extĕrus,	*outside,*	extĕrior,	extrēmus.
intĕrus,	*inward,*	intĕrior,	intĭmus.
postĕrus,	*behind,*	postĕrior,	postrēmus.
		prĭor (*former*),	prīmus (*first*).
		prŏpior (*nearer*),	proxĭmus (*nearest, next*).
		ultĕrior (*further*).	ultĭmus (*furthest, last*).

Declension of Plūs.

	Singular. Neut. only.	Plural. Masc. and Fem.	Neut.
Nom.	Plūs	Plūrēs	Plūră
Acc.	Plūs	Plūrēs	Plūră
Gen.	Plūrĭs	Plūrĭum	(of all genders)
Dat.	[Plūrī]	Plūrĭbŭs	(of all genders)
Abl.	Plūrĕ	Plūrĭbŭs	(of all genders)

RULE 9.—The English word *than* after the Comparative is translated by the Latin quam (indeclinable).

EXERCISE XVIII.

A.—1. Aestate dies longiores sunt quam noctes. 2. Tempore hiberno dies sunt breviores. 3. Lepores timidiores sunt quam canes. 4. Noctes brevissimae sunt aestate. 5. Roma clarissima urbs Italiae erat. 6. Ferrum utilissimum est metallorum. 7. Radices arborum longissimae sunt. 8. Nihil est amabilius quam virtus. 9. Lux est velocior quam sonitus. 10. Nihil in amicitia perniciosius est quam adulatio.

1. Men are stronger than women. 2. Iron is more useful than gold. / 3. The hare is a very timid animal 4. Nothing is more excellent than virtue. 5. The roots of oak-trees are very strong and very long. 6. The Rhine is a very rapid river. 7. The eyes of the eagle are very keen. 8. The days are calmer in summer than in winter. 9. In winter time the light is feebler than in summer. 10. Nothing is more destructive to friendship than flattery.

B.—1. In bello miserrimi sunt agricolae. 2. Filiae matri sunt simillimae. 3. Itinera antiquis temporibus difficillima erant. 4. Pulcherrima est imago regis. 5. Facillimi erant labores militum. 6. Pulcherrima animalia non semper sunt utilissima. 7. Veterrima vina non semper sunt dulcissima. 8. Vultures acerrimos habent oculos. 9. Pulcherrimi sunt colores florum. 10. In Helvetia sunt asperrimi montes.

1. The scent of flowers is very sweet. 2. The work is very difficult. 3. The journey was very long and very rough. 4. The eyes of the vulture are very keen. 5. Helvetia is a very rugged land. 6. The swiftest animals are not always the strongest. 7. The legs of the stag are very slender. 8. The son was very like (his) father (*dat.*). 9. War is the cause of many crimes. 10. In summer the sun is more powerful than in winter.

'**C.**—1. Nihil est melius quam sapientia. 2. Sol major est quam terra. 3. Luna minor est quam terra. 4. Plurima et maxima animalia sunt in mari. 5. Optimae erant leges Romanae. 6. Pessimae sunt consuetudines discipulorum. 7. Melior est certa pax quam sperata victoria. 8. Simulatio amoris est pejor quam odium. 9. Cato optimus erat suae aetatis orator. 10. Aquilae vis maxima est.

1. Hatred is better than flattery. 2. Very many men give the greatest praise to Cato. 3. The best orator is not always the best citizen. 4. The most wicked men slay the most excellent (men). 5. No state was ever more renowned than Rome. 6. The best men are not always the most powerful. 7. They give the honour to the most excellent citizens. 8. Very many islands are larger than Sicily. 9. Sicily is a smaller island than Britain. 10. The Greeks were more learned than the Romans.

XIV.—The Numerals.

Cardinal Numerals denote number simply or absolutely : as, ūnŭs, *one* ; dŭŏ, *two* ; trēs, *three*.

The declension of ūnŭs is given on p. 23.

> *Obs. Unus* is used in the Plural with Plural Nouns which have a singular meaning : as, ūnă castră, *one camp* ; ūnae aedēs, *one house* ; ūnae littĕrae, *one letter*.

Arabic Symbols.	Roman Symbols.	Cardinals.	Ordinals.
1	I	ūnus	prīmus.
2	II	dŭŏ	sĕcundus or altĕr.
3	III	trēs	tertĭus.
4	IV	quattŭŏr (quătŭŏr)	quartus.
5	V	quinquĕ	quintus.
6	VI	sex	sextus.
7	VII	septem	septĭmus.
8	VIII	octŏ	octāvus.
9	IX	nŏvem	nōnus.
10	X	dĕcem	dĕcĭmus.
11	XI	undĕcim	undĕcĭmus.
12	XII	duŏdĕcim	duŏdĕcĭmus.
13	XIII	trĕdĕcim	tertĭus dĕcĭmus.
14	XIV	quattuordĕcim	quartus dĕcĭmus.
15	XV	quindĕcim	quintus dĕcĭmus.
16	XVI	sēdĕcim	sextus dĕcĭmus.
17	XVII	septemdĕcim	septĭmus dĕcĭmus.
18	XVIII	duŏdēvīgintī	duŏdēvīcēsĭmus.
19	XIX	undēvīgintī	undēvīcēsĭmus.
20	XX	vīgintī	vīcēsĭmus.
21	XXI	ūnus et vīgintī or vīgintī ūnus	prīmus et vīcēsĭmus, or vīcēsĭmus prīmus.
22	XXII	dŭŏ et vīgintī or vīgintī duo	alter et vīcēsĭmus, or vīcēsĭmus alter.
23	XXIII	trēs et vīgintī or vīgintī trēs	tertĭus et vīcēsĭmus, or vīcēsĭmus tertĭus.
28	XXVIII	duŏdētrīgintā	duŏdētrīgēsĭmus.
29	XXIX	undētrigintā	undētrīgēsĭmus.
30	XXX	trīgintā	trīgēsĭmus.
40	XL	quadrāgintā	quadrāgēsĭmus.
50	L	quinquāgintā	quinquāgēsĭmus.
60	LX	sexāgintā	sexāgēsĭmus.
70	LXX	septūāgintā	septūāgēsĭmus.
80	LXXX	octōgintā	octōgēsĭmus.
90	XC	nōnāgintā	nōnāgēsĭmus.
100	C	centum	centēsĭmus.
200	CC	dŭcentī, ae, ă	ducentēsĭmus.
300	CCC	trĕcentī, ae, ă	trĕcentēsĭmus.
400	CCCC	quadringentī, ae, ă	quadringentēsĭmus.
500	D or IƆ	quingentī, ae, ă	quingentēsĭmus.
600	DC	sexcentī, ae, ă	sexcentēsĭmus.
700	DCC	septingentī, ae, ă	septingentēsĭmus.
800	DCCC	octingentī, ae, ă	octingentēsĭmus.
900	DCCCC	nongentī, ae, ă	nongentēsĭmus.
1,000	M or CIƆ	millĕ	millēsĭmus.
2,000	MM	dŭŏ milliă	bis millēsĭmus.
100,000	CCCIƆƆƆ	centum milliă	centiēs millēsĭmus.

Dŭŏ, *two*, trēs, *three*, and millĭă, *thousands*, are declined as follows:—

	M.	F.	N.	M. and F.	N.	N.
Nom.	Du-ŏ	du-ae	du-ŏ	Trēs	trĭă	Millĭă
Acc.	Du-ōɟ or duŏ }du-ăs	du-ăs	du-ŏ	Trēs *or* trĭs	trĭă	Millĭă
Gen.	Du-ōrum	du-ărum	du-ōrum	Trĭum (of all genders)		Millĭum
Dat.	Du-ōbŭs	du-ăbŭs	du-ōbŭs	Trĭbŭs (of all genders)		Millĭbus
Abl.	Du-ōbŭs	du-ăbŭs	du-ōbŭs	Trĭbŭs (of all genders)		Millĭbus

    Obs. Ambŏ, *both*, is declined like duo.

Millĕ, *a thousand*, in the singular is an indeclinable adjective; but millĭă, *thousands*, in the plural, is a Substantive: as, millĕ hŏmĭnēs, *a thousand men;* but dŭŏ millĭă hŏmĭnum, *two thousand men*, literally, *two thousands of men.*

The Cardinal Numerals from quattŭŏr, *four*, to centum, *a hundred*, are indeclinable.

Dŭcentī, ae, ă, *two hundred*, and the following hundreds, are declined regularly.

Ordinal Numerals denote numbers regarded as forming parts of a series: as, prīmŭs, *first;* sĕcundŭs, or altĕr, *second.* They are declined regularly as adjectives.

EXERCISE XIX.

1. Homo habet unum ŏs, dnas aures, duos oculos. 2. Magister puero tres libros dat. 3. Sunt (*there are*) sedecim mala, viginti pruna, undeviginti pira, duodeviginti cerasa. 4. In capite hominis sexaginta tria sunt ossa. 5. In exercitu Alexandri Magni duodecim millia Macedonum erant. 6. Xerxes habet classem mille ducentarum navium. 7. In legione Romana erant cohortes decem, manipuli triginta, centuriae sexaginta. 8. Septem erant reges Romani; primus erat Romulus, secundus Numa Pompilius, tertius Tullus Hostilius, quartus Ancus Martius, quintus Tarquinius Priscus, sextus Servius Tullius, septimus Tarquinius Superbus. 9. Augustus octavus est anni mensis. 10. Manipulus erat trigesima pars legionis Romanae.

1. The wise (men) of Greece were seven. 2. The first king of Rome was warlike. 3. They slay the tenth part of the men. 4. In a Roman legion (there) were ten cohorts, thirty maniples, sixty centuries. 5. They slay ten thousand men (*gen.*) in the war. 6. The second king of Rome was just and mild. 7. The seventh king of Rome was unjust and wicked. 8. In the first month of the year (there) are thirty-one days. 9. Rome has two consuls. 10. A Roman legion has five thousand foot-soldiers (*gen.*), three hundred horse-soldiers.*

---

   * The number of soldiers in a legion varied considerably at different periods.

XV.--THE VERB SUM, *I am.*

Sum, fŭi, fŭtūrŭs, essĕ,—*to be.*

VERB FINITE.

INDICATIVE MOOD.

1. PRESENT TENSE.

Sing. Sum,	*I am*		*Plur.* Sŭmŭs,	*We are*
Ĕs,	*thou art*		Estĭs,	*ye are*
Est,	*he is.*		Sunt,	*they are.*

2. FUTURE SIMPLE TENSE.

Sing. Ĕro,	*I shall be*		*Plur.* Ĕrĭmŭs,	*We shall be*
Ĕrĭs,	*thou wilt be*		Ĕrĭtĭs,	*ye will be*
Ĕrĭt,	*he will be.*		Ĕrunt,	*they will be.*

3. IMPERFECT TENSE.

Sing. Ĕram,	*I was*		*Plur.* Ĕrămŭs,	*We were*
Ĕrăs,	*thou wast*		Ĕrătĭs,	*ye were*
Ĕrăt,	*he was.*		Ĕrant,	*they were.*

4. PERFECT TENSE.

Sing. Fŭi,	*I have been, or I was*		*Plur.* Fŭĭmŭs,	*We have been, or we were*
Fuistĭ,	*thou hast been, or thou wast*		Fuistĭs,	*ye have been, or ye were*
Fŭit,	*he has been, or he was.*		Fŭĕrunt or fŭĕrĕ	*they have been, or they were.*

5. FUTURE-PERFECT TENSE.

Sing. Fŭĕro,	*I shall have been*		*Plur.* Fŭĕrĭmŭs,	*We shall have been*
Fŭĕrĭs,	*thou wilt have been*		Fŭĕrĭtĭs,	*ye will have been*
Fŭĕrĭt,	*he will have been.*		Fŭĕrint,	*they will have been.*

6. PLUPERFECT TENSE.

Sing. Fŭĕram,	*I had been*		*Plur.* Fŭĕrămŭs,	*We had been*
Fŭĕrăs,	*thou hadst been*		Fŭĕrătĭs,	*ye had been*
Fŭĕrăt,	*he had been.*		Fŭĕrant,	*they had been.*

IMPERATIVE MOOD.

1. PRESENT TENSE.

Sing. Ĕs,	*Be thou.*		*Plur.* Estĕ,	*Be ye.*

2. FUTURE TENSE.

Sing. Estō,	*Thou shalt or must be*		*Plur.* Estōtĕ,	*Ye shall or must be*
Estō,	*he shall or must be, or let him be.*		Sunto,	*they shall or must be, or let them be.*

SUBJUNCTIVE MOOD.

1. PRESENT TENSE.

Sing. **Sim,**	*I may be*	*Plur.* **Sĭmŭs,**	*We may be*
Sīs,	*thou mayst be*	**Sītĭs,**	*ye may be*
Sīt,	*he may be.*	**Sint,**	*they may be.*

Obs. The first and third Persons singular and plural of the Present
Subjunctive are often used as Imperatives; as, sint cīvēs justī,
let the citizens be just.

2. IMPERFECT TENSE.

Sing. **Essem** or **fŏrem,** }	*I might be*	*Plur.* **Essēmŭs** or **fŏrēmŭs,** }	*We might be*
Essēs or **fŏrēs,** }	*thou mightst be*	**Essētĭs** or **fŏrētĭs,** }	*ye might be*
Essĕt or **fŏrĕt,** }	*he might be.*	**Essent** or **fŏrent,** }	*they might be.*

3. PERFECT TENSE.

Sing. **Fŭĕrim,**	*I may have been*	*Plur.* **Fŭĕrimŭs,**	*We may have been*
Fŭĕrĭs,	*thou mayst have been*	**Fŭĕritĭs,**	*ye may have been*
Fŭĕrĭt,	*he may have been.*	**Fŭĕrint,**	*they may have been.*

4. PLUPERFECT TENSE.

Sing. **Fuissem,**	*I should* }*have*	*Plur.* **Fuissēmŭs,**	*We should* }*have*
Fuissēs,	*thou wouldst* }*been.*	**Fuissētĭs,**	*ye would* }*been.*
Fuissĕt,	*he would*	**Fuissent,**	*they would*

VERB INFINITE.

INFINITIVE PRESENT, AND IMPERFECT, }	**Essĕ,**	*to be.*
INFINITIVE PERFECT, AND PLUPERFECT, }	**Fuissĕ,**	*to have been.*
INFINITIVE FUTURE,	**Fŭtūrŭs essĕ,** or **fŏrĕ,**	*to be about to be.*
PARTICIPLE FUTURE,	**Fŭtūrŭs, -a, -um,**	*about to be.*

NOTE.—A vowel before another vowel is usually short, and will
therefore in future not be marked.

The Verb Sum.—Indicative Mood.

EXERCISE XX.

A.—1. Sum laetus. 2. Es tristis. 3. Non diligens fuisti, Tite.
4. Probi filii gaudium patris erunt. 5. Opera tua multis hominibus
erunt utilia. 6. Dux vester ero : victores erimus. 7. Si contenti
eritis, pauperes non eritis. 8. Multi erunt pauperes, qui (*who*)
divites fuerant. 9. Cives urbis liberae sumus. 10. Custodes
miserae puellae fuistis.

1. We are joyful. 2. Ye are sad. 3. I am a Roman citizen.
4. The contented (*pl.*) are always joyful ; the rich (*pl.*) are often

sad. 5. If ye are good, ye are rich. 6. If thou wilt be diligent, thou wilt be learned. 7. The wicked man is not free. 8. They had been unlearned, now they are learned. 9. Ye will be rich and free. 10. The Roman state was renowned.

Imperative Mood.

B.—1. Judex custos severus juris esto. 2. Probi este, pueri, et felices eritis. 3. Discipuli sunto attenti. 4. Judices justi sunto. 5. Reipublicae salus civibus cara esto. 6. Amici fideles sunto. 7. Reges patres patriae sunto. 8. Attenti este, discipuli. 9. Contenti estote sorte vestra. 10. Praeceptorum memores este.

1. Be diligent, scholars. 2. Praise shall be the reward of diligence. 3. Be faithful, friends! 4. The judge must be just. 5. They are contented; they shall be rich. 6. Let there be no cause of enmity; we are faithful friends. 7. Be just, be upright; thou wilt be successful. 8. Be brave, soldiers! 9. Let the citizens be free, let them be happy! 10. Let the city be the booty of the soldiers.

XVI.—Compounds of Sum.

Absum,	*I am absent.*
Adsum,	*I am present, stand by, side with.*
Dĕsum,	*I am wanting.*
Insum,	*I am in.*
Intersum,	*I am among.*
Obsum,	*I am in the way, am hurtful to, injure.*
Praesum,	*I am before, am at the head of.*
Prōsum,	*I am serviceable, do good to.*
Subsum,	*I am under, or amongst.*
Sŭpersum,	*I remain over, survive.*

All these compounds of Sum are followed by the Dative Case. They are conjugated like Sum, but Prōsum takes *d* before *e* : as

INDICATIVE.

Present.

Sing. Prō-sum	*Plur.* Prō-sŭmŭs
Prōd-ĕs	Prōd-estĭs
Prōd-est.	Prō-sunt.

Future.	*Imperfect.*
Prōd-ĕro.	Prōd-ĕram.

INFINITIVE—*Present.*
Prōd-esse.

EXERCISE XXI.

1. Bonis hominibus non deerunt amici.   2. Cicero reipublicae profuit.   3. Legionibus Romanis duces praefuerunt fortes.   4. Alexander Magnus multis proeliis interfuit.   5. Equitum multitudo exercitui nostro proderit.   6. Miles fortis omnibus aderit periculis.   7. Variae cupiditates animo insunt.   8. Frigus multi plantis non prodest. 9. Militibus deerat animus.   10. Auxilium meum reipublicae non profuit.

1. To good men friends are not wanting.   2. Cicero was serviceable to the commonwealth.   3. A good citizen sides-with his native country in the time of danger.   4. Indolence is hurtful to all men. 5. Alexander the Great survived many battles.   6. The general was amongst his soldiers in the battle.   7. Light is serviceable to all animals.   8. The general is-at-the-head-of the army.   9. Anger has been hurtful to many.   10. The soul survives the body.

XVII.—THE PRONOUNS.

I. PERSONAL PRONOUNS.

1. *Pronoun of the First Person.*

	Sing.		Plur.	
Nom. Ĕgŏ,	I	Nōs,		we
Acc. Mĕ,	me	Nōs,		us
Gen. Mĕ̄ī,	of me	Nostrī and nostrum,		of us
Dat. Mĭhī,	to or for me	Nōbīs,		to or for us
Abl. Mĕ,	by, with, or from me.	Nōbīs,		by, with, or from us.

2. *Pronoun of the Second Person.*

	Sing.		Plur.	
N.V. Tū,	thou	Vōs,		ye
Acc. Tĕ,	thee	Vōs,		you
Gen. Tŭī,	of thee	Vestrī and vestrum,		of you
Dat. Tĭbī,	to or for thee	Vōbīs,		to or for you
Abl. Tĕ,	by, with, or from thee.	Vōbīs,		by, with, or from you.

3. *Pronoun of the Third Person.*

For the Pronoun of the Third Person, *he, she, it,* ĭs, ĕă, ĭd is usually employed.   (See p. 35.)

II. Reflective Pronoun of the Third Person.

The Reflective Pronoun refers to the Subject of the sentence, and cannot therefore have a Nominative case.

Sing. and Plur.

Acc. **Sē** or **sēsē,** *himself, herself, itself,* or *themselves.*
Gen. **Sui,** *of himself, herself, itself,* or *themselves.*
Dat. **Sĭbi,** *to* or *for himself, herself, itself,* or *themselves.*
Abl. **Sē** or **sēsē,** *by* or *from himself, herself, itself,* or *themselves.*

There are no distinct reflective forms in the 1st and 2nd persons; the different cases of *ego* and *tu* being used reflectively: as mei, *of myself;* tĭbi, *to thyself,* etc.

III. Possessive Pronouns.

These are formed from the First and Second Personal and the Third Reflective Pronouns, and are declined as adjectives:

M.	F.	N.	
Meus,	**mea,**	**meum,**	*my* or *mine.*
Tuus,	**tua,**	**tuum,**	*thy* or *thine.*
Noster,	**nostra,**	**nostrum,**	*our, ours.*
Vester,	**vestra,**	**vestrum,**	*your, yours.*
Suus,	**sua,**	**suum,**	*his, her, its, their.*

Example XXII.

1. Ego sum laetus, tu es tristis. 2. Pater mihi librum dat utilem. 3. In me et in te et in nobis omnibus est animus immortalis. 4. Patria mihi carior est quam vita. 5. Omnia tua consilia nobis nota sunt. 6. Parentes vobis cari sunto. 7. Memores sumus tui. 8. Amicus memor est vestri. 9. Memoria nostri nobis grata est. 10. Mihi mea vita, tibi tua (vita) cara est.

1. Thy father is dear to thee; mine to me. 2. Wisdom and counsel are wanting to you, citizens! 3. In thee is all our hope and safety. 4. Let thy native-land be ever most dear to thee. 5. Thine indolence is-in-the-way, Titus! 6. A true friend will be with thee in the time of danger. 7. The memory of our works survives us. 8. In neither battle was the general amongst his soldiers. 9. He was serviceable to his friends; he was hurtful to his enemies. 10. To us the victory is joyful, to you it is most sad.

IV. Demonstrative Pronouns.

1. Hic, haec, hoc, *this (near me)*; pl. *these*.

		Sing.			Plur.	
	M.	**F.**	**N**	**M.**	**F.**	**N.**
Nom.	Hic	haec	hoc	Hī	hae	haec
Acc.	Hunc	hanc	hoc	Hōs	hās	haec
Gen.	Hūjus			Hōrum	hārum	hōrum
Dat.	Huīc			Hīs		
Abl.	Hōc	hāc	hōc	Hīs		

2. Istĕ, istă, istŭd, *that (near you)*, *that of yours*; pl. *those*.

Nom.	Istŏ	istă	istŭd	Istī	istae	istă
Acc.	Istum	istam	istŭd	Istōs	istās	istă
Gen.	Istīus			Istōrum	istārum	istōrum
Dat.	Istī			Istīs		
Abl.	Istō	istă	istō	Istīs		

3. Illĕ, illă, illŭd, *that, that yonder*; pl. *those*.

Nom.	Illĕ	illă	illŭd	Illī	illae	illă
Acc.	Illum	illam	illŭd	Illōs	illās	illă
Gen.	Illīus			Illōrum	illārum	illōrum
Dat.	Illī			Illīs		
Abl.	Illō	illă	illō	Illīs		

Exercise XXIII.

1. Haec carmina suavissima sunt. 2. Hi montes altissimi sunt. 3. Liberi agricolarum illorum diligentes fuerunt. 4. Dat tibi illud carmen pulcherrimum. 5. Hic puer industrius est, ille iners. 6. Demosthenes et Cicero clarissimi oratores fuerunt; ille erat Graecus, hic autem Romanus. 7. Iste tuus amicus vir est optimus. 8. Ista vestra auctoritas est maxima. 9. Memoria harum rerum nobis jucundissima est. 10. Nomen illius poëtae clarissimum est.

1. These mountains are very high and very rugged. 2. That indolence (of yours) is hurtful to you (*sing.*), Titus. 3. The immortal soul will survive this mortal body. 4. That one man has always been hurtful to the commonwealth. 5. The memory of that one day was to Cicero most delightful. 6. That song (of yours) is to me most pleasant. 7. This my son is careful and industrious. 8. This life (of ours) is short; but that-one (ille) is immortal. 9. Those hands (of yours) are always busy. 10. These citizens are serviceable to the commonwealth; those are hurtful.

V. Determinate, Relative, and Interrogative Pronouns.

1. Is, eă, ĭd, *he, she, it, that*, referring to the former part of a sentence.

	Sing.			Plur.		
	M.	F.	N.	M.	F.	N.
Nom.	Ĭs	eă	ĭd	Iĭ	eae	eă
Acc.	Eum	eam	ĭd	Eŏs	eăs	eă
Gen.	Ĕjus			Eŏrum	ĕărum	eŏrum
Dat.	Eī			Iĭs *or* eĭs		
Abl.	Eŏ	eă	eŏ	Iĭs *or* eĭs		

2. Ĭdem, eădem, ĭdem, *the same.*

Nom.	Ĭdem	eădem	ĭdem	Iĭdem	eaedem	eădem
Acc.	Eundem	eandem	ĭdem	Eŏsdem	eăsdem	eădem
Gen.	Ĕjusdem			Eŏrundem	eărundem	eŏrundem
Dat.	Eĭdem			Iĭsdem *or* eisdem		
Abl.	Eŏdem	eădem	eŏdem	Iĭsdem *or* eisdem		

3. Ipsĕ, ipsă, ipsum, *self, himself, herself, itself*

Nom.	Ipsĕ	ipsă	ipsum	Ipsī	ipsae	ipsă
Acc.	Ipsum	ipsam	ipsum	Ipsŏs	ipsăs	ipsă
Gen.	Ipsīus			Ipsŏrum	ipsărum	ipsŏrum
Dat.	Ipsī			Ipsīs		
Abl.	Ipsŏ	ipsă	ipsŏ	Ipsīs		

4. Relative—Quī, quae, quŏd, *who* or *which.*

Nom.	Quī	quae	quŏd	Quī	quae	quae
Acc.	Quem	quam	quŏd	Quŏs	quăs	quae
Gen.	Cūjus			Quŏrum	quărum	quŏrum
Dat.	Cuī			Quībus *or* quīs		
Abl.	Quŏ	quă	quŏ	Quībus *or* quīs		

5. Interrogative—Quĭs or quī, quae, quĭd or quŏd, *who? which? what?*

Nom.	Quĭs & quī	quae	quĭd & quŏd	Quī	quae	quae
Acc.	Quem	quam	quĭd & quŏd	Quŏs	quăs	quae
Gen.	Cūjus			Quŏrum	quărum	quŏrum
Dat.	Cuī			Quībus *or* quīs		
Abl.	Quŏ	quă	quŏ	Quībus *or* quīs		

The forms **quis** and **quid** are used by themselves, without a Noun: as, Quis es? *who art thou?* Quid est? *what is it?* The forms **qui** and **quŏd** are used interrogatively with a Noun: as Quī hŏmo ĕs? *what man art thou?* Quŏd mărĕ, *what sea?*

RULE 10.—The Relative Pronoun agrees with the Antecedent in Gender, Number, and Person, but not in Case : as, Fēlix est rex quem omnēs cīvēs laudant, *Fortunate is the king whom all citizens praise.*

Lĕgĭt, (*he, she, it*) *reads.*   Lĕgunt, (*they*) *read.*

EXERCISE XXIV.

A.—1. Amicum fidum habet; ei addictus est. 2. Sallustius est elegantissimus scriptor; ille ejus libros legit. 3. Qui amico in periculis adest, is verus amicus est. 4. Ii sunt cives boni qui reipublicae prosunt. 5. Ipse labor nobis jucundus est. 6. Fons omnium voluptatum in nobis ipsis est. 7. Melior pars tui ipsius immortalis est. 8. Non minor pugna erat cum mulieribus Cimbrorum quam cum Cimbris ipsis. 9. Idem dies erit initium vitae aeternae. 10. Non omnibus hominibus eadem prosunt.

* In translating this sentence, begin with *is verus amicus est.*

1. He has a faithful friend; he will never injure him. 2. My brother himself is a most elegant writer. 3. (He) who gives honours to the bad is hurtful to the state.* 4. The wives of the Cimbrians were themselves brave. 5. The same (things) injure some, do good to others. 6. (He) who is hurtful to the commonwealth is hurtful to himself.* 7. The same (things) are not pleasing to all (men). 8. Demosthenes himself was not always pleasing to his (fellow) citizens. 9. Cicero is a faithful friend; I am devoted to him. 10. Cicero is a most elegant writer; they read his books.

* In sentences 3 and 6 begin with *qui*, and afterwards use *is :* see Latin sentences, No. 3.

B.—1. Quis habet exercitum? Quis est dux? 2. Cujus est equus? Cujus sunt arma? 3. Quae civitas habet optimas leges? 4. Quod animal est maximum et validissimum? 5. Quorum animalium sunt vires maximae? 6. Qui color pulcherrimus est? 7. Qui orator optimus et dulcissimus est? 8. Quorum arma sunt optima? 9. Cui dat (*does he give*) coronam? 10. Quod tempus felicius est quam praesens?

1. Which constellation is the most beautiful? 2. Which poet is the sweetest? 3. Who is he? what has he? 4. Who gives the book to thee? 5. To whom does he give the greatest praise? 6. Whose (*sing.*) is the victory? Whose (*pl.*) is the booty? 7. Which tax is the greatest? 8. Which king has the greatest taxes? 9. What animal is more sagacious (prudens) than the elephant? 10. What animal is more rapacious than the lion?

XVIII.—The Verb.

Latin Verbs have two Voices :

    I. Active.   II. Passive.

Verbs have two Parts

    I. Finite.   II. Infinite.

I. The Verb Finite has Three Moods :

    (1.) The Indicative Mood.
    (2.) The Subjunctive Mood.
    (3.) The Imperative Mood.

II. The Verb Infinite consists of Verbal Nouns and
    Adjectives :

    (1.) The Infinitive, which is a Verbal Noun.
    (2.) The Participle, which is a Verbal Adjective.
    (3.) The Supine, } which are Verbal Nouns.
    (4.) The Gerund, }

Verbs have Six Tenses :

    I. Three expressing unfinished action :

        Present.
        Future Simple.
        Imperfect.

    II. Three expressing finished action :

        Perfect.
        Future Perfect.
        Pluperfect.

Verbs have two Numbers, Singular and Plural, and
three Persons in each number.

Latin Verbs are arranged in four Classes, called Conjugations, distinguished by the final letter of the Stem,
which is seen in the Infinitive Active. The Stem of

                                       Infinitive.

I. The first Conjugation ends in **A** : ..   .. as, **ămă-rĕ**, *to love.*
II. The Second ,,   ,,   **E** : ..   .. as, **mŏnē-rĕ**, *to advise.*
III. The Third ,,   ,, a **Consonant** or **U** : as, **rĕg-ĕrĕ**, *to rule,*
                                                lu-ĕrĕ, *to pay.*
IV. The Fourth ,,   ,,   **I** : ..   .. as, **audī-rĕ**, *to hear.*

The Present Indicative, the Perfect Indicative, the Present Infinitive, and the Supine are called the *Principal
Parts* of the Verb; because it is necessary to know these
in order to conjugate a Verb.

XIX.—First or **A** Conjugation.—Active Voice.

Amo, ămăvī, ămătum, ămărĕ,—*to love.* Stem : ăma-.

VERB FINITE.

INDICATIVE MOOD.

1. Present Tense.

Sing. Amo,	*I love,* or *am loving*	*Plur.* Am-ămŭs,	*We love,* or *are loving*
Am-ăs,	*thou lovest,* or *art loving*	Am-ătĭs,	*ye love,* or *are loving*
Am-ăt,	*he loves,* or *is loving.*	Am-ant,	*they love,* or *are loving.*

2. Future-Simple Tense.

Sing. Am-ăbo,	*I shall love*	*Plur.* Am-ăbĭmŭs,	*We shall love*
Am-ăbĭs,	*thou wilt love*	Am-ăbĭtĭs,	*ye will love*
Am-ăbĭt,	*he will love.*	Am-ăbunt,	*they will love.*

3. Imperfect Tense.

Sing. Am-ăbam,	*I was loving*	*Plur.* Am-ăbămŭs,	*We were loving*
Am-ăbās,	*thou wast loving*	Am-ăbătĭs,	*ye were loving*
Am-ăbăt,	*he was loving.*	Am-ăbant,	*they were loving.*

4. Perfect Tense.

Sing. Am-ăvī,	*I have loved,* or *I loved*	*Plur.* Am-ăvĭmŭs,	*We have loved,* or *we loved*
Am-ăvistī,	*thou hast loved,* or *thou lovedst*	Am-ăvistĭs,	*ye have loved,* or *ye loved*
Am-ăvĭt,	*he has loved,* or *he loved.*	Am-ăvērunt, or ăm-ăvērĕ }	*they have loved,* or *they loved.*

5. Future-Perfect Tense.

Sing. Am-ăvēro,	*I shall* } *have loved.*	*Plur.* Am-ăvĕrimŭs,	*We shall* } *have loved.*
Am-ăvĕrĭs,	*thou wilt* }	Am-ăvĕritĭs,	*ye will* }
Am-ăvĕrĭt,	*he will* }	Am-ăvĕrint,	*they will* }

6. Pluperfect Tense.

Sing. Am-ăvĕram,	*I had loved*	*Plur.* Am-ăvĕrămŭs,	*We had loved*
Am-ăvĕrās,	*thou hadst loved*	Am-ăvĕrătĭs,	*ye had loved*
Am-ăvĕrăt,	*he had loved.*	Am-ăvĕrant,	*they had loved.*

IMPERATIVE MOOD.

Present Tense.

Sing. Am-ă,	*Love thou.*	*Plur.* Am-ătĕ,	*Love ye.*

Future Tense.

Sing. Am-ăto,	*Thou shalt* or *must love*	*Plur.* Am-ătōtĕ,	*Ye shall* or *must love*
Am-ăto,	*he shall* or *must love.*	Am-anto,	*they shall* or *must love.*

SUBJUNCTIVE MOOD.*

1. PRESENT TENSE.

Sing. **Am-em,** *I may love*
    Am-ēs, *thou mayst love*
    Am-ĕt, *he may love.*

Plur. **Am-ēmŭs,** *We may love*
    Am-ētĭs, *ye may love*
    Am-ent, *they may love.*

2. IMPERFECT TENSE.

Sing. **Am-ārem,** *I might love*
    Am-ārēs, *thou mightst love*
    Am-ārĕt, *he might love.*

Plur. **Am-ārēmŭs,** *We might love*
    Am-ārētĭs, *ye might love*
    Am-ārent, *they might love.*

3. PERFECT TENSE.

S. **Am-āvĕrim,** *I may* ⎫
    Am-āvĕrĭs, *thou mayst* ⎬ *have loved.*
    Am-āvĕrĭt, *he may* ⎭

P. **Am-āvĕrimŭs,** *We may* ⎫
    Am-āvĕritĭs, *ye may* ⎬ *have loved*
    Am-āvĕrint. *they may* ⎭

4. PLUPERFECT TENSE.

S. **Am-āvissem,** *I should* ⎫
    Am-āvissēs, *thou wouldst* ⎬ *have loved.*
    Am-āvissĕt, *he would* ⎭

P. **Am-āvissēmŭs,** *We should* ⎫
    Am-āvissētĭs, *ye would* ⎬ *have loved.*
    Am-āvissent, *they would* ⎭

* The 1st and 3rd Persons of the Present Subjunctive are often used with a kind of Imperative sense : *ămem, let me love ; ămēmus, let us love.* Concerning the translation of the Subjunctive Mood in general, see p. 47.

VERB INFINITE.

INFINITIVES.

PRES. and IMP. } **Am-ārĕ,** *to love.*

PERF. and PLUP. } **Am-āvissĕ,** { *to have loved.*

FUTURE. { **Am-ātūrŭs essĕ,** { *to be about to love.*

GERUND.

Gen. **Am-andī,** *of loving*
Dat. **Am-andō,** *for loving*
Acc. **Am-andum,** *the loving*
Abl. **Am-andō,** *by loving.*

SUPINES.

Am-ătum, *to love.*
Am-ătū, *to be loved.*

PARTICIPLES.

PRESENT. **Am-ans, -antis,** *loving.*
FUTURE. **Am-ātūrŭs (ă, um),** *about [to love.*

NOTE.—In all the Perfect Tenses *vi* and *ve* may be omitted before *s* and *r :* as,

ămāvistī	becomes	ămastī	ămāvĕro	becomes	ămāro
ămāvistĭs	„	ămastĭs	ămāvĕram	„	ămāram
ămāvērunt	„	ămārunt	ămāvĕrim	„	ămārim
but ămāvērĕ does not become			ămāvissem	„	ămassem
ămārĕ, which would be con-			ămāvissĕ	„	ămassĕ
founded with the Present Infin.					

XX.—SECOND OR E CONJUGATION.—ACTIVE VOICE.

Mŏneo, mŏnui, mŏnǐtum, mŏnērĕ,—*to advise.* Stem: mŏne-.

VERB FINITE.

INDICATIVE MOOD.

1. PRESENT TENSE.

S. **Mŏn-eo,**	*I advise,* or *am advising*	*P.* **Mŏn-ēmŭs,**	*We advise,* or *are advising*
Mŏn-ēs,	*thou advisest,* or *art advising*	**Mŏn-ētis,**	*ye advise,* or *are advising*
Mŏn-ĕt,	*he advises,* or *is advising.*	**Mŏn-ent,**	*they advise,* or *are advising.*

2. FUTURE-SIMPLE TENSE.

S. **Mŏn-ēbo,**	*I shall advise*	*P.* **Mŏn-ēbǐmŭs,**	*We shall advise*
Mŏn-ēbǐs,	*thou wilt advise*	**Mŏn-ēbǐtǐs,**	*ye will advise*
Mŏn-ēbǐt,	*he will advise.*	**Mŏn-ēbunt,**	*they will advise.*

3. IMPERFECT TENSE.

S. **Mŏn-ēbam,**	*I was advising*	*P.* **Mŏn-ēbāmŭs,**	*We were advising*
Mŏn-ēbās,	*thou wast advising*	**Mŏn-ēbātǐs,**	*ye were advising*
Mŏn-ēbăt,	*he was advising.*	**Mŏn·ēbant,**	*they were advising.*

4. PERFECT TENSE.

S. **Mŏn-ui,**	*I have advised,* or *I advised*	*P.* **Mŏn-uǐmŭs,**	*We have advised,* or *we advised*
Mŏn-uistī,	*thou hast advised,* or *advisedst*	**Mŏn-uistǐs,**	*ye have advised,* or *ye advised*
Mŏn-uǐt,	*he has advised,* or *he advised.*	**Mŏn-uērunt,** or **-uērĕ,**	*they have advised,* or *they advised.*

5. FUTURE-PERFECT TENSE.

S. **Mŏn-uĕro,**	*I shall*	*P.* **Mŏn-uĕrimŭs,**	*We shall*
Mŏn-uĕrǐs,	*thou wilt* } *have advised.*	**Mŏn-uĕritǐs,**	*ye will* } *have advised.*
Mŏn-uĕrǐt,	*he will*	**Mŏn-uĕrint,**	*they will*

6. PLUPERFECT TENSE.

S. **Mŏn-uĕram,**	*I had advised*	*P.* **Mŏn-uĕrāmŭs,**	*We had advised*
Mŏn-uĕrās,	*thou hadst advised*	**Mŏn-uĕrātǐs,**	*ye had advised*
Mŏn-uĕrăt,	*he had advised.*	**Mŏn-uĕrant,**	*they had advised.*

IMPERATIVE MOOD.

PRESENT TENSE.

S. **Mŏn-ē,**	*Advise thou.*	*P.* **Mŏn-ētĕ,**	*Advise ye.*

FUTURE TENSE.

S. **Mŏn-ēto,**	*Thou shalt* or *must advise*	*P.* **Mŏn-ētōtĕ,**	*Ye must advise*
Mŏn-ēto,	*he shall* or *must advise.*	**Mŏn-ento,**	*they must advise.*

SUBJUNCTIVE MOOD.

1. PRESENT TENSE.

S. **Mŏn-eam,**	*I may advise*	*P.* **Mŏn-eāmŭs,**	*We may advise*
Mŏn-eās,	*thou mayst advise*	**Mŏn-eātĭs,**	*ye may advise*
Mŏn-eāt,	*he may advise.*	**Mŏn-eant,**	*they may advise.*

2. IMPERFECT TENSE.

S. **Mŏn-ērem,**	*I might advise*	*P.* **Mŏn-ērēmŭs,**	*We might advise*
Mŏn-ērēs,	*thou mightst advise*	**Mŏn-ērētĭs,**	*ye might advise*
Mŏn-ērĕt,	*he might advise.*	**Mŏn-ērent,**	*they might advise.*

3. PERFECT TENSE.

S. **Mŏn-uĕrim,**	*I may*	*P.* **Mŏn-uĕrimŭs,**	*We may*
Mŏn-uĕrĭs,	*thou mayst* } *have advised.*	**Mŏn-uĕritĭs,**	*ye may*
Mŏn-uĕrĭt,	*he may*	**Mŏn-uĕrint,**	*they may* } *have advised.*

4. PLUPERFECT TENSE.

S. **Mŏn-uissem,**	*I should*	*P.* **Mŏn-uissēmŭs,**	*We should*
Mŏn-uissēs,	*thou wouldst* } *have advised.*	**Mŏn-uissētĭs,**	*ye would*
Mŏn-uissĕt,	*he would*	**Mŏn-uissent,**	*they would* } *have advised.*

VERB INFINITE.

INFINITIVES.

PRES. and IMP. }	**Mŏn-ērĕ,**	*to advise.*
PERF. and PLUP. }	**Mŏn-uissĕ,**	{ *to have advised.*
FUTURE. {	**Mŏn-ĭtūrŭs essĕ,**	{ *to be about to advise.*

GERUND.

Gen. **Mŏn-endī,**	*of advising*
Dat. **Mŏn-endō,**	*for advising*
Acc. **Mŏn-endum,**	*the advising*
Abl. **Mŏn-endō,**	*by advising.*

SUPINES.

Mŏn-ĭtum,	*to advise.*
Mŏn-ĭtū,	*to be advised.*

PARTICIPLES.

PRESENT.	**Mŏn-ens, -entis,** *advising.*
FUTURE.	**Mŏn-ĭtūrŭs,** (ă, um), *about to advise.*

XXI.—THIRD OR Consonant AND U CONJUGATION.—ACTIVE VOICE.

Rĕgo, rexĭ, rectum, rĕgĕrĕ,—*to rule.* Stem: **rĕg-.**

VERB FINITE.

INDICATIVE MOOD.

1. PRESENT TENSE.

S. **Rĕg-o,**	*I rule,* or *am*	⎫	*P.* **Rĕg-ĭmŭs,**	*We rule,* or *are*	⎫
Rĕg-ĭs,	*thou rulest,* or *art*	⎬ *ruling.*	**Rĕg-ĭtĭs,**	*ye rule,* or *are*	⎬ *ruling.*
Rĕg-ĭt,	*he rules,* or *is*	⎭	**Rĕg-unt,**	*they rule,* or *are*	⎭

2. FUTURE-SIMPLE TENSE.

S. **Rĕg-am,**	*I shall rule*		*P.* **Rĕg-ēmŭs,**	*We shall rule*
Rĕg-ēs,	*thou wilt rule*		**Rĕg-ētĭs,**	*ye will rule*
Rĕg-ĕt,	*he will rule.*		**Rĕg-ent,**	*they will rule.*

3. IMPERFECT TENSE.

S. **Rĕg-ebam,**	*I was ruling*		*P.* **Rĕg-ēbāmŭs,**	*We were ruling*
Rĕg-ēbās,	*thou wast ruling*		**Rĕg-ēbātĭs,**	*ye were ruling*
Rĕg-ēbăt,	*he was ruling.*		**Rĕg-ēbant,**	*they were ruling.*

4. PERFECT TENSE.

S. **Rex-ĭ,**	*I have ruled,* or *I ruled*		*P.* **Rex-ĭmŭs,**	*We have ruled, or we ruled*
Rex-istĭ,	*thou hast ruled,* or *thou ruledst*		**Rex-istĭs,**	*ye have ruled, or ye ruled*
Rex-ĭt,	*he has ruled,* or *he ruled.*		**Rex-ērunt** or **rex-ērĕ,**	*they have ruled, or they ruled.*

5. FUTURE-PERFECT TENSE.

S. **Rex-ĕro,**	*I shall have ruled*		*P.* **Rex-ĕrimŭs,**	*We shall have ruled*
Rex-ĕris,	*thou wilt have ruled*		**Rex-ĕritĭs,**	*ye will have ruled*
Rex-ĕrĭt,	*he will have ruled.*		**Rex-ĕrint,**	*they will have ruled.*

6. PLUPERFECT TENSE.

S. **Rex-ĕram,**	*I had ruled*		*P.* **Rex-ĕrāmŭs,**	*We had ruled*
Rex-ĕrās,	*thou hadst ruled*		**Rex-ĕrātĭs,**	*ye had ruled*
Rex-ĕrăt,	*he had ruled.*		**Rex-ĕrant,**	*they had ruled.*

IMPERATIVE MOOD.

PRESENT TENSE.

S. **Rĕg-ĕ,**	*Rule thou.*		*P.* **Rĕg-ĭtĕ,**	*Rule ye.*

FUTURE TENSE.

S. **Rĕg-ĭto,**	*Thou shalt* or *must rule*		*P.* **Rĕg-ĭtŏtĕ,**	*Ye shall* or *must rule*
Rĕg-ĭto,	*he shall* or *must rule.*		**Rĕg-unto,**	*they shall* or *must [rule.*

SUBJUNCTIVE MOOD.

1. PRESENT TENSE.

S. **Rĕg-am,**	*I may rule*		*P.* **Rĕg-āmŭs,**	*We may rule*	
Rĕg-ās,	*thou mayst rule*		**Rĕg-ātĭs,**	*ye may rule*	
Rĕg-ăt,	*he may rule.*		**Rĕg-ant,**	*they may rule.*	

2. IMPERFECT TENSE.

S. **Rĕg-ĕrem,**	*I might rule*	*P.* **Rĕg-ĕrēmŭs,**	*We might rule*	
Rĕg-ĕrēs,	*thou mightst rule*	**Rĕg-ĕrētĭs,**	*ye might rule*	
Rĕg-ĕrĕt,	*he might rule.*	**Rĕg-ĕrent,**	*they might rule.*	

3. PERFECT TENSE.

S. **Rex-ĕrim,**	*I may*	} *have*	*P.* **Rex-ĕrimŭs,**	*We may*	} *have*
Rex-ĕrĭs,	*thou mayst*	} *ruled.*	**Rex-ĕritĭs,**	*ye may*	} *ruled.*
Rex-ĕrĭt,	*he may*		**Rex-ĕrint,**	*they may*	

4. PLUPERFECT TENSE.

S. **Rex-issem,**	*I should*	} *have*	*P.* **Rex-issēmŭs,**	*We should*	} *have*
Rex-issēs,	*thou wouldst*	} *ruled.*	**Rex-issētĭs,**	*ye would*	} *ruled.*
Rex-issĕt,	*he would*		**Rex-issent,**	*they would*	

VERB INFINITE.

INFINITIVES.

PRES. AND IMP.	} **Rĕg-ĕrĕ,**	*to rule.*
PERF. AND PLUP.	} **Rex-issĕ,**	{ *to have ruled.*
FUTURE.	{ **Rec-tūrŭs essĕ,**	{ *to be about to rule.*

GERUND.

Gen. **Rĕg-endī,**	*of ruling*
Dat. **Rĕg-endō,**	*for ruling*
Acc. **Rĕg-endum,**	*the ruling*
Abl. **Rĕg-endō,**	*by ruling.*

SUPINES.

Rec-tum,	*to rule*
Rec-tū,	*to be ruled.*

PARTICIPLES.

PRESENT.	**Rĕg-ens, -entis,** *ruling.*
FUTURE.	**Rec-tūrŭs (ă, um),** *about [to rule.*

XXII.—Fourth or I Conjugation.—Active Voice.

Audio, audīvī, audītum, audīrĕ,—*to hear.* Stem : **audi-.**

VERB FINITE.

OATIVE MOOD.

1. Present Tense.

S. Aud-io,	I hear, or am		P. Aud-īmŭs,	We hear, or are	
Aud-īs,	thou hearest, or art	*hearing.*	Aud-ītĭs,	ye hear, or are	*hearing.*
Aud-īt,	he hears, or is		Aud-iunt,	they hear, or are	

2. Future-Simple Tense.

S. Aud-iam,	I shall hear		P. Aud-iēmŭs,	We shall hear
Aud-iēs,	thou wilt hear		Aud-iētĭs,	ye will hear
Aud-iĕt,	he will hear.		Aud-ient,	they will hear.

3. Imperfect Tense.

S. Aud-iēbam,	I was hearing		P. Aud-iēbāmŭs,	We were hearing
Aud-iēbās,	thou wast hearing		Aud-iēbātĭs,	ye were hearing
Aud-iēbăt,	he was hearing.		Aud-iēbant,	they were hearing.

4. Perfect Tense.

S. Aud-īvī,	I have heard, or I heard		P. Aud-īvĭmŭs,	We have heard, or we heard
Aud-īvistī,	thou hast heard, or thou heardst		Aud-īvistĭs,	ye have heard, or ye heard
Aud-īvĭt,	he has heard, or he heard.		Aud-īvērunt, or -īvērĕ,	they have heard, or they heard.

5. Future-Perfect Tense.

S. Aud-īvĕro,	I shall		P. Aud-īvĕrimŭs,	We shall	
Aud-īvĕrĭs,	thou wilt	have heard.	Aud-īvĕritĭs,	ye will	have heard.
Aud-īvĕrĭt,	he will		Aud-īvĕrint,	they will	

6. Pluperfect Tense.

S. Aud-īvĕram,	I had heard		P. Aud-īvĕrāmŭs,	We had heard
Aud-īvĕrās,	thou hadst heard		Aud-īvĕrātĭs,	ye had heard
Aud-īvĕrăt,	he had heard.		Aud-īvĕrant,	they had heard.

IMPERATIVE MOOD.

Present Tense.

S. Aud-ī,	Hear thou.		P. Aud-ītĕ,	Hear ye.

Future Tense.

S. Aud-īto,	Thou must hear		P. Aud-ītōtĕ,	Ye must hear
Aud-īto,	he must hear.		Aud-iunto,	they must hear.

SUBJUNCTIVE MOOD.

1. PRESENT TENSE.

S.			P.		
Aud-iam,	I may hear		Aud-iămŭs,	We may hear	
Aud-iăs,	thou mayst hear		Aud-iătĭs,	ye may hear	
Aud-iăt,	he may hear.		Aud-iant,	they may hear.	

2. IMPERFECT TENSE.

S.			P.		
Aud-īrem,	I might hear		Aud-īrēmŭs,	We might hear	
Aud-īrēs,	thou mightst hear		Aud-īrētĭs,	ye might hear	
Aud-īrĕt,	he might hear.		Aud-īrent,	they might hear.	

3. PERFECT TENSE.

S.			P.		
Aud-īvĕrim,	I may		Aud-īvĕrimus,	We may	
Aud-īvĕrĭs,	thou mayst } have heard.		Aud-īvĕritĭs,	ye may } have heard.	
Aud-īvĕrĭt,	he may		Aud-īvĕrint,	they may	

4. PLUPERFECT TENSE.

S.			P.		
Aud-īvissem,	I should		Aud-īvissēmŭs,	We should	
Aud-īvissēs,	thou wouldst } have heard.		Aud-īvissētĭs,	ye would } have heard.	
Aud-īvissĕt,	he would		Aud-īvissent,	they would	

VERB INFINITE.

INFINITIVES.

PRES. AND IMP.	Aud-īrĕ,	to hear.
PERF. AND PLUP.	Aud-īvissĕ,	{ to have heard.
FUTURE.	Aud-ītūrŭs essĕ,	{ to be about to hear.

GERUND.

Gen. Aud-iendī,	of hearing
Dat. Aud-iendō,	for hearing
Acc. Aud-iendum,	the hearing
Abl. Aud-iendō,	by hearing.

SUPINES.

Aud-ītum,	to hear.
Aud-ītū,	to be heard.

PARTICIPLES.

PRESENT.	Aud-iens, -entis, [hearing
FUTURE.	Aud-ītūrŭs (ă um), [about to hear.

NOTE. In all the Perfect Tenses v is frequently omitted before e and i. The two ii are often contracted into i: as,

audīvistī becomes audīistī or audistī			audīvĕram becomes audiĕram		
audīvistĭs	„	audīistĭs or audistĭs	audīvĕrim	„	audiĕrim
audīvĭt	„	audīit	audīvissem	„	{ audīissem or audissem
audīvĕrunt	„	audiĕrunt	audīvissĕ	„	{ audīissĕ or audissĕ.
audīvĕro	„	audiĕro			

First Conjugation.—Active Voice.

Exercise XXV.

The Present, Future-Simple, and Imperfect Tenses, Indicative.

A.—1. Ego te laudabam, tu me vituperabas. 2. Ego te laudabo, tu me vituperabis. 3. Bonos semper laudabo, improbos semper vituperabo. 4. Si virtutem amabitis, omnes boni vos amabunt. 5. Dum nos placidus somnus recreabat, vos vigilabatis. 6. Quum milites urbem intrabant, omnes cives timoris pleni erant. 7. Hieme in urbe habitamus, aestate autem in hortis habitabimus. 8. Probitate, non fraude amicos parabis. 9. Graeci partem praedae Diis dabant. 10. Multi homines aedificant domos, in quibus non habitabunt.

1. He was building a house in the city. 2. I shall always praise the good; I shall always find-fault-with the bad. 3. The Romans gave the greatest honours to good citizens. 4. By virtue they-are-getting to themselves (*sibi*) a renowned name. 5. While the soldiers were refreshing themselves, the enemy (*pl.*) were awake. 6. We (*nos*) build houses; others will dwell in them. 7. The general will give the booty to the soldiers. 8. You (*sing.*) find-fault-with yourself (*te*), I (do) not find-fault-with you. 9. All persons praise diligence and honesty. 10. While the citizens were watching, the soldiers were preparing their arms.

The Perfect, Future-Perfect, and Pluperfect Tenses, Indicative.

Rule 11.—When two Nouns refer to the same person or thing, they are said to be in *Apposition*, and are put in the same case: as, Rŏmŭlŭs rex, *Romulus, the king.*

B.—1. Ego ambulavi, tu vigilavisti, ventus flavit. 2. Ego ambulaveram, tu vigilaveras, ventus flaverat. 3. Ego te laudavero, tu me vituperaveris, frater judicaverit. 4. Praeceptores meos semper amavi. 5. Romani Corinthum, opulentam Graeciae urbem, expugnaverunt. 6. Quum milites urbem intraverant, omnes cives timoris pleni erant. 7. Si unum castigaveris, centum emendabis. 8. Si animum virtutibus ornaveris, semper beatus eris. 9. Quum exercitus urbem oppugnavit, nos jam emigraveramus. 10. Quum hostes agros vastaverint, urbem oppugnabunt.

1. The Romans assaulted the city. 2. The soldiers laid-waste the lands (*agros*) and assaulted the city. 3. Cicero, the orator, got for himself a renowned name. 4. They had adorned the city (of)

Corinth with most splendid buildings. 5. When the army has (*fut. perf.*) laid-waste the lands, the general will assault the city. 6. When thou hast improved (*fut. perf.*) thy life, thou wilt have gained for thyself (*dative*) true praise. 7. I have built for myself a splendid house; I have gained very many friends. 8. I have praised you (*sing.*), not found-fault-with you (*sing.*). 9. The army had entered the city and had laid-waste all (things). 10. If thou hast gained for thyself true friends, thou art happy.

Imperative Mood.

NOTE.—*Not* in prohibitions is always NE.

C.—1. Amato patrem et matrem! 2. Omnes homines ama! 3. Mores vestros mutate, amici! 4. Diligenter cura, amice, valetudinem tuam! 5. Amate litteras, o pueri! 6. Discipulus amato praeceptores! 7. Laudatote probos homines, vituperatote improbos! 8. Omnes homines amanto Deum! 9. Ne nomen muta; muta mores.

1. Enter (*pl.*), O friends! 2. Improve (*pl.*) those ill manners of yours,* scholars! 3. O my son, love (thy) mother! 4. Change not this law, citizens. 5. Praise thou the just and good (*pl.*). 6. Change not (your) friends. 7. While the soldiers are fighting, let the citizens watch. 8. Let good and upright citizens be at-the-head-of the commonwealth. 9. Get not to thyself a name by guilt.

* Translate *those-of-yours*, by *istos*.

THE SUBJUNCTIVE MOOD.

The Indicative Mood speaks of a thing without any condition or doubt: as, aedĭfĭco dŏmum, *I am building a house;* hăbĭtăbo in ĕā, *I shall dwell in it.*

The Subjunctive Mood speaks of a thing with some condition or doubt: as, [aedĭfĭco dŏmum] ŭt in ĕā hăbĭtem, [*I am building a house*] *in order that I may dwell in it.* Here there is no doubt about the act of *building;* but whether the person building will *dwell* in the house or not is uncertain, and depends upon circumstances.

The translation of the Subjunctive Mood with *may* and *might* is only an approximation to its meaning. Very often it has to be rendered in English by the corresponding tense of the Indicative Mood, as in the whole of Exercise E.

NOTE.—The Rule for the sequence of tenses in the Subjunctive Mood is given on p. 95.

Rule 12.—The Conjunctions ŭt, *that, in-order-that*, and nē, *lest, in-order-that-not*, are constructed with the Subjunctive Mood:

The Present and Imperfect Tenses, Subjunctive.

D.—1. Laudat puerum, ut litteras amet. 2. Laudavit puerum, ut litteras amaret. 3. Omnes parentes optant, ut filii litteras diligenter tractent. 4. Saepe majores nostri dimicaverunt, ut patriam suam liberarent. 5. Amo te, ut me redames. 6. Amavi te, ut me redamares. 7. Dux imperavit ut milites stationes suas servarent. 8. Ita judicat judex justus, ut in omni re rectam conscientiam servet. 9. Heri ambulabam, ut tristem animum exhilararem. 10. Exercitus noster pugnabat, ne urbem hostes expugnarent.

1. I often walked in the fields that I might refresh my mind. 2. Who does not fight that he may preserve his country? 3. They were fighting that they might preserve their freedom. 4. He chastises the boy in-order-that he may improve him. 5. He was chastising the boy in-order-that he might improve him. 6. We fight *in-order-that* the enemy (*pl.*) may *not* (ne) lay-waste our lands. 7. The husbandmen were preparing arms *in-order-that* the soldiers might *not* enter their lands. 8. We prepare our arms that we may save the city. 9. We often walked in the garden in order that we might refresh ourselves (nos). 10. We were building and were adorning dwelling-places, in-order-that others might dwell in them.

Rule 13.—Quĭn is used with the Subjunctive Mood after nōn dŭbĭto, *I do not doubt;* nēmo dŭbĭtăt, *no one doubts;* quĭs dŭbĭtăt? *who doubts?* nōn est dŭbĭum, *it is not doubtful,* or, *there is no doubt;* and is translated in English by *that.*

After such expressions as these, the Subjunctive must be translated into English by the corresponding tense of the Indicative: as, nēmo dŭbĭtăt quĭn sĭt justum, *no one doubts that it* IS *just.*

The Perfect and Pluperfect Tenses, Subjunctive.

E.—1. Non dubito, quin milites nostri hostes superaverint. 2. Non dubitabam, quin milites nostri hostes superavissent. 3. Non dubito, quin milites nostri hostes superaturi sint.* 4. Quis dubitat, quin bonos semper laudaverimus? 5. Non est dubium, quin fidem semper servaveritis. 6. Nemo dubitabat quin hostes urbem expugnavissent. 7. Non est dubium, quin malos semper vituperaverimus. 8. Nemo dubitabat, quin Hannibal fortissime pugnavisset.

---

* This is called the *Periphrastic Conjugation,* consisting of the Future Participle in *'urus* with the Verb *sum,* and denotes intention or futurity.

9. Non est dubium, quin terror omnium civium animos occupaverit. 10. Non erat dubium, quin terror omnium civium animos occupavisset.

In the following Exercise the verbs in Italics are to be rendered in Latin by the corresponding Tenses of the Subjunctive.

1. There was no doubt that the enemy *had entered* the city. 2. There is no doubt that our soldiers *have fought* bravely. 3. I do not doubt that *ye have* always *praised* the good. 4. There is no doubt that our (men) *overcame* the enemy. 5. There was no doubt that they *had prepared* arms. 6. Who doubts that the enemy *have prepared* arms? 7. I have no doubt that our soldiers *have taken-by-storm* the city. 8. Who doubts that our men *fought* bravely? 9. There is no doubt that *he has improved* his manners. 10. Who doubts that a good citizen *will fight* (*pres. subj.*) for (prō with abl.) his native-land?

Infinitive Mood and Participles.

RULE 14.—The latter of two verbs is put in the Infinitive Mood: as, Caesăr hostēs sŭpĕrārĕ pŏtest, *Caesar is able to overcome the enemy.*

Pŏtest, (*he, she, it*) *is able.*   Possunt, (*they*) *are able.*

F.—1. Milites urbem expugnare possunt. 2. Caesar sibi amicos parare potest. 3. Naturam mutare difficile est. 4. Errare humanum est. 5. Luscinia cantans animos nostros delectat. 6. Hostes adventant expugnaturi urbem nostram.

1. Caesar is able to take-by-storm the city. 2. Our (men) are able to overcome the enemy. 3. It is difficult to change bad manners. 4. It is easy to overcome the enemies. 5. The general entered the city, carrying (his) sword. 6. They were walking in the garden, singing and adorning themselves with flowers.

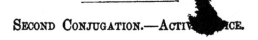

SECOND CONJUGATION.—ACTIVE VOICE.

EXERCISE XXVI.
Indicative and Imperative Moods.

A.—1. Ego te monebam, tu flebas. 2. Ego te moneoo, tu flebis. 3. Arbores vere florent. 4. Tempus omnia opera hominum delet. 5. Romani primis temporibus parebant regibus. 6. Gaudebam quod tu valebas. 7. Praeceptor gaudebat, quod vos ejus praeceptis parebatis. 8. Tibi placebas, aliis displicebas. 9. Omnes boni legibus divinis semper parebunt. 10. Vires vestras semper exercete, pueri!

1. *We* shall rejoice, *you* will weep.   2. The young-man obeys not the laws of the commonwealth.   3. Weep not, O my sons; the commonwealth rejoices.   4. A good king is not always pleasing to his citizens.   5. I rejoice, because the state flourishes.   6. The same (things) do not always please the same persons.   7. The commonwealth was flourishing.   8. The good citizens were rejoicing; the bad were weeping.   9. Obey the laws of your country, citizens.   10. The enemy was destroying the houses.

B.—1. Graecia omnibus artibus floruit.   2. Multum iis debemus, qui nos virtutem docuerunt.   3. Fortes milites! laudem meruistis.   4. Cantus avium maximam nobis praebuerunt voluptatem.   5. Bonae leges Solonis Atheniensibus placuerunt.   6. Divitiae multis homi-nibus nocuerunt.   7. Magistri vos linguam Latinam docuerunt.   8. Equites Caesaris Pompeium ejusque amicos terruerunt.   9. Haec civitas diu floruerat, quia semper legibus paruerat.   10. Tu nobis nocueras, quia temeritatem tuam non coërcueras.

1. Rashness has often been hurtful to generals.   2. We owe very many-things to our parents.   3. Who taught you the Latin language, boy?   4. Curb the tongue; the tongue has been hurtful to very many (persons).   5. Cicero exhibited to his (fellow) citizens a memorable example of integrity.   6. Set (*praebeo*) a good example to thy (fellow) citizens.   7. Destroy ye not the city, soldiers!   8. Solon the Athenian furnished most excellent laws for his (fellow) citizens.   9. That man often curbs his tongue.   10. To whom do not the songs of birds afford pleasure?

Subjunctive and Infinitive Moods and Participles.

C.—1. Curo ut pueri corpus exerceam.   2. Curabam ut pueri corpus exercerem.   3. Cura ut pueri corpus exerceas.   4. Curabam ut pueri corpus exerceres.   5. Nemo dubitat quin ego puerum semper bene monuerim.   6. Nemo dubitavit quin ego puerum semper bene monuissem.   7. Non dubito quin dux temeritatem militum coercuerit.   8. Non dubito, quin dux temeritatem militum coerci-turus sit.   9. Miserum est habuisse, et nihil habere.   10. Bonis placuisse maxima laus est.

1. Who doubts that rashness has been hurtful to generals?   2. It is difficult to curb the tongue; it is more difficult to curb anger.   3. There is no doubt that to curb anger is most difficult.   4. There is no doubt that they entered the city weeping.   5. To do good to very many is true glory.   6. That tongue of yours (*iste*) is destined-to-hurt (*fut. part.*) yourself.   7. I will take care to* set a good example to my children.   8. A son ought to obey (his) father.   9. There is no doubt that the laws of Solon were serviceable to the Athenians.   10. Who doubts that anger has hurt very many?

* *Obs. To set = that I may set: ut with Subjunctive. When the English Infinitive Mood expresses a purpose, it must be translated in Latin by ut and the Subjunctive.*

THIRD CONJUGATION.—ACTIVE VOICE.

EXERCISE XXVII.

Indicative and Imperative Moods.

A.—1. Omnem hunc mundum Deus regit. 2. Hannibal magnum exercitum in Italiam ducet. 3. Semper dicam quod verum est. 4. Dum ego scribebam, tu legebas et frater pingebat. 5. Miles corpus pallio suo teget. 6. Hostes aciem instruebant. 7. Disce, puer! 8. Coelestia semper spectato, humana contemnito. 9. Vos, viri fortissimi, urbem templaque deorum defendetis. 10. Tu exercitum duces, multasque urbes expugnabis.

1. Hannibal will lead his army into the Roman territory (agri, *pl.*). 2. We were leading the army into the Roman territory. 3. We were defending the city and the temples of the gods. 4. I was writing; you were reading; (my) brother was painting. 5. A good citizen will never abandon the commonwealth. 6. The state defends us. 7. I will cover the bodies of the boys with (my) cloak. 8. Learn the song, boys; (it) is very beautiful (*pulcher*). 9. Brave men despise death and danger. 10. Tell * me (*dat.*), (my) son; what has hurt you?

B.—1. Tarquinius Priscus Romam urbem muris cinxit. 2. Xerxes, Persarum rex, Hellespontum ponte junxit. 3. Imperator exercitum duxit, multasque urbes expugnavit. 4. Cicero multas pulcherrimas orationes scripserat. 5. Cicero conjurationem Catilinae detexerat. 6. Simulac litteras scripserimus, ambulabimus. 7. Incendium totam fere urbem absumpserat. 8. Camillum triumphantem albi traxerunt equi. 9. Xerxes, Persarum rex, innumeras copias contraxit. 10. Vix Caesar aciem instruxerat, quum hostes in unum locum convolaverunt.

1. The fire consumed the third part of the city. 2. The general led a great army into Italy. 3. The Cimbri brought-together innumerable forces. 4. Caesar arranged his line-of-battle. 5. Caesar threw a bridge across the river (say, joined the river by a bridge). 6. As soon as I have written (*fut. perf.*) the letter, I will take-a-walk. 7. We discovered the conspiracy of Catiline. 8. I defended the commonwealth (when) a young man. 9. White horses had drawn Camillus triumphing. 10. We have despised human (things) (*neut. pl.*).

* The verbs dīco, dūco, făcio, drop the final *e* in the imperative mood: hence dīc, *tell thou;* dŭc, *lead thou;* fac, *do thou.*

Subjunctive and Infinitive Moods and Participles.

C.—1. Hannibal magnum exercitum in Italiam ducit, ut cum Romanis in hac terra pugnet. 2. Hannibal magnum exercitum in Italiam duxit, ut cum Romanis in hac terra pugnaret. 3. Cura ut pueri animum excolas. 4. Curabam ut pueri animum excoleres. 5. Nemo dubitat quin ego puerum diligenter correxerim. 6. Nemo dubitabat quin ego puerum diligenter correxissem. 7. Narrate nobis, quid parentes scripserint. 8. Quis dubitat, quin hostes urbem obsidione cincturi sint. 9. Difficile est regere hominum animos. 10. Emere facilius est quam solvere.

1. I will take care to cultivate (*ut* and *Subj.*) the boy's mind. 2. There is no doubt that he has carefully cultivated his mind. 3. Take care to be well (*ut* and *Subj.*). 4. Who doubts that it is very difficult to rule the minds of men? 5. Who doubts that we have obeyed the laws? 6. Caesar drew together his forces with-the-intention-of-assaulting (*fut. part.*) the town. 7. White horses drew the chariot of Camillus (when) triumphing. 8. It is difficult to learn many things. 9. There is no doubt that we ought always to-be-learning (*pres. inf.*). 10. I will take care to correct (*ut* and *Subj.*) the boys.

FOURTH CONJUGATION.—ACTIVE VOICE.

EXERCISE XXVIII.

Indicative and Imperative Moods.

A.—1. Mors finiet nostram vitam. 2. Leones non reperitis in Gallia. 3. Discipulos diligentes non puniemus. 4. Persae castra muniebant et custodiebant. 5. Dum tu dormiebas, ego te custodiebam. 6. Scio multas res, quas olim nesciebam. 7. Dum tu dormies, ego te custodiam. 8. Praeceptor puerorum mentes erudito. 9. Liberi parentibus obediunto. 10. Qui Deo obedit, etiam hominibus obediet.

1. The soldiers were fortifying the camp. 2. Cornelia trained her children carefully. 3. My son, obey thy mother. 4. While the citizens were keeping-guard, the soldiers were sleeping. 5. We will keep-guard, and you shall sleep. 6. Now 1 know these things; yesterday I was-ignorant-of them. 7. You will not easily find a lion in Europe. 8. Death puts-an-end-to all the hopes of this life. 9. Carefully train your children; praise the good; punish the bad. 10. Thou shalt not bury (*fut. imper.*) a dead man within (in) the city.

B.—1. Natura Italiam Alpibus munivit. 2. Cicero domum suam muniverat et firmaverat. 3. Magister puniebat eos discipulos, qui non obediverant. 4. Vincīte eos, qui non obediverunt. 5. Claram vocem hujus avis non audivisti? eam non audivi. 6. Servi dominum sepeliverunt. 7. Vix milites castra muniverant, quum Caesar aciem instruxit. 8. Quum milites castra muniverint, dormient. 9. Natura oculos membranis tenuissimis vestivit. 10. Parentes mei pauperem hunc puerum nutriverant.

1. A good father will nurture, clothe, (and) train-up his children. 2. Who did not hear that very clear (*sup.*) song of the nightingale? 3. Nature has fortified the earth with mountains. 4. They bound the men with the hardest chains. 5. Lictor, bind the man! 6. Very delicate membranes clothe the eyes. 7. Punish thou the bad; give honour to the good; in-that-way thou wilt be serviceable to the commonwealth. 8. He will bind the citizens with the strongest (validissimus) chains. 9. That cruel mother did not nurture her own children. 10. Bind not the man, soldier, he is a Roman citizen.

Subjunctive and Infinitive Moods and Participles.

C.—1. Curo ut pueri mentem erudiam. 2. Curabam, ut pueri mentem erudirem. 3. Obedit aliis, ut sibi quoque alii obediant. 4. Obediebam aliis, ut mihi quoque alii obedirent. 5. Nemo dubitat quin ego puerum gnaviter custodi(v)erim. 6. Nemo dubitabat quin puerum gnaviter custodi(v)isses. 7. Non dubito quin longinquitas temporis dolorem tuum mollitura sit. 8. Milites urbem custodire debent. 9. Nihil scire turpe est. 10. Venio auditurus, quid pater scripserit.

1. There is no doubt that length of time will assuage your grief. 2. It is easy to exercise the body; it is difficult to train the mind. 3. Who doubts that the father carefully trained the mind of his son? 4. I will take pains to assuage (*ut* and *Subj.*) the pain of the wound. 5. I have no doubt that he is going-to-train-up (*fut. part.*) the boy most carefully. 6. To punish is not to train-up. 7. He bound the men with chains, that they might learn to obey. 8. It is easy to obey the feelings (animus*). 9. There is no doubt that length of time assuages both grief and anger (dolorem iramque). 10. (He) who knows not (nescio) (how) to obey, knows not (how) to command.

* Use the Singular.

XXIII.—FIRST OR A CONJUGATION.—PASSIVE VOICE.

Ămŏr, ămātŭs sum *or* fŭi, ămārĭ,—*to be loved.*

VERB FINITE.

INDICATIVE MOOD.

1. PRESENT TENSE.

S. Am-ŏr,	*I am loved*	*P.* Am-āmŭr,	*We are loved*
Am-ārĭs *or* ăm-ārĕ,	*thou art loved*	Am-āmĭnĭ,	*ye are loved*
Am-ātŭr,	*he is loved.*	Am-antŭr,	*they are loved*

2. FUTURE-SIMPLE TENSE.

S. Am-ābŏr,	*I shall be loved*	*P.* Am-ābĭmŭr,	*We shall be loved*
Am-ābĕrĭs *or* ămābĕrĕ,	*thou wilt be loved*	Am-ābĭmĭnĭ,	*ye will be loved*
Am-ābĭtŭr,	*he will be loved.*	Am-ābuntŭr,	*they will be loved.*

3. IMPERFECT TENSE.

S. Am-ābăr,	*I was being loved*	*P.* Am-ābāmŭr,	*We were being loved*
Am-ābārĭs *or* ăm-ābārĕ,	*thou wast being loved*	Am-ābāmĭnĭ,	*ye were being loved.*
Am-ābātŭr,	*he was being loved.*	Am-ābantŭr,	*they were being loved.*

4. PERFECT TENSE

S. Am-ātŭs sum *or* fŭi,	*I have been loved, or was loved*	*P.* Am-ātĭ sŭmŭs *or* fŭimŭs,	*We have been loved, or were loved*
Am-ātŭs ĕs *or* fŭistĭ,	*thou hast been loved, or wast loved*	Am-ātĭ estĭs *or* fŭistĭs,	*ye have been loved, or were loved*
Am-ātŭs est *or* fŭĭt,	*he has been loved, or was loved.*	Am-ātĭ sunt, fŭĕrunt, *or* fŭĕrĕ,	*they have been loved, or were loved.*

5. FUTURE-PERFECT TENSE.

S. Am-ātŭs ĕro *or* fŭĕro,	*I shall have been loved*	*P.* Am-ātĭ ĕrĭmŭs *or* fŭĕrimŭs,	*We shall have been loved.*
Am-ātŭs ĕrĭs *or* fŭĕrĭs,	*thou wilt have been loved*	Am-ātĭ ĕrĭtĭs *or* fŭĕrĭtĭs,	*ye will have been loved*
Am-ātŭs ĕrĭt *or* fŭĕrĭt,	*he will have been loved.*	Am-ātĭ ĕrunt *or* fŭĕrint,	*they will have been loved.*

6. PLUPERFECT TENSE.

S. Am-ātŭs ĕram *or* fŭĕram,	*I had been loved*	*P.* Am-ātĭ ĕrāmŭs *or* fŭĕrāmŭs,	*We had been loved*
Am-ātŭs ĕrās *or* fŭĕrās,	*thou hadst been loved*	Am-ātĭ ĕrātĭs *or* fŭĕrātĭs,	*ye had been loved*
Am-ātŭs ĕrăt *or* fŭĕrăt,	*he had been loved.*	Am-ātĭ ĕrant *or* fŭĕrant,	*they had been loved.*

IMPERATIVE MOOD.

PRESENT TENSE.

S. **Am-ărĕ,**   *Be thou loved.* | *P.* **Am-ămĭnĭ,**   *Be ye loved.*

FUTURE TENSE.

S. **Am-ātŏr,**   *Thou must be loved*
Am-ātŏr,   *he must be loved.* | *P.* **Am-antŏr,**   { *They must be loved.*

SUBJUNCTIVE MOOD.

1. PRESENT TENSE.

S. **Am-ĕr,**   *I may be loved* | *P.* **Am-ĕmŭr,**   *We may be loved*
Am-ērĭs or } *thou mayst be*   **Am-ēmĭnĭ,**   *ye may be loved*
ăm-ērĕ, } *loved*
Am-ētŭr,   *he may be loved.* | **Am-entŭr,**   *they may be loved.*

2. IMPERFECT TENSE.

S. **Am-ărĕr,**   *I might be loved* | *P.* **Am-ărēmŭr,** *We might be loved*
Am-ărērĭs or } *thou mightst be*   **Am-ărēmĭnĭ,** *ye might be loved*
ăm-ărērĕ, } *loved*
Am-ărētŭr,   *he might be loved.* | **Am-ărentŭr,** *they might be loved.*

3. PERFECT TENSE.

S. **Am-ātŭs sim** } *I may have been* | *P.* **Am-ătĭ sīmŭs** } *We may have*
or **fuĕrim,** } *loved*   or **fuĕrimŭs,** } *been loved*
Am-ātŭs sīs } *thou mayst have*   **Am-ătĭ sītĭs** } *ye may have*
or **fuĕrĭs,** } *been loved*   or **fuĕritĭs,** } *been loved*
Am-ātŭs sīt } *he may have been*   **Am-ătĭ sint** } *they may have*
or **fuĕrĭt,** } *loved.*   or **fuĕrint,** } *been loved.*

4. PLUPERFECT TENSE.

S. **Am-ātŭs essem** } *I should have* | *P.* **Am-ătĭ essēmŭs** } *We should have*
or **fuissem,** } *been loved*   or **fuissēmŭs,** } *been loved*
Am-ātŭs essēs } *thou wouldst*   **Am-ătĭ essētĭs** } *ye would have*
or **fuissēs,** } *have been loved*   or **fuissētĭs,** } *been loved*
Am-ātŭs essĕt } *he would have*   **Am-ătĭ essent** } *they would have*
or **fuissĕt,** } *been loved.*   or **fuissent,** } *been loved.*

VERB INFINITE.

INFINITIVES.

PRES. AND IMP.   **Am-ărĭ,**   *to be loved.*
PERF. AND PLUP.   **Am-ātŭs (a, um) essĕ** or **fuissĕ,**   *to have been loved.*
FUTURE.   **Am-ātum īrĭ** (not declined),   *to be about to be loved.*

PARTICIPLES.

PERFECT.   **Am-ātŭs (a, um),**   *loved* or *having been loved.*
GERUNDIVE.   **Am-andŭs (a, um),**   *meet to be loved.*

XXIV.—SECOND OR E CONJUGATION.—PASSIVE VOICE.

Mŏneŏr, mŏnĭtŭs sum *or* **fuī, mŏnērī,**—*to be advised.*

VERB FINITE.

INDICATIVE MOOD.

1. PRESENT TENSE.

S. **Mŏn-eŏr,**	*I am advised*	*P.* **Mŏn-ēmŭr,**	*We are advised*
Mŏn-ērĭs *or* **mŏn-ērĕ,**	} *thou art advised*	**Mŏn-ēmĭnī,**	*ye are advised*
Mŏn-ētŭr,	*he is advised*	**Mŏn-entŭr,**	*they are advised.*

2. FUTURE-SIMPLE TENSE.

S. **Mŏn-ēbŏr,**	{ *I shall be advised*	*P.* **Mŏn-ēbĭmŭr,**	{ *We shall be advised*
Mŏn-ēbĕrĭs *or* **mŏn-ēbĕrĕ,**	{ *thou wilt be advised*	**Mŏn-ēbĭmĭnī,**	{ *ye will be advised*
Mŏn-ēbĭtŭr,	{ *he will be advised.*	**Mŏn-ēbuntŭr,**	{ *they will be advised.*

3. IMPERFECT TENSE.

S. **Mŏn-ēbăr,**	{ *I was being advised*	*P.* **Mŏn-ēbāmŭr,**	{ *We were being advised*
Mŏn-ēbărĭs *or* **mŏn-ēbārĕ,**	{ *thou wast being advised*	**Mŏn-ēbāmĭnī,**	{ *ye were being advised*
Mŏn-ēbātŭr,	{ *he was being advised.*	**Mŏn-ēbantŭr,**	{ *they were being advised.*

4. PERFECT TENSE.

S. **Mŏn-ĭtŭs sum** *or* **fuī,**	{ *I have been advised, or was advised*	*P.* **Mŏn-ĭtī sŭmŭs** *or* **fuĭmŭs,**	{ *We have been advised, or were advised*
Mŏn-ĭtŭs ĕs *or* **fuistī,**	{ *thou hast been advised, or wast advised*	**Mŏn-ĭtī estĭs** *or* **fuistĭs,**	{ *ye have been advised, or were advised*
Mŏn-ĭtŭs est *or* **fuĭt,**	{ *he has been advised, or was advised.*	**Mŏn-ĭtī sunt, fuĕrunt,** *or* **fuĕrĕ,**	{ *they have been advised, or were advised.*

5. FUTURE-PERFECT TENSE.

S. **Mŏn-ĭtŭs ĕro** *or* **fuĕro,**	} *I shall have been advised*	*P.* **Mŏn-ĭtī ĕrimŭs** *or* **fuĕrimŭs,**	} *We shall have been advised*
Mŏn-ĭtŭs ĕrĭs *or* **fuĕrĭs,**	} *thou wilt have been advised*	**Mŏn-ĭtī ĕrĭtĭs** *or* **fuĕritĭs,**	} *ye will have been advised*
Mŏn-ĭtŭs ĕrĭt *or* **fuĕrĭt,**	} *he will have been advised.*	**Mŏn-ĭtī ĕrunt** *or* **fuĕrint,**	} *they will have been advised.*

6. PLUPERFECT TENSE.

S. **Mŏn-ĭtŭs ĕram** *or* **fuĕram,**	} *I had been advised*	*P.* **Mŏn-ĭtī ĕrāmŭs** *or* **fuĕrāmŭs,**	} *We had been advised*
Mŏn-ĭtŭs ĕrās *or* **fuĕrās,**	} *thou hadst been advised*	**Mŏn-ĭtī ĕrātĭs** *or* **fuĕrātĭs,**	} *ye had been advised*
Mŏn-ĭtŭs ĕrăt *or* **fuĕrăt,**	} *he had been advised.*	**Mŏn-ĭtī ĕrant** *or* **fuĕrant,**	} *they had been advised.*

IMPERATIVE MOOD.
PRESENT TENSE.

S. **Mŏn-ērĕ,**   *Be thou advised.* | *P.* **Mŏn-ēmĭnĭ,**   *Be ye advised.*

FUTURE TENSE.

S. **Mŏn-ētŏr,** *Thou must be advised* | *P.* **Mŏn-entŏr,**   { *They must be ad-*
   Mŏn-ētŏr, *he must be advised.* | *vised.*

SUBJUNCTIVE MOOD.
1. PRESENT TENSE.

S. **Mŏn-eăr,**   { *I may be ad-*   *P.* **Mŏn-eămŭr,**   { *We may be ad-*
                 vised   *vised*
   Mŏn-eărĭs *or* { *thou mayst be*   **Mŏn-eămĭnĭ,**   { *ye may be ad-*
    mŏn-eărĕ,   { *advised*   *vised*
   Mŏn-eătŭr,   { *he may be ad-*   **Mŏn-eantŭr,**   { *they may be ad-*
                 vised.   *vised.*

2. IMPERFECT TENSE.

S. **Mŏn-ērĕr,**   { *I might be ad-*   *P.* **Mŏn-ērēmŭr,**   { *We might be*
                 vised   *advised*
   Mŏn-ērērĭs *or* { *thou mightst be*   **Mŏn-ērēmĭnĭ,**   { *ye might be ad-*
    mŏn-ērērĕ,   { *advised*   *vised*
   Mŏn-ērētŭr,   { *he might be ad-*   **Mŏn-ērentŭr,**   { *they might be*
                 vised.   *advised.*

3. PERFECT TENSE.

S. **Mŏn-ĭtŭs sim**   } *I may have been*   *P.* **Mŏn-ĭtĭ sīmŭs**   } *We may have*
   or **fuĕrim,**   }   *advised*   *or* **fuĕrimŭs,**   }   *been advised*
   Mŏn-ĭtŭs sīs   } *thou mayst have*   **Mŏn-ĭtĭ sītĭs**   } *ye may have*
   or **fuĕrĭs,**   }   *been advised*   *or* **fuĕritĭs,**   }   *been advised*
   Mŏn-ĭtŭs sĭt   } *he may have been*   **Mŏn-ĭtĭ sint**   } *they may have*
   or **fuĕrĭt,**   }   *advised.*   *or* **fuĕrint,**   }   *been advised*

4. PLUPERFECT TENSE.

S. **Mŏn-ĭtŭs essem** } *I should have*   *P.* **Mŏn-ĭtĭ essēmŭs** } *We should have*
   or **fuissem,**   }   *been advised*   *or* **fuissēmŭs,** }   *been advised*
   Mŏn-ĭtŭs essēs } *thou wouldst*   **Mŏn-ĭtĭ essētĭs** } *ye would have*
   or **fuissēs,**   } *ha{}ve been ad-*   *or* **fuissētĭs,** }   *been advised*
                 vised
   Mŏn-ĭtŭs essĕt } *he would have*   **Mŏn-ĭtĭ essent** } *they would have*
   or **fuissĕt,**   }   *been advised.*   *or* **fuissent,**   }   *been advised.*

VERB INFINITE.
INFINITIVES.

PRES. AND IMP.   **Mŏn-ērĭ,**   *to be advised.*
PERF. AND PLUP.   **Mŏn-ĭtŭs (a, um) essĕ** *or* **fuissĕ,** *to have been advised.*
FUTURE.   **Mŏn-ĭtum ĭrĭ** (not declined), *to be about to be ad-*
                                                  [*vised.*

PARTICIPLES.

PERFECT.   **Mŏn-ĭtŭs (a, um),**   *advised,* or *having been advised.*
GERUNDIVE.   **Mŏn-endŭs (a, um),**   *meet to be advised.*

XXV.—Third or Consonant and U Conjugation.
—Passive Voice.

Rĕgŏr, rĕctŭs sum or fŭi, rĕgī,—*to be ruled.*

VERB FINITE.

INDICATIVE MOOD.

1. Present Tense.

S.		P.	
Rĕg-ŏr,	*I am ruled*	Rĕg-ĭmŭr,	*We are ruled*
Rĕg-ĕrĭs *or* rĕg-ĕrĕ,	*thou art ruled*	Rĕg-ĭmĭnī,	*ye are ruled*
Rĕg-ĭtŭr,	*he is ruled.*	Rĕg-untŭr,	*they are ruled.*

2. Future-Simple Tense.

S.		P.	
Rĕg-ăr,	*I shall be ruled*	Rĕg-ēmŭr,	*We shall be ruled*
Rĕg-ērĭs *or* rĕg-ērĕ,	*thou wilt be ruled*	Rĕg-ēmĭnī,	*ye will be ruled*
Rĕg-ētŭr,	*he will be ruled.*	Rĕg-entŭr,	*they will be ruled.*

3. Imperfect Tense.

S.		P.	
Rĕg-ēbăr,	*I was being ruled*	Rĕg-ēbāmŭr,	*We were being ruled*
Rĕg-ēbārĭs *or* rĕg-ēbārĕ,	*thou wast being ruled*	Rĕg-ēbāmĭnī,	*ye were being ruled*
Rĕg-ēbātŭr,	*he was being ruled.*	Rĕg-ēbantŭr,	*they were being ruled.*

4. Perfect Tense.

S.		P.	
Rĕc-tŭs sum *or* fŭi,	*I have been ruled, or was ruled*	Rĕc-tī sŭmŭs *or* fŭimŭs,	*We have been ruled, or were ruled*
Rĕc-tŭs ĕs *or* fuistī,	*thou hast been ruled, or wast ruled*	Rĕc-tī estĭs *or* fuistĭs,	*ye have been ruled, or were ruled*
Rĕctŭs est *or* fŭit,	*he has been ruled, or was ruled.*	Rĕc-tī sunt, fŭĕrunt, *or* fŭĕrĕ,	*they have been ruled, or were ruled.*

5. Future-Perfect Tense.

S.		P.	
Rĕc-tŭs ĕro *or* fŭĕro,	*I shall have been ruled*	Rĕc-tī ĕrĭmŭs *or* fŭĕrimŭs,	*We shall have been ruled*
Rĕc-tŭs ĕrĭs *or* fŭĕrĭs,	*thou wilt have been ruled*	Rĕc-tī ĕrĭtĭs *or* fŭĕritĭs,	*ye will have been ruled*
Rĕc-tŭs ĕrĭt *or* fŭĕrĭt,	*he will have been ruled.*	Rĕc-tī ĕrunt *or* fŭĕrint,	*they will have been ruled.*

6. Pluperfect Tense.

S.		P.	
Rĕc-tŭs ĕram *or* fŭĕram,	*I had been ruled*	Rĕc-tī ĕrāmŭs *or* fŭĕrāmŭs,	*We had been ruled*
Rĕc-tŭs ĕrās *or* fŭĕrās,	*thou hadst been ruled*	Rĕc-tī ĕrātĭs *or* fŭĕrātĭs,	*ye had been ruled*
Rĕc-tŭs ĕrăt *or* fŭĕrăt,	*he had been ruled.*	Rĕc-tī ĕrant *or* fŭĕrant,	*they had been ruled.*

IMPERATIVE MOOD.

PRESENT TENSE.

S. **Rĕg-ĕrĕ,** *Be thou ruled.* | *P.* **Rĕg-ĭmĭnĭ,** *Be ye ruled.*

FUTURE TENSE.

S. **Rĕg-ĭtŏr,** *Thou must be ruled* | *P.* **Rĕg-untŏr,** *They must be ruled.*
Rĕg-ĭtŏr, *he must be ruled.*

SUBJUNCTIVE MOOD.

1. PRESENT TENSE.

S. **Rĕg-ăr,** *I may be ruled* | *P.* **Rĕg-ămŭr,** *We may be ruled*
Rĕg-ărĭs *or* }thou mayst be | **Rĕg-ămĭnĭ,** *ye may be ruled*
   rĕg-ărĕ,   *ruled*
Rĕg-ătŭr, *he may be ruled.* | **Rĕg-antŭr,** *they may be ruled.*

2. IMPERFECT TENSE.

S. **Rĕg-ĕrĕr,** *I might be ruled* | *P.* **Rĕg-ĕrēmŭr,** *We might be ruled*
Rĕg-ĕrērĭs *or*}thou mightst be | **Rĕg-ĕrēmĭnĭ,** *ye might be ruled*
  reg-ĕrērĕ, } *ruled*
Rĕg-ĕrētŭr *he might be ruled.* | **Rĕg-ĕrentŭr,** *they might be ruled.*

3. PERFECT TENSE.

S. **Rec-tŭs sim** *or*}*I may have been* | *P.* **Rec-tĭ sīmŭs** }*We may have*
  fuĕrim, } *ruled*   *or* **fuĕrĭmŭs,**} *been ruled*
Rec-tŭs sīs *or*}*thou mayst have* | **Rec-tĭ sītĭs** *or*}*ye may have been*
  fuĕrĭs, } *been ruled*   **fuĕrĭtĭs,** } *ruled*
Rec-tŭs sĭt *or*}*he may have been* | **Rec-tĭ sint** *or*}*they may have*
  fuĕrĭt, } *ruled.*   **fuĕrint,** } *been ruled.*

4. PLUPERFECT TENSE.

S. **Rec-tŭs essem**}*I should have been* | *P.* **Rec-tĭ essēmŭs**}*We should have*
  or **fuissem,** } *ruled*   *or* **fuissēmŭs,**} *been ruled*
Rec-tŭs essēs}*thou wouldst have* | **Rec-tĭ essētĭs**}*ye would have*
  or **fuissēs,** } *been ruled*   *or* **fuissētĭs,** } *been ruled*
Rec-tŭs essĕt}*he would have been* | **Rec-tĭ essent**}*they would have*
  or **fuissĕt,** } *ruled.*   *or* **fuissent,** } *been ruled.*

VERB INFINITE.

INFINITIVES.

PRES. AND IMP. **Rĕg-ī,**   *to be ruled.*
PERF. AND PLUP. **Rec-tŭs (a, um) essĕ** *or* **fuissĕ,** *to have been ruled.*
FUTURE.   **Rec-tum īrĭ** (not declinēd),   *to be about to be ruled.*

PARTICIPLES.

PERFECT.   **Rec-tŭs (a, um),**   *ruled* or *having been ruled,*
GERUNDIVE.   **Rĕg-endŭs (a, um),**   *meet to be ruled.*

XXVI.—Fourth or I Conjugation.—Passive Voice.

Audiŏr, audītŭs sum *or* fuī, audīrī,—*to be heard.*

VERB FINITE.

INDICATIVE MOOD.

1. Present Tense.

S. Aud-iŏr,	*I am heard*	*P.* Aud-īmŭr,	*We are heard*
Aud-īrĭs *or* aud-īrĕ,	*thou art heard*	Aud-īmĭnī,	*ye are heard*
Aud-ītŭr,	*he is heard.*	Aud-iuntŭr,	*they are heard.*

2. Future-Simple Tense.

S. Aud-iăr,	*I shall be heard*	*P.* Aud-iēmŭr,	*We shall be heard*
Aud-iērĭs *or* aud-iērĕ,	*thou wilt be heard*	Aud-iēmĭnī,	*ye will be heard*
Aud-iētŭr,	*he will be heard.*	Aud-ientŭr,	*they will be heard.*

3. Imperfect Tense.

S. Aud-iēbăr,	*I was being heard*	*P.* Aud-iēbămŭr,	*We were being heard*
Aud-iēbārĭs *or* aud-iēbārĕ,	*thou wast being heard*	Aud-iēbāmĭnī,	*ye were being heard*
Aud-iēbātŭr,	*he was being heard.*	Aud-iēbantŭr,	*they were being heard.*

4. Perfect Tense.

S. Aud-ītŭs sum *or* fuī,	*I have been heard, or was heard*	*P.* Aud-ītī sŭmŭs *or* fuĭmŭs,	*We have been heard, or were heard*
Aud-ītŭs ĕs *or* fuistī,	*thou hast been heard, or wast heard*	Aud-ītī estĭs *or* fuistĭs,	*ye have been heard, or were heard*
Aud-ītŭs est *or* fuĭt,	*he has been heard, or was heard.*	Aud-ītī sunt, fuĕrunt, *or* fuĕrĕ,	*they have been heard, or were heard.*

5. Future-Perfect Tense.

S. Aud-ītŭs ĕro *or* fuĕro,	*I shall have been heard*	*P.* Aud-ītī ĕrĭmŭs *or* fuĕrĭmŭs,	*We shall have been heard*
Aud-ītŭs ĕrĭs *or* fuĕrĭs,	*thou wilt have been heard*	Aud-ītī ĕrĭtĭs *or* fuĕrĭtĭs,	*ye will have been heard*
Aud-ītŭs ĕrĭt *or* fuĕrĭt,	*he will have been heard.*	Aud-ītī ĕrunt *or* fuĕrint,	*they will have been heard.*

6. Pluperfect Tense.

S. Aud-ītŭs ĕram *or* fuĕram,	*I had been heard*	*P.* Aud-ītī-ĕrāmŭs *or* fuĕrāmŭs,	*We had been heard*
Aud-ītŭs ĕrās *or* fuĕrās,	*thou hadst been heard*	Aud-ītī ĕrātĭs *or* fuĕrātĭs,	*ye had been heard*
Aud-ītŭs ĕrăt *or* fuĕrăt,	*he had been heard.*	Aud-ītī ĕrant *or* fuĕrant,	*they had been heard.*

IMPERATIVE MOOD.

PRESENT TENSE.

S. **Aud-īrĕ,** *Be thou heard.* | *P.* **Aud-īmīnī** *Be ye heard.*

FUTURE TENSE.

S. **Aud-ītŏr,** *Thou must be heard*
Aud-ītŏr, *he must be heard.* | *P.* **Aud-iuntŏr,** *They must be heard.*

SUBJUNCTIVE MOOD.

1. PRESENT TENSE.

S. **Aud-iăr,** *I may be heard* | *P.* **Aud-iāmŭr,** *We may be heard*
Aud-iārīs *or*)*thou mayst be* |
aud-iārĕ,) *heard* | **Aud-iāmīnī,** *ye may be heard*
Aud-iātŭr, *he may be heard.* | **Aud-iantŭr,** *they may be heard.*

2. IMPERFECT TENSE.

S. **Aud-īrĕr,** *I might be heard* | *P.* **Aud-īrēmŭr,** *We might be heard*
Aud-īrērīs *or*)*thou mightst be* |
aud-īrērĕ,) *heard* | **Aud-īrēmīnī,** *ye might be heard*
Aud-īrētŭr, *he might be heard.* | **Aud-īrentŭr,** *they might be heard.*

3. PERFECT TENSE.

S. **Aud-ītŭs sim**)*I may have been* | *P.* **Aud-ītī sīmŭs**)*We may have*
or **fuĕrim,**) *heard* | *or* **fuĕrimŭs,**) *been heard*
Aud-ītŭs sīs)*thou mayst have* | **Aud-ītī sītīs**)*ye may have*
or **fuĕrīs,**) *been heard* | *or* **fuĕritīs,**) *been heard*
Aud-ītŭs sīt)*he may have been* | **Aud-ītī sint**)*they may have*
or **fuĕrĭt,**) *heard.* | *or* **fuĕrint,**) *been heard.*

4. PLUPERFECT TENSE.

S. **Aud-ītŭs essem**)*I should have* | *P.* **Aud-ītī essēmŭs**)*We should have*
or **fuissem,**) *been heard* | *or* **fuissēmŭs,**) *been heard*
Aud-ītŭs essēs)*thou wouldst have* | **Aud-ītī essētīs**)*ye would have*
or **fuissēs,**) *been heard* | *or* **fuissētīs,**) *been heard*
Aud-ītŭs essĕt)*he would have* | **Aud-ītī essent**)*they would have*
or **fuissĕt,**) *been heard.* | *or* **fuissent,**) *been heard.*

VERB INFINITE.

INFINITIVES.

PRES AND IMP. **Aud-īrī,** *to be heard.*
PERF. AND PLUP. **Aud-ītŭs (a, um) essĕ** *or* **fuissĕ,** *to have been heard.*
FUTURE. **Aud-ītum īrī** (not declined), *to be about to be heard.*

PARTICIPLES.

PERFECT. **Aud-ītŭs (a, um),** *heard* or *having been heard.*
GERUNDIVE. **Aud-iendŭs (a, um),** *meet to be heard.*

First Conjugation.—Passive Voice.

Rule 15.—A proposition in the active voice may also be expressed by the passive voice, the accusative being changed into the nominative, and the nominative into the ablative. If the ablative denotes a living being, the preposition ā or ăb is prefixed. Thus măgistĕr puĕrum laudăt, *the master praises the boy*, becomes in the passive, puĕr ă măgistrō laudătŭr, *the boy is praised by the master*.

Exercise XXIX.

A.—1. Multi milites in proelio vulnerabantur. 2. Pueri attenti a magistris laudabantur. 3. Troja a Graecis expugnata est. 4. Leges egregiae a Lycurgo datae sunt. 5. Duces exercitus nostri in proelio vulnerati sunt. 6. Antiocho regi pax a Romanis data est. 7. Fugari et superari dulce non est. 8. Puer bene educator. 9. Puer, bene educatus, omnibus placet. 10. Quum rex urbem intravit, omnium civium domus floribus ornatae erant.

1. The good (men) are praised; the bad are blamed. 2. He was severely wounded. 3. In the first battle the Romans were overcome. 4. Immense forces had been raised (paro) by the enemy. 5. The temple of Vesta was built by Numa Pompilius. 6. Antiochus was overcome by the Roman general. 7. The town was assaulted. 8. The city was not taken-by-storm by Hannibal. 9. It is a small-thing to be adorned with gold and silver. 10. The whole land (ager) was laid-waste by the enemy.

B.—1. Pater curat ut ego bene edŭcer. 2. Pater curabat, ut ego bene educarer. 3. Curo, ut puer bene educetur. 4. Curabăm, ut puer bene educaretur. 5. Non dubito quin hostes a militibus nostris superati sint. 6. Non dubitabam, quin hostes a militibus nostris superati essent. 7. Nemo dubitat quin urbs ab hostibus expugnata sit. 8. Nemo dubitabat, quin urbs ab hostibus expugnata esset. 9. Exercitus noster pugnat, ut urbs servetur. 10. Exercitus noster pugnabat, ut urbs servaretur.

1. Cornelia took-care that her children snould be well educated. 2. Who doubts that the boy has been carefully educated? 3. I will take-care that the girl may be adorned with good-qualities. 4. There is no doubt that the city has been assaulted. 5. To be put-to-flight is not always to be overcome. 6. Let arms be made-ready; let the gates of the city be strengthened. 7. The general takes-care that the gates may be strengthened. 8. Let not the good be blamed; let not the bad be praised! 9. We were put to flight, but we were not overcome. 10. There is no doubt that Pompey was overcome by Caesar.

SECOND CONJUGATION.—PASSIVE VOICE.

EXERCISE XXX.

A.—1. Discipuli a magistro docentur. 2. Amari major est laus quam timeri. 3. Fortis vir nullis periculis movebitur. 4. Nero ab omnibus Romanis timebatur. 5. Incolae illius urbis hostium adventu territi sunt. 6. Moniti sumus, ut diligentiores essemus. 7. Puer strenue exercetor. 8. Hostes territi in urbe manserunt. 9. Pueri in litterarum studiis gnaviter exerciti sunt. 10. Monemini ut diligentiores sitis.

1. The pupil is taught by the màster. · 2. The walls were destroyed. 3. The citizens had been terrified. 4. You have been taught by your father. 5. It is a great thing to be well taught. 6. All the citizens werè terrified (at) his (ejus) arrival (*abl.*). 7. Nero was grievously feared by all the citizens. 8. It is not pleasant to be feared by the good; it is very-pleasant to be feared by the bad. 9. Let the bodies of the children be actively exercised. 10. You had been warned, but you did not obey.

B.—1. Pater curat, ut ego strenue exercear. 2. Pater curabat, ut ego strenue exercerer. 3. Curo, ut strenue exerceare. 4. Curabam, ut strenue exercerere. 5. Curo ut puer strenue exerceatur. 6. Curabam ut puer strenue exerceretur. 7. Nemo dubitat quin puer a me semper bene monitus sit. 8. Nemo dubitavit quin puer a me semper bene monitus esset. 9. Non est dubium quin milites subito periculo territi sint. 10. Non erat dubium quin milites subito periculo territi essent.

1. He-was-taking-care that his body might be vigorously exercised. 2. I will take care that the boys are (*subj.*) carefully taught. 3. A good mother will take-care that her daughter is carefully taught. 4. I do not doubt that the whole city was terrified at his arrival. 5. There is no doubt that the citizens were alarmed by the sudden danger. 6. Let not the citizens be troubled (moved) by the arrival of the enemy. 7. (Our) father took care that we might be carefully taught. 8. I have taken care that my sons should (*pres. sub.*) be carefully taught. 9. Brave men will not be suddenly terrified. 10. Virtue is the most beautiful (*fem.*) of (all) things; take care that it is diligently exercised (*pres. subj.*).

THIRD CONJUGATION.—PASSIVE VOICE.

EXERCISE XXXI.

A.—1. Omnis hic mundus a Deo regitur. 2. Respublica Romana a consulibus regebatur. 3. Ripae Rheni ponte junguntur. 4. Urbs muro cincta erat. 5. Graecia perversis suis consiliis afflicta est. 6. Si semper bene vixeris, ab omnibus diligēre. 7. Quum urbs ab hostibus oppugnabatur, a civibus defendebatur. 8. Conjuratio Catilinae a Cicerone detecta est. 9. Multae fabulae a poetis fictae sunt. 10. Vix acies a Caesare instructa erat, quum hostes in unum locum convolaverunt.

1. Hannibal was conquered by Scipio. 2. The commonwealth was severely cast-down. 3. He was esteemed and was loved by all. 4. This story was invented by the poets. 5. The memory of the man will always be cherished (colo) by his fellow-citizens. 6. The conspiracy is discovered; the commonwealth is preserved. 7. You will be loved by many. 8. The town is being assaulted indeed (quidem), but it is not taken. 9. In that most celebrated (nobilis) battle Carthage was cast-down. 10. A bridge was thrown over the Rhine by Caesar. (Say, the river Rhine was joined with a bridge by Caesar.)

B.—1. Pater curat, ut ego probe excolar. 2. Pater curabat, ut ego probe excolerer. 3. Curo, ut puer probe excolatur. 4. Curabam, ut puer probe excoleretur. 5. Phaethon vehementer optat, ut patris curru vehatur. 6. Phaethon vehementer optavit, ut patris curru veheretur. 7. Dicit mihi, quid tibi a sorore scriptum sit.* 8. Dixit mihi, quid tibi a sorore scriptum esset.* 9. Puer probe excolitor. 10. Sapientes semper ratione rĕgi student.

1. I will take-care that he may be rightly cultivated. 2. He took-care that the boy might be rightly cultivated. 3. We vehemently wish that the enemy may be conquered. 4. Cicero vehemently desired that all (things) might be disco___. 5. Let-us-be-zealous to be ruled by reason. 6. All are ze___ rule, not to be ruled. 7. Tell me (dat.) what (quae, neu___) was written (perfect subj.*) to thee. 8. He told me ___ what (quae) had been written (pluperf. subj.*). 9. The ___ wishes that he may ride in the chariot. 10. The boy was wis___ at he might ride in the chariot.

* The rule for this use of the Subjunctive is ___ equently. See p. 95.

FOURTH CONJUGATION.—PASSIVE VOICE.

EXERCISE XXXII.

A.—1. Pueri a magistris erudiuntur. 2. Improbi homines Deo punientur. 3. Bellum Punicum secundum finitum est a Scipione Africano. 4. Omnes dolores morte finientur. 5. Pisces in mari, aves in aëre a Deo nutriuntur. 6. Oculi tenuissimis membranis a natura vestiti sunt. 7. Veteres Britanniae incolae pellibus vestiebantur. 8. Corpora eorum, qui in pugna ceciderunt, sepeliuntor. 9. Urbes munitae ab hostibus non expugnabantur. 10. Non prius dormiemus, quam negotia vestra finita erunt (*prius quam*, before that).

1. The Britons used-to-clothe-themselves (*imperf. pass.*) with skins. 2. The cities had been fortified with stone (*adj.*) walls. 3. The sons of Tiberius Gracchus had been carefully trained by their mother. 4. The bodies were buried with the highest honours. 5. The generals were punished because they had not buried the bodies. 6. These two boys had been trained by their mother carefully. 7. The camp had not been fortified. 8. This life of-ours (nostra) will be found exceedingly-short (*sup.*). 9. When the city has been fortified (*fut. perf.*), the citizens will defend it. 10. The city is fortified and made strong with guards.

B.—1. Pater curat, ut ego diligenter erudiar. 2. Pater curabat, ut ego diligenter erudirer. 3. Curo, ut diligenter erudiare. 4. Curabam, ut diligenter erudirere. 5. Curabam, ut puer bene educaretur, strenue exerceretur, probe excoleretur, diligenter erudiretur. 6. O puer, diligenter eruditor! 7. Bonus discipulus litterarum cognitione erudiri studet. 8. Homo eruditus non solum sibi, sed etiam aliis prodest. 9. Nemo dubitat, quin puer a me gnaviter custoditus sit. 10. Nemo dubitavit, quin puella a me gnaviter custodita sit.

1. Let the boys be carefully trained. 2. Let not the boys be trained by wicked men. 3. I will take care that my son is carefully trained. 4. I took care that my son should not be trained by a wicked master. 5. There is no doubt that the boys have been carefully trained. 6. Who doubts that it is better to be trained by a good master than by a bad one? 7. Who doubts that Socrates was unjustly punished? 8. It is not disgraceful to be unjustly punished. 9. Take care that the boy is well trained. 10. Well trained boys love their master.

PR. L. I.

XXVII.—THIRD CONJUGATION (WITH I IN CERTAIN TENSES).

Căpĭo, cēpī, captum, căpĕrĕ,—*to take.* Stem: **căp-** or **căpi-.**

I. ACTIVE VOICE.

INDICATIVE MOOD.

Present.	**Căp-io,** *I take*	**Căp-ĭmŭs,**	*We take*
	Căp-ĭs, *thou takest*	**Căp-ĭtĭs,**	*ye take*
	Căp-ĭt, *he takes.*	**Căp-iunt,**	*they take.*

Future.	**Căp-iam,**	*I shall take.*
Imperfect.	**Căp-iēbam,**	*I was taking.*

SUBJUNCTIVE MOOD.

Present.	**Căp-iam,**	*I may take.*
Imperfect.	**Căp-ĕrem,**	*I might take.*

IMPERATIVE MOOD.

Present.	**Căp-ĕ,**	*take thou.*
Future.	**Căp-ĭto,**	*thou shalt* or *must take.*

INFINITIVE MOOD.

Present.	**Căp-ĕrĕ,**	*to take.*

PARTICIPLE.

Present.	**Căp-iens,**	*taking.*

GERUND.

Căp-iendi,	*of the taking.*

II. PASSIVE VOICE.

INDICATIVE MOOD.

Present.	**Căp-ĭŏr,** *I am taken*	**Căp-ĭmŭr,**	*We are taken*
	Căp-ĕrĭs \ *thou art*	**Căp-ĭmĭnī,**	*ye are taken*
	or **-ĕrĕ,** / *taken*		
	Căp-ĭtŭr, *he is taken.*	**Căp-iuntŭr,**	*they are taken.*

Future.	**Căp-iăr,**	*I shall be taken.*
Imperfect.	**Căp-iēbar,**	*I was being taken.*

Subjunctive Mood.

Present.	**Căp-iăr,**	*I may be taken.*
Imperfect.	**Căp-ĕrĕr,**	*I might be taken.*

Imperative Mood.

Present.	**Căp-ĕrĕ,**	*be thou taken.*
Future.	**Căp-ĭtŏr,**	*thou must be taken.*

Infinitive Mood.

Present.	**Căp-I,**	*to be taken.*

Obs. 1. The Perfect Tenses are not given, as their conjugation is quite regular, cĕp-ī, cĕp-ĕro, cĕp-ĕram, etc.

Obs. 2. The Verbs conjugated like căpio are:

făcio,	fēcī,	factum,	făcĕrĕ,	*to make.*
jăcio,	jēcī,	jactum,	jăcĕrĕ,	*to throw.*
fŭgio,	fŭgī,	fŭgĭtum,	fŭgĕrĕ,	*to flee.*
fŏdio,	fŏdī,	fossum,	fŏdĕrĕ,	*to dig.*
răpio,	răpuī,	raptum,	răpĕrĕ,	*to seize.*
părio,	pĕpĕrī,	partum,	părĕrĕ,	*to bring forth.*
quătio,	no perfect,)	quassum,	quătĕrĕ,	*to shake.*
cŭpio,	cŭpīvī,	cŭpĭtum,	cŭpĕrĕ,	*to desire.*
săpio,	săpīvī,	—	săpĕrĕ,	*to savour of, be wise.*
lăcio,	—	—	lăcĕre,	*to draw* } only in com-
spĕcio,	—	—	spĕcĕrĕ,	*to look* } pounds.

Exercise XXXIII.

1. Urbs capitur; fugiunt cives, rapiuntur omnia. 2. Curabit dux strenuus ne milites sui fugiant. 3. Scribebam ego versus, tu pingebas, et frater in horto fodiebat. 4. Quis dubitat quin absurdum sit malos versus facere? 5. Poeta versus faciebat quum hostes urbem intrabant. 6. Ne fugiant milites, saepe tutius est pugnare quam fugere. 7. Non omnes eadem cupimus. 8. Curavit ut oratio sua Ciceronem saperet. 9. Quis dubitat quin milites bona nostra rapturi sint? 10. Ne facite absurda, cives! Sapite et iram coercete.

1. Birds make their nests in trees. 2. An eagle had made her nest in a tall tree. 3. We desire very many things which are not needful to us. 4. It is easy to make verses; it is not easy to make good (ones). 5. The enemy flee, and the camp is taken. 6. Flee not, soldiers! It is safer to fight than to flee. 7. We will dig in the earth, in order that we may find metals. 8. Men do not dig in the ground to (ut) find (*subj.*) pearls. 9. A strong wind was shaking the trees. 10. That whole oration savours-of the poets (*acc.*).

Deponent Verbs have a Passive form,

I. Hortĕr, hortātŭs sum, hortārī, *to exhort*, like ămŏr.
II. Vĕreŏr, vĕrĭtŭs sum, vĕrērī, *to fear*,   ,,   mŏneŏr.

		I.		**II.**	
INDICATIVE MOOD.	*Present.*	Hort-ŏr,	I exhort, or am exhorting.	Vĕr-eŏr,	I fear, or am fearing.
		Hort-ārīs (ārĕ),	thou exhortest.	Vĕr-ērīs (ērĕ),	thou fearest.
		&c.	&c.		&c.
	Future Simple.	Hort-ābŏr,	I shall exhort.	Vĕr-ĕbŏr,	I shall fear.
	Imperfect.	Hort-ābăr,	I was exhorting.	Vĕr-ĕbăr,	I was fearing.
	Perfect.	Hort-ātŭs sum,	I have exhorted, or I exhorted.	Vĕr-ĭtŭs sum,	I have feared, or I feared.
	Fut. Perfect.	Hort-ātŭs ĕro,	I shall have exhorted.	Vĕr-ĭtŭs ĕro,	I shall have feared.
	Pluperfect.	Hort-ātŭs ĕram,	I had exhorted.	Vĕr-ĭtŭs ĕram.	I had feared.
SUBJUNCTIVE MOOD.	*Present.*	Hort-ĕr,	I may exhort.	Vĕr-eăr,	I may fear.
	Imperfect.	Hort-ārĕr,	I might exhort.	Vĕr-ĕrĕr,	I might fear.
	Perfect.	Hort-ātŭs sim,	I may have exhorted.	Vĕr-ĭtŭs sim,	I may have feared.
	Pluperfect.	Hort-ātŭs essem,	I should have exhorted.	Vĕr-ĭtŭs ĕssem,	I should have feared.
IMPERATIVE.	*Present.*	Hort-ārĕ,	Exhort thou.	Vĕr-ērĕ,	Fear thou.
	Future.	Hort-ātŏr,	thou shalt or must exhort.	Vĕr-ĕtŏr,	thou shalt or must fear.
INFINITIVE.	*Pres. & Imperf.*	Hort-ārī,	to exhort.	Vĕr-ērī,	to fear.
	Perf. & Plup.	Hort-ātŭs esse,	to have exhorted.	Vĕr-ĭtŭs essĕ,	to have feared.
	Future.	Hort-ātūrŭs essĕ,	to be about to exhort.	Vĕr-ĭtūrŭs essĕ,	to be about to fear.
PARTICIPLES.	*Present.*	Hort-ans,	exhorting.	Vĕr-ens,	fearing.
	Future.	Hort-ātūrŭs,	about to exhort.	Vĕr-ĭtūrŭs,	about to fear.
	Perfect.	Hort-ātŭs,	having exhorted.	Vĕr-ĭtŭs,	having feared.
	Gerundive.	Hort-andŭs,	meet to be exhorted.	Vĕr-endŭs,	meet to be feared.
SUPINES.		Hort-ātum,	to exhort.	Vĕr-ĭtum,	to fear.
		Hort-ātŭ,	to be exhorted.	Vĕr-ĭtŭ,	to be feared.
GERUND.		Hort-andī, &c.	of exhorting. &c.	Vĕr-endī, &c.	of fearing. &c.

Besides the Passive forms, the Deponents have the two Active Participles, the Supines, and the Gerunds.

Deponents are the only Latin Verbs that have a Perfect Participle Active: as, hortātŭs, *having exhorted.*

but an Active meaning.

III. Lŏquŏr, lŏcūtŭs sum, lŏquī,   *to speak*, like rĕgŏr.
IV. Partĭŏr, partītŭs sum, partīrī, *to divide*, „   audĭŏr.

III.		IV.		
Present.	Lŏqu-ŏr,	{ *I speak, or am speaking.*	Part-ĭŏr,	{ *I divide, or am dividing.*	**INDICATIVE MOOD.**
	Lŏqu-ĕrĭs (ĕrĕ), &c.	} *thou speakest.*	Part-ĭrĭs (īrĕ),	} *thou dividest.*	
		&c.		&c.	
Fut. Simple.	Lŏqu-ăr,	*I shall speak.*	Part-ĭăr,	*I shall divide.*	
Imperfect.	Lŏqu-ēbăr,	*I was speaking.*	Part-ĭēbăr,	*I was dividing.*	
Perfect.	Lŏcū-tŭs sum,	} *I have spoken, or I spoke.*	Part-ītŭs sum,	} *I have divided, or I divided.*	
Fut. Perfect.	Lŏcū-tŭs ĕro,	} *I shall have spoken.*	Part-ītŭs ĕro,	} *I shall have divided.*	
Pluperfect.	Lŏcū-tŭs ĕram,	} *had spoken.*	Part-ītŭs ĕram,	} *I had divided.*	
Present.	Lŏqu-ăr,	*I may speak.*	Part-ĭăr,	*I may divide.*	**SUBJUNCTIVE MOOD.**
Imperfect.	Lŏqu-ĕrĕr,	*I might speak.*	Part-ĭrĕr,	*I might divide.*	
Perfect.	Lŏcū-tŭs sim,	} *I may have spoken.*	Part-ītŭs sim,	} *I may have divided.*	
Pluperfect.	Lŏcū-tŭs essem,	} *I should have spoken.*	Part-ītŭs essem,	} *I should have divided.*	
Present.	Lŏqu-ĕrĕ,	*speak thou.*	Part-ĭrĕ,	*Divide thou.*	**IMPERATIVE.**
Future.	Lŏqu-ĭtŏr,	{ *thou shalt or must speak.*	Part-ītŏr,	{ *thou shalt or must divide.*	
Pres. & Imp.	Lŏqu-ī,	*to speak.*	Part-īrī,	*to divide.*	**INFINITIVE.**
Perf. & Plup.	Lŏcū-tŭs essĕ,	} *to have spoken.*	Part-ītŭs essĕ,	} *to have divided.*	
Future.	Lŏcū-tūrŭs essĕ,	} *to be about to speak.*	Part-ītūrŭs essĕ,	} *to be about to divide.*	
Present.	Lŏqu-ens,	*speaking.*	Part-ĭens,	*dividing.*	**PARTICIPLES.**
Future.	Lŏcū-tūrŭs,	*about to speak.*	Part-ītūrŭs,	*about to divide.*	
Perfect.	Lŏcū-tŭs,	*having spoken.*	Part-ītŭs,	*having divided.*	
Gerundive.	Lŏqu-endŭs,	*meet to be spoken.*	Part-ĭendŭs,	*meet to be divided.*	
SUPINES.	Lŏcū-tum,	*to speak.*	Part-ītum,	*to divide.*	
	Lŏcū-tū,	*to be spoken.*	Part-ītū,	*to be divided.*	
GERUND.	Lŏqu-endī, &c.	*of speaking.* &c.	Part-ĭendī, &c.	*of dividing.* &c.	

The Gerundive, and occasionally the Perf. Participle, are the only forms in the Deponent that ever have a passive meaning.

Intransitive Deponents have no Supine in *u* and no Gerundive.

EXERCISE XXXIV.

Deponent Verbs of the First Conjugation.

1. Admiramur cantum avium illarum. 2. Admiramini Dei potentiam. 3. Animalia quaedam vocem humanam imitantur. 4. Caesar milites hortatus est, ut fortiter pugnarent. 5. Hannibal Alpes superare conatus est. 6. Hortabor patrem ut pueri mentem probe excolat. 7. Quid meditaris, carissime amice? 8. Contemplor pulchram hanc imaginem. 9. Venerare Deum, venerare parentes. 10. Tum demum beatus eris, quum aspernatus eris voluptatem.

1. Who does not admire the song of the nightingale? 2. Meditate on these things. 3. Observe (carefully) this beautiful image. 4. It does-good to the mind to contemplate lofty things. 5. Contemplate, citizens, the examples of the ancients! 6. Then at length will ye be happy when ye have learnt (*fut. perf.*) to despise pleasure. 7. I will encourage the boy to (ut) contemplate those things. 8. Attempt great things; thou wilt do great things. 9. I will take care that my son may admire those things (ea, *n. pl.*) which are fit-to-be-admired. 10. There is no doubt that the Romans admired Cicero.

EXERCISE XXXV.

Deponent Verbs of the Second Conjugation.

RULE 16.—Verbs signifying *to remember, to forget, to pity,* are in Latin commonly followed by the Genitive.

1. Veremini, O pueri, senectutem! 2. Darius Alexandro magnam partem Asiae pollicitus est. 3. Plinius scribit : nunc pueri omnia sciunt, neminem verentur, imitantur neminem. 4. Tuebimur miseros, quorum agros vastavistis. 5. Incolae hoc facinus fatebuntur. 6. Comites, qui salutem regis tuiti erant, maximum praemium acceperunt. 7. Scelerum suorum recordabuntur. 8. Reus facinus confessus est. 9. Jucundum est mare a terra intueri. 10. Semper miserorum hominum miserebimur.

1. We reverence the power of God. 2. Guard the king, soldiers! 3. Confess the truth (true things), boy ; it is better to be punished than to deceive. 4. Look-into these things carefully. 5. The general has promised rewards to the soldiers. The generals have promised (*subj.*) rewards to the soldiers. 6. He has confessed the crime, and will be punished. 7. It is pleasant to call-to-mind past dangers. 8. Ye will call-to-mind these things, citizens, when I am cast forth (*fut. perf.*) from the city. 9. Have-pity-on the accused (man), judges! 10. He reverences the gods.

EXERCISE XXXVI.

Deponent Verbs of the Third Conjugation.

RULE 17.—**Utor, fruor, vescor, fungor,** govern the Ablative Case. To these add **pŏtior,** *I obtain-possession-of* (4 Conj.).

A.—1. Si morimur, corpus tantum moritur, non animus. 2. Dux maximam adeptus est gloriam. 3. Cives, libertatem adepti, summa laetitia fruentur. 4. Virtutis viam semper sequemur. 5. Cura ut bene moriaris. 6. Audi multa, loquere pauca. 7. Per multos annos pace usi sunt. 8. Lacte, caseo, carne vescuntur. 9. Munere tuo bene fungĕre! 10. Aliquando oculi non funguntur munere suo.

. 1. By this death he obtained the freedom of his country. 2. By this death he has obtained immortal glory. 3. It is a small-thing to enjoy life; it is a great-thing to discharge the duties of life. 4. Take care that you always follow (*subj.*) the path (way) of virtue. 5. You 'will enjoy all these good (things). 6. When the body has died (*fut. perf.*), ' then indeed shall we enjoy true life. 7. The Britons used-to-feed (*imperfect*) on milk, flesh, (and) cheese. 8. He used the greatest freedom in his oration. 9. Use riches, do not abuse (them). 10. Follow us; *we* will protect you.

B.—1. Sapienter utimini tempore. 2. Clarissimus hic dux consulatu functus est. 3. Qui nimis cupit honores, raro eos adipiscitur. 4. Caesar duas legiones ad Labienum proficisci jubet, ipse in Menapiorum fines profectus est. 5. Bellum gerimus, ut pace fruamur. 6. Alexander immortalitatis gloriam adeptus est. 7. Augustus omnes cives benigne alloquebatur. 8. Eodem die, quo Dianae templum deflagravit, Alexander Magnus natus est. 9. Regulus omnes cruciatus Poenorum fortiter passus est. 10. Hannibal milites adhortatus est, ut reminiscerentur pristinae virtutis suae, neve (*and not*) liberorum obliviscerentur.

1. Thou hast wisely dischargĕd thine office-of-consul. 2. Generals often exhort their soldiers to (ut) remember their wives and children. 3. Remember (your) ancient valour, soldiers! 4. Caesar orders these two legions to set out. 5. It is a small thing to speak kindly (benigne) to (one's) fellow-citizens. 6. That most famous (nobilis) battle was fought near the lake Trasimenus. 7. Caesar himself set out for (into) the territories of the Menapii. 8. Now we have peace; shortly we shall carry-on war. 9. Regulus endured bravely the utmost tortures. 10. On the same day (see Latin No. 8), on which that most famous battle was fought, the poet Euripides was born.

EXERCISE XXXVII.

Deponent Verbs of the Fourth Conjugation.

1. Milites belli fortunam experiuntur. 2. Epaminondas nunquam mentiebatur. 3. Senes multa experti sunt in longa vita. 4. Magnos viros virtute metimur, non fortuna. 5. Voluptas blanditur sensibus

nostris. 6. Frons, oculi, vultus saepe mentiuntur. 7. Tarquinius Superbus potitus est regno. 8. Puniemini, quod mentiti estis. 9. Bellum civile in Italia orsum est. 10/ Patres bona sua cum liberis partiunturl

1. We will try the fortune of war. 2. The Romans often tried the fortune of war. 3. It is extremely-base (*superl.*) to lie. 4. We will share our goods with our children. 5. There is no doubt that the enemy (*pl.*) have-obtained-possession-of the city. 6. Let us try our valour; let us obtain-possession-of the camp of the enemy. 7. There is no doubt that pleasure wins-upon our senses. 8. We ought to measure men by (their) virtue, not by (their) fortune. 9. Very many (people) measure all things by fortune. 10. The consuls will measure (out) lands to the soldiers.

XXIX.—Prepositions.

Of the Prepositions some govern the Accusative Case, some the Ablative, and some either the Accusative or Ablative.

I. *With the Accusative alone.*

Ad,	to.	Ŏb,	on account of
Adversŭs, Adversum,	} towards, against.	Pĕnĕs,	in the power of.
		Pĕr,	through
Antĕ,	before.	Pŏnĕ,	behind.
Apŭd,	at, near.	Post,	after.
Circă, circum,	around.	Praetĕr,	beside.
Circĭtĕr,	about.	Prŏpĕ,	near.
Cis & citră,	on this side of.	Proptĕr,	on account of.
Contră,	against, contrary to.	Sĕcundum,	{following, in accordance with.
Ergă,	towards (only of the		
Extră,	outside of. [feelings).	Supră,	above.
Infră,	below.	Trans,	across.
Intĕr,	between, among.	Ultră,	on the farther side of.
Intră,	inside of, within.	Versŭs,	towards (only of place
Juxtă,	near, hard by, next to.		[or direction).

Versŭs is put after the word it governs.

Exercise XXXVIII.

1. Exercitus hostium ad portas urbis venit. 2. Multi homines contra naturam vivunt. 3. Judices secundum leges hunc hominem puniverunt. 4. Multae aves ante hiemem in alias terras migrant. 5. Hac aestate extra urbem habitabimus. 6. Romani trans Rhenum multa oppida vastaverunt. 7. Hoc bellum intra paucos dies finitum erit. 8. Vir sapiens non propter metum legibus parebit. 9. Rhodanus primo occidentem versus fluit. 10. Equitatum praeter fluminis ripas contra hostem ducit.

1. Hannibal led (his) army to the gates of the city. 2. Who doubts that it is contrary-to virtue to lie? 3. All these things are in-the-power-of the consuls. 4. The general led his army towards the river. 5. Very many birds migrate into Britain in the summer. 6. The river Rhone flows through the lake. 7. A good judge will judge according to the laws. 8. We (nos) shall dwell within the city, but you (vos) will depart into the country (agri). 9. The camp of Hannibal was near the walls of the city. 10. The night-ingale migrates across the sea in winter.

II. With the Ablative alone.

A, ăb, *or* abs,	*by or 'from*	Ex *or* ĕ,	*out of.*
Absquĕ (rare),	*without.*	Prae,	*before, in comparison with.*
Cŏram,	*in the presence of.*	Prŏ,	*before, for, on behalf of.*
Cum,	*with.*	Sĭnĕ,	*without.*
Dĕ,	*down 'from, 'from, concerning.*	Tĕnŭs,	*reaching to, as far as.*

Tĕnŭs is put after the word it governs.

Exercise XXXIX.

1. Magna cum voluptate avium cantum audivimus. 2. A Cicerone liber de senectute scriptus est. 3. Rhenus agrum Helvetium a Germanis dividit. 4. Romani ex Gallia trans Rhenum veniunt. 5. Pro salute reipublicae et pro liberis pugnabimus. 6. Magna gloria nemini venit sine virtute. 7. Coram parentibus dixi quae scripseram. 8. Incolae urbis de pace legatos ad Caesarem miserunt. 9. Cato in senectute prae ceteris floruit. 10. Alexander omnes terras Oceano tenus vicit.

1. The songs of birds are heard with pleasure by all. 2. Cicero has written a very beautiful book concerning old age. 3. The ocean separates Britain from Gaul. 4. He said these things in-the-presence-of all the soldiers. 5. The general marched (duco) his army out of the city. 6. Before all others Demosthenes and Cicero are the most renowned orators. 7. There is no true glory without virtue. 8. Along with thee (tecum*) we will depart into another land. 9. We are fighting for (pro) our country, for our wives, for our children. 10. He has said this in the presence of his father.

III. With the Accusative or Ablative.

In,	*in, into.*	Sŭper,	*over.*
Sŭb,	*up to, under;* of time, *about.*	Subter,	*under.*

Clam, *secretly, without the knowledge of.*

In and *Sub* with the *Acc.* answer to the question *Whither?* with the *Abl.*, the question *Where?*

* *Mecum, tecum, secum, nobiscum, vobiscum,* are used instead of *cum me, cum te,* etc.

Exercise XL.

1. Multi homines in varias terras itinera faciunt. 2. In magno flumine magni capiuntur pisces. 3. In hortum meum non venisti, in urbe autem fuisti. 4. Sub terra est magna rerum utilium multitudo. 5. Equitatus hostium sub noctem in castra venit. 6. Plurimae aves sub hiemem in alias terras volant. 7. Pompeius in Aegypto sub oculis uxoris et liberorum mortuus est. 8. Caesar super Indos proferet imperium. 9. Super tabernaculum Darii imago solis fulgebat. 10. Etiam sub marmore et auro habitat servitus.

1. We were coming into the city; you were dwelling in it. 2. The camp of Hannibal was under the walls of Rome. 3. We were walking in the garden. 4. It is not pleasant to all to dwell in the city. 5. Large fishes are not caught in a small river. 6. The nightingale does not always remain in the same lands. 7. They slay Pompey beneath the very (ipse) eyes of his wife. 8. The Romans will extend their empire beyond the boundaries of Europe. 9. Beneath the earth there are many beautiful things. 10. Towards winter these birds migrate into other lands.

XXX.—Adverbs.

Adverbs are formed from Adjectives and Participles, by means of the terminations -ē and -tĕr. Adverbs derived from Adjectives and Participles of the First and Second Declensions end in -ē, as doctē, *learnedly*, from doctus. Adverbs derived from Adjectives and Participles of the Third Declension end in -tĕr, as fortĭtĕr, *bravely*, from fortis.

The *Comparative* of the Adverb is the same as the Neuter Nominative Singular of the Comparative Adjective, and consequently ends in iŭs.

The *Superlative* of the Adverb is formed from the Superlative of the Adjective by changing the final syllable of the latter into ē.

ADJECTIVES.		Positive.	ADVERBS.	Comparative.	Superlative.
doctus,	*learned.*	doctē,	*learnedly.*	doctius	doctissĭmē
lĭber,	*free.*	lĭbĕrē,	*freely.*	lĭbĕrius	lĭberrĭmē
pulcher,	*beautiful.*	pulchrē,	*beautifully.*	pulchrius	pulcherrĭmē
fortis,	*brave.*	fortĭtĕr,	*bravely.*	fortius	fortissĭmē
sĭmĭlis,	*like.*	sĭmĭlĭtĕr,	*alike.*	sĭmĭlius	sĭmillĭmē
ācĕr,	*keen.*	ācrĭtĕr,	*keenly.*	ācrius	ācerrĭmē
fēlix,	*lucky.*	fēlĭcĭtĕr,	*luckily.*	fēlĭcius	fēlĭcissĭmē
prūdens,	*prudent.*	prūdenter,	*prudently.*	prūdentius	prūdentissĭmē

Adverbs are irregular in their Comparison, if the Adjectives from which they are derived are also irregular.

Adjectives.		Adverbs.			
		Positive.		Comp.	Sup.
bŏnus,	good.	bĕnĕ,	well.	mĕlius	optĭmē
mălus,	bad.	mălē,	badly, ill.	pājus	pessĭmē
multus,	much, many.	multum,	much.	plŭs	plūrĭmum
magnus,	great,	magnŏpĕrĕ,	greatly.	măgĭs	maxĭmē
prŏpinquus,	near.	prŏpĕ,	near, nearly.	prŏpius	proxĭmē
(prŏ)	before.	———		prius	primum &
					[primō

EXERCISE XLI.

A.—1. Germani cum Romanis fortiter pugnavērunt. 2. Milites audacius resistere ac fortius pugnare incipiunt. 3. Miles hostibus fortissime restitit. 4. Galli Italiam longe lateque vastaverunt. 5. Cicero Roscium audacissime defendit. 6. Judicem ii timere debent, qui male egerunt. 7. Deus mundum sapientissime regit. 8. Leones facilius vincuntur quam tigres. 9. Nunquam jucundius viximus quam nunc. 10. Orationes Demosthenis ab Atheniensibus attentissime audiebantur.

1. Fight bravely, soldiers; ye are fighting for your country. 2. Now we shall live most delightfully. 3. The Germans fought very bravely. 4. Hear the speech more attentively, citizens! 5. The Gauls laid waste the lands (ager) of the Romans far and wide. 6. Ye have acted most wisely, citizens! 7. Who doubts that the soldiers have fought most bravely? 8. In this matter (res) Cicero acted most prudently. 9. The Gauls were not easily conquered. 10. Who doubts that God rules the world most wisely?

B.—1. Non satis est vivere, debemus bene vivere. 2. Multum prodest juventuti libros veterum legere. 3. Eo tempore Cicero maxime omnium reipublicae profuit. 4. Quis reipublicae plus quam Cicero profuit? 5. Orator est (he is) magis quam poeta. 6. Hannibal, dux Poenorum, proxime ad urbem accessit. 7. Primum Latinam linguam discere incipiam. 8. Propius ad portas urbis accessit Hannibal quam Hasdrubal. 9. Pessime omnium egisti! bonos cives perdidisti; improbis bene fecisti. 10. Prius linguam Latinam quam Graecam didicit.

1. It is easy to write; it is not easy to write well. 2. (He) who does not read attentively, reads ill. 3. It was difficult to approach near to the gates. 4. Hannibal approached very-near to the gates of Rome. 5. There is no doubt that you have acted very-ill. 6. You have acted worse than all the others. 7. It is not a great thing to write much, it is a very-great thing to write well. 8. First of all (things), reverence the celestial gods. 9. We have lived most pleasantly. 10. There is no doubt that to write well is extremely-difficult.

XXXI.—Irregular Verbs.

1. Possum, pŏtuī, posse,—*to be able ; can.*

Indicative.	Subjunctive.	Indicative.	Subjunctive.
1. Present.		*4. Perfect.*	
S. Pos-sum	Pos-sim	*S.* Pŏt-uī	Pŏt-uĕrim
Pŏt-ĕs	Pos-sīs	Pŏt-uistī	Pŏt-uĕrīs
Pŏt-est	Pos-sīt	Pŏt-uīt	Pŏt-uĕrīt
P. Pos-sŭmŭs	Pos-sīmŭs	*P.* Pŏt-uīmŭs	Pŏt-uĕrimŭs
Pŏt-estīs	Pos-sītīs	Pŏt-uistīs	Pŏt-uĕritīs
Pos-sunt	Pos-sint	Pŏt-uĕrunt (ĕrĕ)	Pŏt-uĕrint
2. Future-Simple.		*5. Future-Perfect.*	
S. Pŏt-ĕro	(wanting.)	*S.* Pŏt-uĕro	(wanting.)
Pŏt-ĕrīs		Pŏt-uĕrīs	
Pŏt-ĕrīt		Pŏt-uĕrīt	
P. Pŏt-ĕrimŭs		*P.* Pŏt-uĕrimŭs	
Pŏt-ĕritīs		Pŏt-uĕritīs	
Pŏt-ĕrunt		Pŏt-uĕrint	
3. Imperfect.		*6. Pluperfect.*	
S. Pŏt-ĕram	Pos-sem	*S.* Pŏt-uĕram	Pŏt-uissem
Pŏt-ĕrās	Pos-sēs	Pŏt-uĕrās	Pŏt-uissēs
Pŏt-ĕrāt	Pos-sĕt	Pŏt-uĕrāt	Pŏt-uissĕt
P. Pŏt-ĕrāmŭs	Pos-sēmŭs	*P.* Pŏt-uĕrāmŭs	Pŏt-uissēmŭs
Pŏt-ĕrātīs	Pos-sētīs	Pŏt-uĕrātīs	Pŏt-uissētīs
Pŏt-ĕrant	Pos-sent	Pŏt-uĕrant	Pŏt-uissent

Infinitive.

Pres. and Imp.—**Posse.** *Perf. and Plup.*—**Pŏtuisse.** *Future*—wanting.
(Participle **pŏtens,** used only as Adjective, *powerful.*)

Exercise XLII.

1. Ego possum legere, tu potes scribere, soror potest acu pingere.
2. Tyrannus animum sapientis infringere non poterat. 3. Cur heri nobiscum ambulare non poteras? 4. Cura, ut possis aequo animo vitam relinquere. 5. Nemo dubitat, quin milites urbem defendere possint. 6. Mores tyranni ei amicos parare non potuerunt. 7. Non dubitamus, quin urbs a civibus defendi potuerit. 8. Vix Caesar milites e castris educere potuerat, quum hostes impetum fecerunt. 9. Quid melius hominibus dari potuit quam ratio? 10. Virtutis splendor nunquam obscurari poterit.

1. We are all able to be serviceable to (our) friends. 2. You will not be able to be a friend to all. 3. Hannibal was not able to obtain-possession-of the city. 4. Cornelia was able to train her sons

most wisely. 5. No one doubted that the soldiers were able to defend the city. 6. We cannot all be kings; we can all be good citizens. 7. You will not be able to read Sallust easily : he is a difficult author. 8. Caesar was able to conquer his enemies; he was not able to conquer envy. 9. Those wicked men will not be able to quit life with even mind. 10. Restrain (thy) tongue; so thou wilt be able to restrain also thy temper (animus).

---

2. Vŏlo, vŏluī, vellĕ,—*to be willing, to wish.*

3. Nōlo, nōluī, nollĕ,—*to be unwilling, not to wish.*

4. Mālo, māluī, mallĕ,—*to be more willing, to prefer, to have rather.*

INDICATIVE.

1. *Present.*

Sing.	Vŏlo	Nōlo	Mālo
	Vīs	Nōn vīs	Māvīs
	Vult	Nōn vult	Māvult
Plur.	Vŏlŭmŭs	Nōlŭmŭs	Mālŭmŭs
	Vultĭs	Nōn vultĭs	Māvultĭs
	Vŏlunt	Nōlunt	Mālunt

2. *Future-Simple*

Sing.	Vŏl-am	Nōl-am	Māl-am
	Vŏl-ĕs	Nōl-ĕs	Māl-ĕs
	Vŏl-ĕt	Nōl-ĕt	Māl-ĕt
Plur.	Vŏl-ēmŭs	Nōl-ēmŭs	Māl-ēmŭs
	Vŏl-ētĭs	Nōl-ētĭs	Māl-ētĭs
	Vŏl-ent	Nōl-ent	Māl-ent

3. *Imperfect*

Sing.	Vŏl-ēbam	Nōl-ēbam	Māl-ēbam
	Vŏl-ēbăs	Nōl-ēbăs	Māl-ēbăs
	Vŏl-ēbăt	Nōl-ēbăt	Māl-ēbăt
Plur.	Vŏl-ēbāmŭs	Nōl-ēbāmŭs	Māl-ēbāmŭs
	Vŏl-ēbātĭs	Nōl-ēbātĭs	Māl-ēbātĭs
	Vŏl-ēbant	Nōl-ēbant	Māl-ēbant

4. *Perfect.*

Sing.	Vŏl-uī	Nōl-uī	Māl-uī
	Vŏl-uistī	Nōl-uistī	Māl-uistī
	Vŏl-uĭt	Nōl-uĭt	Māl-uĭt
Plur.	Vŏl-uĭmŭs	Nōl-uĭmŭs	Māl-uĭmŭs
	Vŏl-uistĭs	Nōl-uistĭs	Māl-uistĭs
	Vŏl-uērunt *or* -uērĕ	Nōl-uērunt *or* uērĕ	Māl-uērunt *or* -uērĕ

5. *Future-Perfect.*

Sing.	Vŏl-uĕro	Nŏl-uĕro	Māl-uĕro
	Vŏl-uĕrīs	Nŏl-uĕrīs	Māl-uĕrīs
	Vŏl-uĕrĭt	Nŏl-uĕrĭt	Māl-uĕrĭt
Plur.	Vŏl-uĕrimŭs	Nŏl-uĕrimŭs	Māl-uĕrimŭs
	Vŏl-uĕritĭs	Nŏl-uĕritĭs	Māl-uĕritĭs
	Vŏl-uĕrint	Nŏl-uĕrint	Māl-uĕrint

6. *Pluperfect.*

Sing.	Vŏl-uĕram	Nŏl-uĕram	Māl-uĕram
	Vŏl-uĕrās	Nŏl-uĕrās	Māl-uĕrās
	Vŏl-uĕrăt	Nŏl-uĕrăt	Māl-uĕrăt
Plur.	Vŏl-uĕrāmŭs	Nŏl-uĕrāmŭs	Māl-uĕrāmŭs
	Vŏl-uĕrātĭs	Nŏl-uĕrātĭs	Māl-uĕrātĭs
	Vŏl-uĕrant	Nŏl-uĕrant	Māl-uĕrant

SUBJUNCTIVE.

1. *Present.*

Sing.	Vĕl-im	Nŏl-im	Māl-im
	Vĕl-īs	Nŏl-īs	Māl-īs
	Vĕl-ĭt	Nŏl-ĭt	Māl-ĭt
Plur.	Vĕl-īmŭs	Nŏl-īmŭs	Māl-īmŭs
	Vĕl-ītĭs	Nŏl-ītĭs	Māl-ītĭs
	Vĕl-int	Nŏl-int	Māl-int

2. *Imperfect.*

Sing.	Vel-lem	Nol-lem	Mal-lem
	Vel-lēs	Nol-lēs	Mal-lēs
	Vel-lĕt	Nol-lĕt	Mal-lĕt
Plur.	Vel-lēmŭs	Nol-lēmŭs	Mal-lēmŭs
	Vel-lētĭs	Nol-lētĭs	Mal-lētĭs
	Vol-lent	Nol-lent	Mal-lent

3. *Perfect.*

Sing.	Vŏl-uĕrim	Nŏl-uĕrim	Māl-uĕrim
	Vŏl-uĕrīs	Nŏl-uĕrīs	Māl-uĕrīs
	Vŏl-uĕrĭt	Nŏl-uĕrĭt	Māl-uĕrĭt
Plur.	Vŏl-uĕrimŭs	Nŏl-uĕrimŭs	Māl-uĕrimŭs
	Vŏl-uĕritĭs	Nŏl-uĕritĭs	Māl-uĕritĭs
	Vŏl-uĕrint	Nŏl-uĕrint	Māl-uĕrint

4. *Pluperfect.*

Sing.	Vŏl-uissem	Nŏl-uissem	Māl-uissem
	Vŏl-uissēs	Nŏl-uissēs	Māl-uissēs
	Vŏl-uissĕt	Nŏl-uissĕt	Māl-uissĕt
Plur.	Vŏl-uissēmŭs	Nŏl-uissēmŭs	Māl-uissēmŭs
	Vŏl-uissētĭs	Nŏl-uissētĭs	Māl-uissētĭs
	Vŏl-uissent	Nŏl-uissent	Māl-uissent

IMPERATIVE.

Present.

(wanting.) Nŏl-ī (wanting.)
Nŏl-ĭtŏ

Future.

Nŏl-ĭto
Nŏl-ĭto
Nŏl-ĭtŏtŏ
Nŏl-unto

INFINITIVE.

Present and Imperfect.

Vel-lĕ Nŏl-lĕ Mal-lĕ

Perfect and Pluperfect.

Vŏl-uissĕ Nŏl-uissĕ Māl-uissĕ

PRESENT PARTICIPLE.

Vŏl-ens Nŏl-ens (wanting.)

EXERCISE XLIII.

A.—1. Ego volo legere, tu vis scribere, frater vult pingere. 2. Ego domi sedere nolo, tu ambulare non vis. 3. Tu ambulare mavis quam domi sedere. 4. Soror saltare mavult quam ambulare. 5. Oro te, ut mecum ludere velis. 6. Dic, cur me comitari nolis. 7. Orabam te, ut mecum ludere velles. 8. Nesciebam, cur me comitari nolles. 9. Si beati esse volumus, sorte nostra contenti esse debemus. 10. Si vis amari, ama!

1. We do not wish to walk in the fields; we prefer to remain at home. 2. We wished to read, you wished to write, (our) brother wished to paint. 3. I knew-not (how) to dance; I preferred to write and to read. 4. I wished to read; but my sister wished to sing and to dance. 5. If you wish to be happy, imitate the examples of good men. 6. Alexander wished to extend his empire beyond the Indi. 7. We do not all obtain those-things which we wish. 8. I had-rather (*pres.*) fight (*inf.*) against enemies than against envy. 9. Pompey was unwilling to depart from the city. 10. I entreat you to (ut) be willing to accompany me.

B.—1. Ego tibi prodesse malo quam obesse. 2. Non dubito, quin mihi prodesse malis quam obesse. 3. Non dubitabam, quin prodesse mihi malles quam obesse. 4. Amicus maluit diligi quam metui. 5. Secundum naturam volent vivere. 6. Cato esse quam videri bonus malebat. 7. Boni esse mavultis quam nobiles et divites. 8. Pythagoras Apollini hostiam immolare noluit. 9. Nolite dolori nimis indulgere. 10. Amici eadem velle debent.

1. I prefer to be good (rather) than to seem (so). 2. Do not deceive; do not* lie; those things (res) very greatly injure friendship. 3. Epaminondas was unwilling to lie. 4. You wish the same things which I (wish). 5. We had-rather (*pres.*) be (*inf.*) useful to our country than be (*inf.*) rich. 6. A good man will prefer to be loved (rather) than to be feared. 7. I had-rather be loved by true friends than be rich. 8. The ancient Romans sacrificed very many victims to the gods. 9. Pythagoras was unwilling to indulge anger: he preferred to restrain it. 10. Be unwilling to follow bad examples, my son!

* Say, *Be unwilling to lie.* Compare No. 9 of the Latin sentences.

---

5. **Fĕro, tŭlī, ferrĕ, lātum,**—*to bear, carry, endure.*

I. ACTIVE VOICE.

INDICATIVE.	SUBJUNCTIVE.	INDICATIVE.	SUBJUNCTIVE.
1. *Present.*		**4. *Perfect.***	
S. Fĕr-o	Fĕr-am	*S.* Tŭl-ī	Tŭl-ĕrim
Fer-s	Fĕr-ās	Tŭl-istī	Tŭl-ĕrīs
Fer-t	Fĕr-ăt	Tŭl-ĭt	Tŭl-ĕrĭt
P. Fĕr-ĭmŭs	Fĕr-āmŭs	*P.* Tŭl-ĭmŭs	Tŭl-ĕrimŭs
Fer-tĭs	Fĕr-ātĭs	Tŭl-istĭs	Tŭl-ĕritĭs
Fĕr-unt	Fĕr-ant	Tŭl-ĕrunt *or* ĕrĕ Tŭl-ĕrint
2. *Future-Simple.*		**5. *Future-Perfect.***	
S. Fĕr-am	(wanting.)	*S.* Tŭl-ĕro	(wanting.)
Fĕr-ĕs		Tŭl-ĕrĭs	
Fĕr-ĕt		Tŭl-ĕrĭt	
P. Fĕr-ĕmŭs		*P.* Tŭl-ĕrimŭs	
Fĕr-ētĭs		Tŭl-ĕritĭs	
Fĕr-ent		Tŭl-ĕrint	
3. *Imperfect.*		**6. *Pluperfect.***	
S. Fĕr-ĕbam	Fer-rem	*S.* Tŭl-ĕram	Tŭl-issem
Fĕr-ĕbās	Fer-rēs	Tŭl-ĕrās	Tŭl-issēs
Fĕr-ĕbăt	Fer-rĕt	Tŭl-ĕrăt	Tŭl-issĕt
P. Fĕr-ĕbāmŭs	Fer-rēmŭs	*P.* Tŭl-ĕrāmŭs	Tŭl-issēmŭs
Fĕr-ĕbātĭs	Fer-rētĭs	Tŭl-ĕrātĭs	Tŭl-issētĭs
Fĕr-ĕbant	Fer-rent	Tŭl-ĕrant	Tŭl-issent

IMPERATIVE.		PARTICIPLES.	
Present.	Fĕr	*Present.*	Fĕr-ens
	Fer-tŏ	*Future.*	Lātūrŭs (a, um)
Future.	Fer-to		
	Fer-to	SUPINES.	
	Fer-tōtĕ		Lātum
	Fĕr-unto		Lātū
INFINITIVE.			
Pres. and Imp.	Fer-rĕ	GERUND.	
Perf. and Plup.	Tŭl-issĕ	*Gen.*	Fĕr-endī
Future.	Lātūrŭs essĕ		&c.

II. PASSIVE VOICE.

INDICATIVE.	SUBJUNCTIVE.	INDICATIVE.	SUBJUNCTIVE.

1. *Present.*

S. Fĕr-ŏr   Fĕr-ăr
Fer-rĭs, -rĕ   Fĕr-ārĭs, -ārĕ
Fer-tŭr   Fĕr-ātŭr
P. Fĕr-ĭmŭr   Fĕr-ămŭr
Fĕr-ĭmĭnī   Fĕr-āmĭnī
Fĕr-untŭr   Fĕr-antŭr

4. *Perfect.*

S. Lātŭs sum   Lātŭs sim
Lātŭs ĕs   Lātŭs sīs
Lātŭs est   Lātŭs sīt
P. Lātī sŭmŭs   Lātī sīmŭs
Lātī estīs   Lātī sītĭs
Lātī sunt   Lātī sint

2. *Future-Simple.*

S. Fĕr-ăr   (wanting.)
Fĕr-ērĭs, -ērĕ
Fĕr-ētŭr
P. Fĕr-ēmŭr
Fĕr-ēmĭnī
Fĕr-entŭr

5. *Future-Perfect.*

S. Lātŭs ĕro   (wanting.)
Lātŭs ĕrĭs
Lātŭs ĕrĭt
P. Lātī ĕrĭmŭs
Lātī ĕrĭtĭs
Lātī ĕrunt

3. *Imperfect.*

S. Fĕr-ēbăr   Fer-rĕr
Fĕr-ēbārĭs, -ārĕ   Fer-rērĭs, -ērĕ
Fĕr-ēbātŭr   Fĕr-rētŭr
P. Fĕr-ēbāmŭr   Fer-rēmŭr
Fĕr-ēbāmĭnī   Fer-rēmĭnī
Fĕr-ēbantŭr   Fer-rentŭr

6. *Pluperfect.*

S. Lātŭs ĕram   Lātŭs essem
Lātŭs ĕrās   Lātŭs essēs
Lātŭs ĕrăt   Lātŭs essēt
P. Lātī ĕrāmŭs   Lātī essēmŭs
Lātī ĕrātĭs   Lātī essētĭs
Lātī ĕrănt   Lātī easent

IMPERATIVE.

Present.   Fer-rĕ
    Fĕr-ĭmĭnī

Future.   Fer-tŏr
    Fer-tŏr
    Fĕr-untŏr

INFINITIVE.

Pres. and Imp.   Fer-ri
Perf. and Plup.   Lātŭs essĕ
Future.   Lātum īrī

PARTICIPLES.

Perfect.   Lātŭs (a, um)
Gerundive.   Fĕr-endŭs (a, um)

Obs. The compounds of fĕro are conjugated in the same way : *e. g.*

Affĕro	(ad, | fero),	attŭlī,	allātum,	afferrĕ,	*bring to.*
Aufĕro	(ab, | fero),	abstŭlī,	ablātum,	aufferrĕ,	*carry away.*
Effĕro	(ex, | fero),	extŭlī,	ēlātum,	efferrĕ,	*carry out.*
Infĕro	(in, | fero),	intŭlī,	illātum,	inferrĕ,	*carry into.*
Offĕro	(ob, | fero),	obtŭlī,	oblātum,	offerrĕ,	*present.*
Perfĕro	(per, | fero),	pertŭlī,	perlātum,	perferrĕ,	*bear through, endure.*
Praefĕro	(prae, | fero),	praetŭlī,	praelātum,	praeferrĕ,	*prefer.*
Rĕfĕro	(re, | fero),	{ rĕtŭlī / rettŭlī }	rēlātum,	rĕferrĕ,	*bring back.*

EXERCISE XLIV.

1. Senectus affert prudentiam. 2. Laudo vos, quod misero atque inopi auxilium fertis. 3. Ferre laborem consuetudo docet. 4. Nihil potest praeferri virtuti. 5. Curabamus, ut vobis auxilium ferremus. 6. Rex curabat, ut inopibus civibus auxilium ferretur. 7. Non omnis ager, qui seritur, fert fruges. 8. Agricola paupertatis

˙ PR. L. I.   G

onus patienter tulit. 9. Fer patienter laborem. 10. Milites in itineribus multas aerumnas pertulerunt.

1. Socrates bore hardships most patiently. 2. Learn thou to bear well pleasure and pain. 3. Cato bore old age excellently-well (*superl.* of bene). 4. There is no doubt that old age brings many sorrows with it (secum). 5. Caesar ordered two cohorts to bring assistance to the cavalry. 6. I have learned to bring assistance to the wretched. 7. A sailor ought to be able to bear patiently the hardships of the sea. 8. A good man is able to bear with even mind the hardships of life. 9. Who can endure the discourse of this unlearned man? 10. The Romans knew (how) to bear with even mind the greatest disasters.

6. Ĕo, Ĭvĭ, Ĭrĕ, Ĭtum,—*to go.*

Indicative.	Subjunctive.		Indicative.	Subjunctive.
1. Present.			**4. Perfect.**	
S. Ĕ-o	E-am		S. I-vĭ or Ĭ-ĭ	I-vĕrim or Ĭ-ĕrim
I-s	E-ās		I-vistĭ &c.	I-vĕrĭs &c.
Ĭ-t	E-ăt		I-vĭt &c.	I-vĕrĭt &c.
P. I-mŭs	E-āmŭs		P. I-vĭmŭs &c.	I-vĕrimŭs &c.
I-tis	E-ātĭs		I-vistĭs &c.	I-vĕritĭs &c.
E-unt	E-ant		I-vĕrunt &c.	I-vĕrint &c.
			or I-vĕrĕ	
2. Future-Simple.			**5. Future-Perfect.**	
S. I-bo	Ĭ-tūrŭs sim		S. I-vĕro or Ĭ-ĕro (wanting.)	
I-bĭs	Ĭ-tūrŭs sĭs		I-vĕrĭs &c.	
I-bĭt	Ĭ-tūrŭs sĭt		I-vĕrĭt &c.	
P. I-bĭmŭs	Ĭ-tūrĭ sĭmŭs		P. I-vĕrimŭs &c.	
I-bĭtĭs	Ĭ-tūrĭ sĭtĭs		I-vĕritĭs &c.	
I-bunt	Ĭ-tūrĭ sint		I-vĕrint &c.	
3. Imperfect.			**6. Pluperfect.**	
S. I-bam	I-rem		S. I-vĕram or I-vissem, I-issem,	
I-bās	I-rēs		I-ĕram	or I-ssem.
I-băt	I-rĕt		I-vĕrās &c. I-vissēs &c.	
P. I-bāmŭs	I-rēmŭs		I-vĕrăt &c. I-vissĕt &c.	
I-bātĭs	I-rētis		P. I-vĕrāmŭs &c. I-vissēmŭs &c.	
I-bant	I-rent		I-vĕrātĭs &c. I-vissētĭs &c.	
			I-vĕrant &c. I-vissent &c.	

	IMPERATIVE.		PARTICIPLES.	
Present.	I	*Present.*	I-ens (*Gen.* ĕ-untĭs)	
	I-tŏ	*Future.*	Ĭ-tūrŭs (ă, um)	
Future.	I-to			
	I-to		GERUND.	
	I-tōtŏ	*Gen.*	Ĕ-undi, &c.	
	Ĕ-unto			
	INFINITIVE.		SUPINE.	
Pres. and Imp. I-rĕ			Ĭ-tum	
Perf. and Plup. I-vissĕ, Ĭissĕ, or issĕ				
Future. Ĭ-tūrus essĕ				

The Compounds of *ĕo* are conjugated in the same way.
The following are the principal :—

ăb-ĕo,	ăb-ĭi,	ăb-ĭtum,	*to go away.*
ăd-eo,		&c.	*to go to.*
cŏ-eo,		&c.	*to join together.*
ex-eo,		&c.	*to go out.*
ĭn-eo, intro-eo,		&c.	*to go into, enter.*
intĕr-eo,		&c.	*to perish.*
ŏb-eo,		&c.	*to meet ; esp. to meet death ; to die.*
pĕr-eo,		&c.	*to perish.*
prae-eo,		&c.	*to go before.*
praetĕr-eo,		&c.	*to pass by.*
rĕd-eo,		&c.	*to return.*
sŭb-eo,		&c.	*to go up to.*
trans-eo,		&c.	*to cross over.*

N.B. In the Compounds the form *ii* is used in preference to *iri*.

EXERCISE XLV.

1. Ego abeo, tu ex itinere redis.   2. Post mortem corpus interit,
animus nunquam interibit.   3. Quum animi nostri ex corporibus
exierint, non interibunt.   4. In pugna atrocissima multi fortissimi
milites perierunt.   5. Curare debemus, ne vitam ignave transe-
amus.   6. Milites e castris redeuntes occisi sunt.   7. Socrates aequo
atque hilari animo diem supremum obiit.   8. Magna pars militum
fame et frigore interiit.   9. Alpes nemo unquam ante Hannibalem
cum exercitu transierat.   10. Alexander adire ad Jovis oraculum
statuit.

1. Very many (persons) pass their life indolently.   2. Let us go-
out from the camp; let us return into the city.   3. Caesar threw
a bridge over the river, in-order-that his soldiers might cross on foot
(*pedibus*).   4. A brave man will meet his last day with even mind.
5. Fifteen thousand of the Romans perished in that desperate battle.
6. We ought all to be able to meet (our) last day with even mind.
7. After the battle very many perished of hunger (*abl.*) and cold
(*abl.*).   8. Let us go to the temples of the gods.   9. I pass-by
very many things in silence.   10. Italy is fortified by the Alps,
(those) most lofty mountains, which an army will not easily cross.

7. Fīo, factŭs sum, fīĕrī,—*to become, or be made, to happen.*

INDICATIVE.	SUBJUNCTIVE.		INDICATIVE.	SUBJUNCTIVE.
	1. Present.			*3. Imperfect.*
S. Fī-o	Fī-am		S. Fī-ēbam	Fī-ērem
Fī-s	Fī-ās		Fī-ēbās	Fī-ērēs
Fī-t *or* fĭ-t	Fī-ăt		Fī-ēbăt	Fī-ērĕt
P. [Fī-mŭs]	Fī-āmŭs		P. Fī-ēbāmŭs	Fī-ērēmŭs
[Fī-tĭs]	Fī-ātĭs		Fī-ēbātĭs	Fī-ērētĭs
Fī-unt	Fī-ant		Fī-ēbant	Fī-ērent
	2. Future.			*4. Perfect.*
S. Fī-am	(wanting.)		Factŭs sum, &c.	Factŭs sim, &c.
Fī-ēs				*5. Future-Perfect.*
Fī-ĕt			Factŭs ĕro, &c.	(wanting.)
P. Fī-ēmŭs				*6. Pluperfect.*
Fī-ētĭs			Factŭs ĕram, &c.	Factŭs essem, &c.
Fī-ent				

	IMPERATIVE.		INFINITIVE.	
Present.	FĪ, Fī-tŏ		*Pres. and Imp.*	Fī-ĕrī
	PARTICIPLES.		*Perf. and Plup.*	Factŭs essĕ
Perfect.	Factŭs (a, um)		*Future.*	Factum īrī
Gerundive.	Făciendŭs (a, um)			

Fio is used as the Passive of făcio.

EXERCISE XLVI.

1. Nemo fit casu bonus. 2. Ex amico inimicus, ex inimico amicus fieri potest. 3. Senectute prudentior fis. 4. Nemo ignaviā immortalis factus est. 5. Deus dixit: fiat, et factus est mundus. 6. Apud veteres Romanos ex agricolis fiebant consules. 7. Themistoclis consilio factum est, ut Athenienses urbem relinquerent. 8. Onus quod bene fertur leve fit. 9. Quod factum est, infectum fieri non potest. 10. Qui noxium adjuvabit, fiet socius culpae.

1. No one becomes altogether-base (*sup.*) by chance. 2. This heavy burden was made light by patience. 3. There is no doubt that the heaviest sorrows become lighter by patience. 4. Bear these things through, citizens: (things) done cannot be made undone. 5. In time our soldiers will be made more daring. 6. Two consuls were appointed (made). 7. There is no doubt that the danger has become more severe with time. 8. In the winter time the days become shorter and the nights. longer. 9. In the time of Philip, the Athenians had become the allies of the Romans. 10. Do not assist a guilty-person; in-that-way you will become a partner in (= of) his fault.

8. NEUTER-PASSIVE VERBS.

Besides Fio several other Intransitive Verbs form their Perfect tenses after the manner of Passives. The principal of these are the following:—

Audeo, ausus sum, audēre,	*to dare, venture.*
Fido, fisus sum, fīdēre (usu. with *Dat.*),	*to trust.*
Gaudeo, gāvīsus sum, gaudēre,	*to rejoice.*
Sōleo, sōlĭtus sum, sōlēre,	*to be accustomed.*

So too coeno, *to sup* or *dine*, often takes coenātus sum, and jūro, *to swear*, jurātus sum, instead of coenāvi, jurāvi. Such Verbs are called Semi-Deponents or Neuter-Passives.

EXERCISE XLVII.

1. Nonnullae aves prope ad domicilia hominum accedere audent. 2. Optimus ille vir mori ausus est; non autem mentiri. 3. Canes solebant currentes bibere in flumine Nilo. 4. Jam coenati eramus, et in horto ambulabamus. 5. Maxime gavisi sunt cives quod urbs servata erat. 6. In has leges jurati estis, et debetis jusjurandum vestrum conservare. 7. Solitus est Solon aliquid quotidie addiscere. 8. Multum gavisi sunt Romani quod Poenos navali praelio vicerant. 9. Caesar fisus est rebus suis. 10. Gavisus est consul quod illum tam fidelem socium repererat.

1. The ancient Britons were accustomed to clothe themselves with skins. 2. Some animals are accustomed to dwell both (et) in the water and on (in) land. 3. The Helvetii were accustomed to receive hostages, not to give (them). 4. The Romans rejoiced when Cicero returned to the city. 5. The general trusted to himself. 6. Dare to die, citizens! 7. When you return (*fut.-perf.*) we shall already have dined. 8. All the magistrates had sworn to (*in* with *acc.*) the laws. 9. We ought to rejoice because the war has been brought-to-an-end (finio). 10. The whole city rejoiced that (quod) the conspiracy had been discovered.

XXXII.—IMPERSONAL VERBS.

Impersonal Verbs are such as cannot have a Personal subject (I, thou, he), and are used only in the Third Person Singular.

The following are the principal Impersonal Verbs :—

I. VERBS WHICH DENOTE MENTAL STATES.

Děcět, děcuĭt, děcěrě,	it is seemly, become
Dĕdĕcět, dĕdĕcuĭt, dĕdĕcěrě,	it is unseemly.
Lĭbět, lĭbuĭt & lĭbĭtum est, lĭbĕrě,	it pleases.
Lĭcět, lĭcuĭt & lĭcĭtum est, lĭcěrě,	it is lawful, it is allowed.
Lĭquět, lĭquěrě,	it is clear.
Mĭsěrět or mĭsěrětŭr, mĭsěrĭtum est, mĭsěrěrě,	it excites pity.
Ŏportět, ŏportuĭt, ŏportěrě,	it behoves ; (one) ought.
Pĭgět, pĭguĭt & pĭgĭtum est, pĭgěrě,	it vexes.
Plăcět, plăcuĭt or plăcĭtum est, plăcěrě,	it pleases.
Poenĭtět, poenĭtuĭt, poenĭtěrě,	it causes sorrow, repents.
Pŭdět, pŭduĭt or pŭdĭtum est, pŭděrě,	it shames.
Taedět, (pertaesum est,) taeděrě,	it disgusts, wearies.

The Persons are expressed in the following way :—

INDICATIVE.

Present. **Pŭdět mě,** *it shames me,* or *I am ashamed.*
    Pŭdět tě, *it shames thee,* or *thou art ashame*
    Pŭdět eum, *it shames him,* or *he is ashamed.*
    Pŭdět nōs, *it shames us,* or *we are ashamed.*
    Pŭdět vōs, *it shames you,* or *ye are ashamed.*
    Pŭdět eōs, *it shames them,* or *they are ashamed.*

Fut.-Simp. **Pŭdēbĭt mě,** tě, eum, &c., *it will shame me, thee, him, &c.,* or *I, thou, he, &c., will be ashamed.*

Imperfect. **Pŭdēbăt mě,** tě, eum, nōs, vōs, eōs, *it shamed me, thee, him, us, &c.,* or *I, thou, he, we, &c., were ashamed.*

Perfect. **Pŭduĭt mě,** tě, eum, &c., *I, thou, he, &c., was ashamed.*

Fut.-Perf. **Pŭduěrĭt mě,** tě, eum, &c., *I, thou, he, &c., will have been ashamed.*

Pluperfect. **Pŭduěrăt mě,** tě, eum, &c., *I, thou, he, &c., had been ashamed.*

And similarly for the Subjunctive Mood. The Imperative is not found; the Pres. of the Subjunctive being used instead; as, pudeat te, *let it shame thee,* or *be ashamed!*

All these Verbs govern the subject in the Accusative Case, except lĭbet, lĭcet, lĭquet, and plăcet, which govern the Dative: as, mĭhĭ lĭbět, *it pleases me;* mĭhĭ lĭcět, *it is lawful for me, I am at liberty, &c.*

II. Verbs which denote Atmospherical Phenomena.

Grandĭnăt, ăvĭt, ărĕ,	*it hails.*
Ningĭt, ninxĭt, ningĕrĕ,	*it snows.*
Plŭĭt, plŭĭt *or* plŭvĭt, plŭĕrĕ,	*it rains.*
Tŏnăt, tŏnuĭt, tŏnărĕ,	*it thunders.*
Lūcescĭt, (illūxit,) lūcescĕrĕ,	*it becomes light.*
Vespĕrascĭt vespĕrăvĭt, vespĕrascĕrĕ,	*evening comes on.*

Exercise XLVIII.

1. Me pudet poenitetque stultitiae meae. 2. Homines infamiae suae neque pudet neque taedet. 3. Nos oportet hoc facere. 4. Nobis non licebit castris exire. 5. Me civitatis morum piget taedetque. 6. Oratorem irasci minime decet. 7. Non libet mihi deplorare vitam. 8. Placuit Caesari, ut ad Ariovistum legatos mitteret. 9. Pueros decet tacere. 10. Si forte tonuerat, veteres tribuere solebant Jovi.

1. That wicked man (*acc.*) repents not of his crime (scelus). 2. What does it behove us to do? 3. It behoved you to maintain the laws. 4. It-is-unbecoming-in a citizen to deceive his fellow-citizens. 5. I am vexed and disgusted at the folly (*gen.*) of these men. 6. In the winter it seldom thunders; in the summer it seldom snows. 7. Evening-is-coming-on; let us go-out-from the fields and let us return to the city. 8. On the same day it thundered, hailed, snowed (and) rained. 9. You may (it is allowed to you) go forth (*inf.*) from the city, citizens! 10. Dare to be free, Romans! it is allowed to all to die!

PART II.

SOME SYNTACTICAL RULES.

The pupil should repeat the Syntactical Rules already given:—

XXXIII.—THE ABLATIVE AFTER THE COMPARATIVE.

RULE 18.—After Adjectives in the Comparative degree *quam* may be omitted and the Ablative used instead of the Nominative or Accusative: as, vīlius argentum est auro, *silver is more common than gold.*

EXERCISE XLIX.

1. Vilius argentum est auro, virtutibus aurum. 2. Deus major et potentior est cunctis. 3. Nihil est majus amicitiā, nihil jucundius. 4. Homini Deus nihil mente praestabilius dedit. 5. Ignoratio futurorum malorum utilior esse videtur scientiā. 6. Elephanto nulla belluarum prudentior est. 7. Tullus Hostilius non solum proximo regi dissimilis, sed ferocior etiam Romulo fuit 8. Humana omnia inferiora sunt virtute. 9. Phidiae simulacris nihil est perfectius. 10. Sol major et splendidior est lunā.

1. What is brighter than the sun? What more excellent than virtue? 2. Who doubts that the sun is larger than the moon? 3. The earth is greater than the moon; the sun than the earth. 4. Silver and gold are brighter than iron. 5. The elephant is more sagacious than all (other) beasts. 6. There is no doubt that the knowledge of these things is better than the ignorance (of them). 7. Caesar was more powerful than all (the rest of) the citizens,

8. What is commoner than water? yet (autem) what is more useful? 9. Hatred is better than pretence of friendship. 10. No-one of the Athenians is more renowned than Socrates.

XXXIV.—ABLATIVE ABSOLUTE.

RULE 19.—When a subordinate clause has a different subject from the subject of the principal clause, the English Verb in the subordinate clause is in Latin expressed by a Substantive and Participle in the Ablative Case. This construction is called the ABLATIVE ABSOLUTE: as, sōlĕ ortō, Rōmānī hostēs vīdērunt, *when the sun had risen* [lit. *the sun having risen*] *the Romans saw the enemy.*

There is no Perfect Participle Active in Latin, except in the case of Deponent Verbs. But the English Perfect Participle Active may often be expressed by means of the Latin Perfect Participle Passive, in the Ablative Absolute: as, Caesăr, expŏsĭtō exercĭtū, ăd hostēs contendĭt, *Caesar, having landed the army* [lit. *the army having been landed*], *hastens against the enemy.*

N.B. The pupil must carefully observe that it is not the Subject of the principal sentence, but the Accusative after the Verb which becomes the Ablative Absolute.

EXERCISE L.

A.—1. Sole oriente, nox fugit. 2. Recuperatā pace, artes efflorescunt. 3. Alpibus superatis, Hannibal in Italiam venit. 4. Labitur aetas, nobis non sentientibus. 5. Pompeius, ineunte vere, bellum suscepit. 6. His paratis rebus, Caesar milites naves conscendere jubet. 7. Cognito hostium adventu, Caesar naves ex portu educit. 8. Caesar, exposito exercitu, ad hostes contendet. 9. Nivibus solutis, intumescere solent flumina. 10. Solon et Pisistratus, Serviŏ Tullio regnante, vixerunt.

NOTE.—In the two following Exercises, the words which are to be expressed by the Ablative Absolute·are put in italics.

1. *When the sun rises* (*the sun rising*), all (things) become brighter. 2. *When the moon had risen*, the night was made brighter. 3. *When Cato was slain*,.the commonwealth perished. 4. *When these things were done*, Caesar orders his soldiers to embark. 5. Caesar, *after he had overcome the Gauls*, waged war with Pompeius. 6. *Having heard these things*, he led his army to the banks of the river. 7. *Whilst Servius Tullius was king* (*Serv. Tull. being-king*), the city was fortified with a wall of-stone. 8. *Having learned these things*, he hastened into the territory of the enemy.

9. *Having thrown a bridge across the river (the river being joined by a bridge)*, he orders the soldiers to cross. 10. *Having disembarked his soldiers*, he began to lay waste the lands of the enemy.

B.—1. Bello Punico confecto, triumphavit Scipio cum summo honore. 2. Dario apud Arbelam victo, Alexander Asia potitus est. 3. His literis perlectis, consul comprehendi eos jubet. 4. Conjuratione detecta, jam servata esse videbatur civitas. 5. Senatu convocato, Cicero literas recitat quas de conjuratione acceperat. 6. His rebus paratis, contendit Caesar maximis itineribus in agros Helvetiorum. 7. Delectu habito, consul ad exercitum statim proficiscitur. 8. Catone mortuo, nulla jam erat respublica. 9. Caesare occiso, gravissime vexata est respublica bello civili. 10. Proelio commisso, conantur Galli aciem Romanorum perrumpere.

1. *Having learned these things*, Caesar orders his soldiers to embark immediately. 2. *Having learned their* (eorum) *plan*, Caesar led his army into the territories of Cassivellaunus. 3. Caesar, *having sent forward his cavalry*, ordered the legions immediately to follow up. 4. Our men, *having slain many of* (ex) *the enemy*, returned to the camp. 5. Cassivellaunus, *having heard of this disaster*, sends ambassadors to (ad) Caesar concerning peace. 6. *Having extended (his) empire* as far as the Indus, Alexander returned towards the west. 7. *When this war is finished*, we shall be able to enjoy peace. 8. (*With*) *you* (*for*) *our leader*, we shall be safe. 9. *When old age is attained* (adeptus *), our bodies become more feeble. 10. *Having slain many of* (ex) *the enemy*, he led his army into winter quarters.

* *Adeptus*, with a few other Perf. Participles of Deponent Verbs, is used both in an Active and Passive sense.

XXXV.—The Accusative expressing Duration or Extent of Time, Distance, and Dimension.

RULE 20.—The answers to the questions, *How long? How far? How high? How deep? How broad? How old?* are put in Latin in the Accusative case: as, sex ĕt vīgintī annōs regnāvĭt, *he reigned twenty-six years;* aggĕrem lātum pĕdēs trĕcentōs, altum pĕdēs quinquāgintā exstruxērunt, *they heaped up a mound* 300 *feet broad and* 50 *feet high.*

The Accusative, answering the question *How long?* is called the accusative of *duration of time.*

Exercise LI.

1. Romulus septem et triginta annos regnavit. 2. Quaedam bestiolae unum diem vivunt. 3. Augustus septem horas dormiebat. 4. Troja decem annos a Graecis obsessa est. 5. Cato annos quinque et octoginta natus excessit e 'ta. 6. Dionysius annos quinque et

viginti natus dominatum occupavit. 7. Turris pedes ducentos alta est. 8. Saguntini aggerem duxerunt trecentos pedes longum et viginti pedes altum. 9. Hanno tria passuum millia ab ipsa urbe castra posuit. 10. Campus Marathon abest ab oppido Atheniensium circiter millia passuum decem.

1. Tarquinius Superbus, the seventh king of the Romans, reigned twenty-four years. 2. They build a wall fifty feet high, and eight feet broad. 3. The walls of Athens were-distant about four thousand paces (*gen.*) from the sea. 4. The towers were about a hundred feet high. 5. Socrates was put-to-death, aged seventy years. 6. Plato lived eighty-one years. 7. It is not enough to have lived many years; it behoves (us) to have lived (them) well. 8. The city (of) Troy was besieged ten years on-account-of (ob) a single (unus) woman. 9. Socrates lived seventy years. 10. Some men live a hundred years.

XXXVI.—CONSTRUCTION OF THE NAMES OF TOWNS.

RULE 21.—In answer to the question *Whither?* names of towns and small islands are put in the Accusative case without prepositions: as, Consul Rōmam prŏfectŭs est, *the Consul set out for Rome.*

> In like manner are used, dŏmum (*to one's*) *home;* rūs, *to the country.*

In answer to the question *Whence?* names of towns and small islands are put in the Ablative case without prepositions: as, Consŭl Rōmā Athēnās prŏfectŭs est, *the Consul set out from Rome to Athens.*

> In like manner are used, dŏmō, *from home;* rūrĕ, *from the country.*

EXERCISE LII.

1. Curius primus Romam elephantos quattuor duxit. 2. Pompeius Luceriā proficiscitur Canusium. 3. Lycurgus Cretam profectus est, ibique perpetuum exilium egit. 4. Aeschines cessit Athenis et se Rhodum contulit. 5. Legati Atheniensium Lacedaemonem profecti sunt, ut auxilium contra Persas peterent. 6. Acceptis mandatis, Roscius cum Lucio Caesare Capuam pervenit. 7. Alcibiades, maximis rebus gestis, domum reversus est. 8. Leonidas cum trecentis iis, quos eduxerat Spartā, se opposuit hostibus. 9. Tiberius domo cessit, et se rus contulit. 10. Alexander, Dario apud Arbelam victo, Babylonem profectus est.

1. In the summer I shall set out for Venusia. 2. He departed from Athens and returned to Rome. 3. We will go to Crete, you to Rhodes, but the others will remain in the city. 4. Caesar having done these things (*ablative absolute*), returned immediately home. 5. He departed from Rome and set out for Luceria. 6. I

will betake myself to Lacedaemon; there I shall be safe. 7. Do not set out to the country. 8. The consuls had already arrived at Luceria. 9. The ambassadors of the Carthaginians came to Rome in-order-to (ut) seek-for peace. 10. Pompeius having been slain (*abl. absol.*), Caesar was unwilling to return immediately to Rome.

RULE 22.—In answer to the question *Where?* names of towns and small islands are put in the Genitive case, if the Noun be of the First or Second Declension and Singular; in all other cases in the Ablative without a preposition; as,

Rōmae Consŭlĕs, Athēnīs Archontēs, Carthāgĭnĕ Suffĕtēs, sive jŭdĭcĕs, quŏtannīs creābantur, *At Rome Consuls, at Athens Archons, at Carthage Suffetes, or judges, were elected annually.*

Diŏnȳsiŭs Cŏrinthī puĕrōs dŏcēbăt, *Dionysius taught boys at Corinth.*

In like manner are used hŭmī, *on the ground;* dŏmī, *at home;* rūrī, *in the country.*

EXERCISE LIII.

1. Pompeius hiemare Dyrrachii et Apolloniae constituerat. 2. Delphis Apollinis oraculum fuit. 3. Conon plurimum Cypri vixit, Timotheus Lesbi. 4. Multos annos domi nostrae vixit. 5. Alexander Magnus Babylone morbo consumptus est. 6. Dionysius multos annos Corinthi vixit. 7. Horatius Venusiae natus est. 8. Catilina humi jacet. 9. Talis (*such*) Romae Fabricius, qualis (*as*) Aristides Athen's fuit. 10. Lycurgus Cretae perpetuum exilium egit.

1. Marius and Cicero were born at Arpinum. 2. Atticus, a friend of Cicero, lived many years at Athens. 3. Your friend lived many years at my house. 4. Dionysius, having been driven-out-of Syracuse, used-to-teach (*imperf.*) boys at Corinth. 5. Many apples and pears lay on the ground. 6. At Cannae a sanguinary battle was fought (committo) between the Romans and Hannibal. 7. I had-rather dwell* at home than in the country. 8. Tiberius retired from Rome and lived in exile at Rhodes. 9. Very many great generals, few poets were born at Rome. 10. At Lacedaemon, both (et) boys and girls were most carefully trained up (*imperf.*).

* Say, *I prefer to dwell.*

XXXVII.—THE ACCUSATIVE CASE AND INFINITIVE MOOD.

RULE 23.—The Accusative Case and the Infinitive Mood are used:

> After words of *saying, hearing, seeing, feeling, perceiving, thinking, knowing:* as, histŏriă narrăt Rōmam ā Rōmŭlō condĭtam essĕ, *history relates that Rome was founded by Romulus:* sentīmŭs călērĕ ignem,

nĭvem essĕ albam, dulcĕ (essĕ) mĕl, *we perceive that
fire is hot, that snow is white, that honey is sweet.*

II. After such expressions as nōtum est, *it is known ;*
justum est, *it is just ;* vērĭsĭmĭlĕ est, *it is probable ;*
constăt, *it is agreed, it is certain,* &c.: as, constăt
Rōmam ā Rōmŭlō condĭtam essĕ, *it is agreed that
Rome was founded by Romulus.*

EXERCISE LIV.

A.—1. Equitatum Caesaris advenire videmus.' 2. Thales aquam
dixit esse initium rerum. 3. Solon rempublicam praemiis et poenis
contineri dixit. 4. Nemo negabit mundum a Deo conservari. 5.
Vox quondam audita est, Romam a Gallis captum iri. 6. Epaminondas animadvertebat, totum exercitum propter ducum impru-
dentiam periturum esse. 7. Pollicebaris te venturum esse. |8. Hel-
vetii polliciti sunt se Caesari obsides daturos. 9. Videmus aves
auctumno in alias terras migrare. 10. Scio haec vera esse.

1. We know that the sun is larger than the moon. 2. Caesar learns
that the enemy are-gathering-together all their forces. 3. The oracle
of Delphi said that Socrates was (*infin. pres.*) the wisest of all men.
4. We see that the flowers blossom forth. 5. We know that the
body perishes, but that the soul is immortal. 6. Socrates thought
(*imperf.*) that knowledge was more excellent than all (other) things.
7. Who has not heard that the Romans were conquered by Hannibal
at (*apud*) Cannae? 8. We see that all things are done by the wisdom of God. 9. We know that the sun is very-far distant (*absum*)
from the earth. 10. We promise that we will be faithful to you.

B.—1. Credibile est hominum causā factum esse mundum. 2.
Verum est amicitiam nisi inter bonos esse non posse. 3. Traditum
est Homerum caecum fuisse. 4. Hannibalem in Asia mortuum
esse constat. 5. Bestiis rationem deesse manifestum est. 6. Omnes
cives legibus parere aequum est. 7. Certum est liberos a parentibus amari. 8. Sororem tuam hac aestate reversuram esse non veri-
simile est. 9. Constat Romanos eodem anno duas urbes floren-
tissimas, Carthaginem et Corinthum, delevisse. 10. Memoriae
proditum est Latonam confugisse Delum atque ibi Apollinem
Dianamque peperisse.

1. It is just that you (should) punish me. 2. It is probable that
the stars are suns. 3. It is true that we have been conquered.
4. It has been handed down to us that Socrates was the wisest of
all the Greeks. 5. It is manifest that the world was not made by
chance. 6. It is agreed amongst all writers that Romulus was
(*perf.*) the first king of the Romans. 7. It is manifest that you
make-a-mistake. 8. It is handed down (*perf.*) to us by the poets
that a woman was the cause of the Trojan war. 9. It is certain
that the soul ought to obey reason. 10. It is manifest that we
shall be conquered unless we remain (*fut.-perf.*) in the city.

XXXVIII.—DIRECT QUESTIONS.

RULE 24.—Questions are usually put in Latin with the help of Interrogative words or particles: as, Quĭd ăgĭs? *What are you doing?* Pŭtas-nĕ? *Do you think?* Non-nĕ pŭtăs? *Do you not think?*

The principal Interrogative particles are nĕ, num, utrum, ăn. Of these nĕ is always written as an enclitic like the Conjunction que. Utrum and an are used only when two alternatives are spoken of; and an always with the second alternative.

Nĕ does not need to be expressed by any English word, as Visnĕ? *Do you wish?* Nonnĕ pŭtăs? *Do you not think?*

Utrum . . . ăn may be translated by *whether . . . or*, as Utrum sōl ăn lūnă măjŏr est? *Whether is the sun or the moon the greater?*

Num has a negative force, as Num ĭtă pŭtăs = *You don't think so, do you?* and is to be used when the answer *No* is looked for.

EXERCISE LV.

A.—1. Estne voluptas summum bonum? 2. Nonne fuit Socrates antiquorum sapientissimus? 3. Nonne sol longe major est quam luna? 4. Num ita audes dicere? 5. Utrum est aurum gravius an argentum? 6. Utrum Socrates an Plato sapientior fuit? 7. Suntne haec vera bona? 8. Num tu has res melius quam magister tuus intelligis? 9. Nonne omnes discere oportet vitam tranquillo animo relinquere? 10. Num putas argentum et aurum cariora esse virtute et prudentiă?

1. Are these things true? 2. Do you believe that pain is the greatest evil? 3. Was not (begin with *nonne*) Pythagoras a very great (*summus*) philosopher? 4. You don't think that I am a liar, do you? 5. Is gold more excellent than wisdom? (No.) 6. Are you wiser than (your) father? (No.) 7. Whether is iron or gold more useful? 8. Is not (begin with *nonne*) iron far more useful than gold? 9. Whether do you prefer this or that? 10. Is not (begin with *nonne*) the world governed by the Divine wisdom?

B.—1. Nonne urbs Roma a Gallis capta et direpta est? 2. Nonne omnes consentiunt Scipionem primarium fuisse virum? 3. Num audes dicere haec benevolo animo facta esse? 4. Utrum Romae an ruri hibernis mensibus manere mavis? 5. Utrum est turpitudo omnium malorum maximum an non? 6. Utrum haec benevolo an malevolo animo fecisti? 7. Utrum Cato an Caesar tibi praestantior et clarior vir esse videtur? 8. Utrum esse an videri bonus mavis?

9. Num audes dicere, Lucreti, haec casu facta esse? tunc ita credis?
10. Estne verum, quod nonnulli dicunt, animos ex aliis (*corporibus*) in alia córpora migrare?

1. Is it true that the sun is made-of-fire? 2. Is not Plato the most eloquent of philosophers? 3. Are not Livy and Sallust most elegant writers? 4. Does it not do good to all to read the works [books] of that (*ille*) most excellent writer? 5. Are you so foolish that (*ut*) you should believe all these things to have been made by chance? 6. Is the body mortal? Is the soul immortal? 7. Are not the books of Plato full of these subjects (*res*)? 8. Is Sallust or Livy (begin with *utrum*) the more elegant writer? Are-you-able to answer? 9. Does it (*num*) become a philosopher to lament-over his life? Does it not behove him to act bravely? 10. Do all the philosophers agree concerning these subjects?

XXXIX.—INDIRECT QUESTIONS.

RULE 25.—Indirect questions are those which are quoted as having been asked, or are dependent upon some word expressing doubt, uncertainty, or wonder, in the former part of the sentence, as Rŏgābo quĭd factum sĭt, *I will ask what has been done;* Mīrum est quae fŭĕrĭt causă, *It is strange what the reason may have been;* Vĭdēbo num rĕdĭĕrĭt, *I will see whether he has returned.* The dependent verb is always put in the Subjunctive Mood.

RULE 26.—The Tense of the Verb in the Subjunctive Mood is determined by that of the verb in the former part of the sentence upon which it depends. (1.) If the verb in the former clause expresses *Present* or *Future Time*, the verb in the dependent clause is put in the Present or Present-Perfect Tense Subjunctive. (2.) If the verb in the principal clause expresses *Past Time*, the verb in the dependent clause is put in the Past Tense Subjunctive.

Present and Future Time.

PRESENT. Scio quĭd ăgās,	*I know what you are doing.*
Scio quĭd ēgĕrĭs,	*I know what you have done.*
Scio quĭd actūrŭs sīs,	*I know what you are going to do.*
PRESENT PERFECT. Cognōvī quĭd ăgās,	*I have learnt what you are doing.*
Cognōvī quĭd ēgĕrĭs,	*I have learnt what you have done.*
Cognōvī quĭd actūrŭs sīs,	*I have learnt what you are going to do.*

	Audiam quĭd ăgās,	I shall hear what you are doing.
FUTURE.	Audiam quĭd ēgĕris,	I shall hear what you have done.
	Audiam quĭd actūrŭs sīs,	I shall hear what you are going to do.

Past Time.

	Sciēbam quĭd ăgĕrēs,	I knew what you were doing.
IMPERF.	Sciēbam quĭd ēgissēs,	I knew what you had done.
	Sciēbam quĭd actūrŭs essēs,	I knew what you were going to do.

	Cognōvī quĭd ăgĕrēs,	I learnt what you were doing.
PAST INDEFNL.	Cognōvī quĭd ēgissēs,	I learnt what you had done.
	Cognōvī quĭd actūrŭs essēs,	I learnt what you were going to do.

	Cognōvĕram quĭd ăgĕrēs,	I had learnt what you were doing.
PAST PERFECT.	Cognōvĕram quĭd ēgissēs,	I had learnt what you had done.
	Cognōvĕram quĭd actūrŭs essēs,	I had learnt what you were going to do.

The same Rule is applicable to the sequence of Tenses in the Subjunctive Mood universally. See Exercises **xxv., xxvi., xxvii., xxviii.** (the Subjunctive Mood).

N.B. In single Indirect Questions *whether* is generally expressed by **num**, which then ceases to have a negative force. In double Indirect Questions it is expressed either by **utrum** or **-ne**.

EXERCISE LVI.

N.B. In the following examples the Subjunctive must in English be rendered by the Indicative.

A.—1. Rogo quid agatis. 2. Rogavit quid agerent. 3. Rogavit quid egissent. 4. Roga tu quid acturi sint. 5. Nescio quare me ex civitate expuleritis. 6. Cognoscere non potuit quantae essent hostium copiae. 7. Speculabimur quot homines in urbem ineant et quot exeant. 8. Dic mihi, Catilina, cur patriam prodere volueris. 9. Dic mihi, Blaese, ubi corpus abjeceris. 10. Chaerephon ex oraculo quaesivit quis omnium Graecorum sapientissimus esset.

1. I will ask how great the forces of the enemy are. 2. Xenophon inquired of (ex) the oracle what it behoved him to do. 3. I wish to learn where the camp of the enemy is. 4. I do-not-know what it behoves me to do. 5. Tell me, my son, what you are going to do. 6. The son was unwilling to tell what he was going-to-do. 7. Count how many darts have been thrown (*conjicio*) into the tent. 8. I will inquire which-of-the-two has conquered. 9. Socrates used-to-inquire (*imperf.*) what was just, what unjust. 10. It is a great thing to know what things are just, what unjust.

B.—1. Quaeram num omnia feliciter evenerint. 2. Jussit eos speculari num hostes ex castris exirent. 3. Visam num advenent hostes. 4. Subdifficilis est-quaestio num unquam novi amici sint veteribus anteponendi? 5. Rogavit nonne haec improba et infamia essent? 6. Rogabo num credat-omnia casu facta esse? 7. Quaesivit ex oraculo Croesus, utrum ipse an Cyrus superaturus esset. 8. Saepe-numero quaerebant antiqui philosophi mortalisne esset animus an immortalis. 9. Num dubium est casune an consilio factus sit mundus? 10. Plane incertum est vicerintne hostes an victi sint.

1. Inquire of (*ex*) him.·whether he knows these things. 2. It is doubtful whether these things are true. 3. It is uncertain whether (*utrum* or *ne*) he is a good man or a wicked (one). 4. It is doubtful whether he deserve praise (*laudemne*) or blame. 5. He asked whether the dead felt cold and hunger. 6. I know not whether you are-sleeping or waking. 7. I doubt whether he will return (*subj.-pres.*) immediately. 8. He asked whether the city was very strongly fortified. 9. This I ask you, whether you were or not (*nonne*) that (*ille*) night in the house of M. Laeca,? 10. Do you doubt whether it behoves a good citizen to·side-with his country in time of danger?

XL.—Additional Exercises on the Subjunctive Mood.

Rule 27.—Besides ŭt, nē, and quīn (see Ex. xxv., &c.), the Conjunctions quō, *that*, and quōmĭnŭs, *that not*, are constructed with the Subjunctive Mood.

1. Ut = *that, in order that, granting that*, is used to express either a *purpose* or a *consequence ;* as, ĕo ŭt spectem lūdōs, *I am going in order that I may look at the games ;* accĭdĭt ŭt nōn dŏmĭ essem, *it happened that I was not at home.*

2. Nĕ = *that not*, is used to express a *purpose*, but not a mere consequence: as, Haec făcĭo nē mē ĭnĭmĭcum tĭbi pŭtēs, *these things I do that you may not think me your enemy ;* but, sĕquĭtŭr *ŭt* haec *nōn* vera sint, *it follows that these things are not true.*

> *Obs.* After verbs of *fearing*, ŭt has the meaning of *that not*, and nĕ of *that :* as, tĭmĕo ŭt dux mĭlĭtēs ē castrīs ēdūcăt, *I fear that the general will not lead the soldiers out of the camp :* tĭmĕo nē dux mĭlĭtēs ē castrīs ēdūcăt, *I fear that the general will lead the soldiers out of the camp.*

3. Quīn is used after *negative propositions and propositions expressing doubt :* as, dĭēs nullŭs est, quĭn littĕras scrĭbam,

there is no day that I do not write a letter; nōn dŭbĭto quĭn vērum dixĕris, *I do not doubt you have spoken the truth.* (See Ex. xxv, C, &c.)

4. Quō is used for ŭt ĕŏ, and signifies *that thereby, in order that, so that :* haec lex dătă est, quō mălĕfĭcī dĕterrērentŭr, *this law was given (enacted) that thereby evil-doers might be deterred;* portăs oppĭdī obstruxĭt, quō făcĭliŭs impĕtum hostium rĕtardărĕt, *he barricaded the gates of the town in order that he might more easily retard the attack of the enemy.*

5. Quōmĭnŭs, *that not,* is used after verbs of *hindering, preventing, resisting,* &c., and must be frequently translated in English by *from* with a verbal substantive : as, aetăs nōs non impĕdĭt quōmĭnŭs littĕras tractēmus, *age does not prevent us from cultivating literature.*

Exercise LVII.

A.—1. Enitar ut in omnibus rebus tibi prosim.   2. Hoc te rogo atque oro, ne rempublicam deseras.   3. Contendit Caesar maximis itineribus in fines Neryiorum ut consilia eorum praeveniret. 4. Magnopere tibi suadeo ne improbis illis hominibus confidas. 5. Accidit ut milites impransi essent quum signum datum est. 6. Milites cohortatus est ut fortiter castra defenderent.   7. Nonne omnes cives oportet eniti ut reipublicae prosint?   8. Accidit ut inter Labienum et hostes esset flumen praealtum.   9. Sequitur ut non possim tibi confidere.   10. Enitar ne possis mihi diffidere.

1. I will strive-hard to (*ut*) persuade him.   2. It follows that pleasure is not the highest good.   3. I entreat you to (*ut*) learn to bear patiently bad fortune.   4. We ought to strive-hard that we may be serviceable to (our) native-country.   5. The Helvetii determined to depart from their own territories, in order that they-might-obtain possession of all Gaul.   6. Does it not follow that these things are unjust?   7. So it came to pass (*fio*) that out of (them) all, no one returned to the city.   8. The Helvetii have been so trained (*instituo*) by their ancestors that they are accustomed to receive hostages, not to give them.   9. I will strive earnestly that you may be able to think me a friend.   10. The Carthaginians sent ambassadors to Rome to (*ut*) beg-for peace.

> N.B. In future the pupil will be left to himself to discover when the English infinitive denotes a purpose, and must therefore be translated with ut.

B.—1. Constituit Caesar pontem in flumine Rheno facere, quo copias suas transduceret.   2. Milites cohortatus est quo mortem fortius obirent.   3. Quid obstat quominus moenia statim oppugnemus? 4. Nullo modo introire possum quin me videant. 5. Nullo modo exire potuit quin eum viderent. 6. Minimum abest quin sim miserrimus. 7. Dies fere nullus est quin Satrius domum meam ventitet. 8. Facere non possum quin tibi dolores meos enarrem. 9. Quis dubitat quin omnes oporteat patriae suae adesse? 10. Recusare non possum quin me comiteris.

1. He resolved to carry a wall round the camp that (*quo*)* the army might be more secure (*tutus*). 2. He fortified the camp that he might the more easily keep off the enemy. 3. There is no day that I do not hear many wonderful things. 4. Who can doubt that Hannibal was a very great (*summus*) general? 5. There was nobody who did not (*quin*) rejoice greatly. 6. I cannot but hope that we shall be conquerors. 7. Nobody is so brave but (*quin*) he sometimes feels fear. 8. We are preparing arms, not that (*ut*) we may attack others, but that (*quo*) we may better defend our country. 9. There was nothing wanting *that* I should be very wretched. 10. Our soldiers could not go forth from the camp *but* they were overwhelmed with missiles.

* **Quo** is used in preference to **ut** when there is a comparative in the clause which it introduces.

C.—1. Per Trebonium stetit quominus oppido potirentur. 2. Me infirmitas valetudinis tenuit quominus ad ludos venirem. 3. Hiems prohibuit quominus a te literas haberemus. 4. Bibulum deterruerunt quominus domo exiret. 5. Deterrent me latrones quominus in illam partem urbis eam. 6. Quid tibi obstabat quominus nobiscum adesses? 7. Quis audebit miseros prohibere quominus fleant? 8. Legem brevem esse oportet quo facilius ab imperitis teneatur. 9. Unum vereor ne senatus Pompeium nolit dimittere. 10. Quis est quin cernat quanta vis sit in sensibus?

1. It was owing to you that we did not obtain-possession-of the town. 2. No weakness of health shall prevent me *from* coming to you. 3. Nothing ought to deter a citizen *from* siding with his country in time of danger. 4. They attempted to deter Cato *from* appearing (*adsum*) in the forum. 5. Nothing shall prevent me *from* siding-with you. 6. Nobody can prohibit us *from* worshipping God. 7. Nothing ought to deter children *from* obeying their parents. 8. I fear *that* we may be cast out of the city. 9. I fear *that* we may *not* be able to defend ourselves and our country. 10. I cannot but think that Caesar was the greatest of the Romans.

XLI.—USE OF THE SUPINES.

RULE 28.—The Supine in **um** is used after verbs of motion: as, Lăcĕdaemŏnĭï Ăgēsĭlāum *bellātum* ĭn Ăsiam mīsērunt, *the Lacedaemonians sent Agesilaus into Asia to make war.*

The Supine in **ū** is used after many adjectives: as, făcĭlĭs, *easy,* diffĭcĭlĭs, *difficult,* dulcĭs, *sweet,* &c., and with fās est, *it is lawful,* nĕfās est, *it is unlawful,* ŏpŭs est, *it is necessary;* as, rēs diffĭcĭlĭs factū est, *the thing is difficult to be done.*

EXERCISE LVIII.

1. Ingens hominum multitudo in urbem convenit, ludos publicos spectatum. 2. Veientes, pacem petitum, oratores Romam mittunt. 3. Aedui legatos ad Caesarem mittunt, rogatum auxilium. 4. Milites pabulatum et aquatum longius progressi erant. 5. Divitiacus Romam ad senatum venit, auxilium postulatum. 6. Athenienses miserunt Delphos consultum, quidnam facerent de rebus suis. 7. Pira dulcia sunt gustatu. 8. Difficile dictu est. 9. Quod optimum factu videbitur, facies. 10. Nefas est dictu, miseram fuisse Fabii Maximi senectutem.

1. We will set out for Rome, to look-at the games. 2. Croesus sent ambassadors to Delphi to inquire concerning the fortune of the war. 3. Chaerephon went to Delphi to ask who was (*subj.*) the wisest of men. 4. The general dismissed the soldiers to forage and get-water. 5. These things are very difficult to be done. 6. Very many things are easier to be said than done. 7. Old wines are not always sweet to taste. 8. The Romans sent ambassadors to Carthage to inquire concerning Hannibal and the Saguntines. 9. It would be impious to say that the life of a good man can be miserable. 10. We have come to consult you (as to) what may be best to be done.

XLII.—USE OF THE GERUND.

RULE 29.—The Gerund is a Neuter Verbal Substantive, governing the same case as the Verb from which it comes. It corresponds to the English Verbal Substantives in *ing;* as *writing, walking.*

It is declined in the Singular only, and is not used in

the Nominative case, the Present of the Infinitive mood taking the place of the Nominative : as,

Nom. Lĕgĕre pulchra carmĭna suāve est,   *reading (to read) beautiful poems is delightful.*

Gen. Ars pŭĕrōs ēdŭcandī diffĭcĭllĭs est,   *the art of educating boys is difficult.*

Dat. Scrībendō ŏpĕram dăt,   *he devotes his care to writing.*
Acc. Nātŭs ăd ăgendum,   *born for acting.*
Abl. Littĕras tractandō mens ăcŭĭtŭr,   *the wits are sharpened by dealing with letters.*

> *Obs.* The Accusative Case of the Gerund is used only with Prepositions; otherwise the Present Infinitive is used: as, disco nătăre, *I learn swimming.*

EXERCISE LIX.

1. Saepissime perniciosa est plura habendi cupiditas. 2. Vehementer ardebat juvenis studio omnia cognoscendi et experiendi. 3. Quidam canes venandi gratia comparantur. 4. Beate vivendi studiosi sumus omnes, 5. Aqua marina haud utilis est bibendo. 6. Mores puerorum se inter ludendum detegunt. 7. Hominis mens discendo et cogitando alitur. 8. Caesari dare jucundissimum erat. 9. Inter bibendum de variis rebus colloquebamur. 10. Quid potest esse jucundius quam inter ambulandum libere de variis rebus colloqui?

1. Very many persons burn with the desire of having more (*pl.*). 2. Epaminondas was eager-after hearing (*gen.*). 3. All are not zealous of living well. 4. He got together very many horses and (que) dogs for the sake of hunting. 5. Do not attempt to obtain friends by flattering. 6. Do not attempt to preserve your life by lying. 7. Bodies are nourished by eating and drinking. 8. The soul is nourished by thinking (*cogito*), feeling, acting. 9. Conversing (*infin.*) about (de) these things is most delightful. 10. It is becoming a youth to burn with a zeal for knowledge (*gerund*).

XLIII.—USE OF THE GERUNDIVE.

RULE 30.—The Gerundive is a Passive Verbal Adjective: as, scrĭbendus, a, um, *to be written, necessary* or *fit to be written.*

When the Verb from which the Gerundive comes governs an Accusative Case, the Gerundive agrees with the Nominative Case of its Substantive: as, scrĭbenda est mihi ĕpistŏla, *a letter must be* or *ought to be written by me*, or *I must* or *ought to write a letter.*

The person by whom the thing is *to be done* is put in the Dative (see preceding example).

Exercise LX.

1. Diligenter sunt emendandi puerorum mores. 2. Sapientia non solum paranda est nobis, sed etiam fruenda. 3. Prae omnibus rebus adhibenda est prudentia. 4. Agenda est omnibus aetas non sine periculis. 5. Ciceroni in arduis temporibus gerenda erat respublica. 6. Strenue nobis excolenda sunt corpus, mens, animus. 7. Habendus est delectus, comparandae sunt naves. 8. Non sunt ea nobis contemnenda; sunt diligentissime providenda. 9. Prae omnibus aliis observandi et colendi sunt pueris parentes. 10. Utrum amandi an timendi reges sunt?

1. Virtue must be cultivated. 2. Who doubts that the gods are to be feared? 3. A parent (*dat.*) ought so to train-up (his) son that he may obey the laws of virtue. 4. Those persons are to be admired who have dared to die for (pro) their-country. 5. (We) must preserve the state; (we) must crush the conspiracy. 6. Virtue must not only be cultivated, but also loved. 7. These things must not be passed over by us (*dat.*). 8. Before (prae) all other things (res) the war must be carried on vigorously. 9. We (*dat.*) ought to read the orators and poets. 10. A man (*dat.*) should not despise death.

RULE 31.—But when the Verb from which the Gerundive comes is intransitive or governs any other Case than the Accusative, the Gerundive is used impersonally in the Nominative Case Singular Neuter. The Object is put in the case which the Verb governs, and the Subject in the Dative Case: as, obtemperandum est nōbīs (*dative*) virtūtĭs praeceptĭs (*dative*), *we must obey the lessons of virtue:* cuīque (*dative*) ūtendum est judĭciō suō (*ablative*), *each one must use his own judgment.*

N.B. The Dative of the Agent is not always expressed.

Exercise LXI.

1. Omnibus moriendum est. 2. Ita bellandum est ut pax peti videatur. 3. Mihi utendum est judicio meo. 4. Nobis quoque ingrediendum est istuc quo pervenisti. 5. Ita nobis vivendum est ut ad mortem parati simus. 6. Non longius progrediendum est, commilitones, ne commeatibus nostris intercludamur. 7. Non dubium est quin bono civi legibus sit obtemperandum. 8. Proficiscendum mihi erat illo ipso die. 9. Magnopere est curandum ne nobis consilium defuisse videatur. 10. Cognoscendum est quid de illo homine factum sit.

1. Must (we) not (nonne) all die? 2. We must die bravely, fellow-soldiers! 3. Boys ought to strive-hard to please their

parents. 4. We must strive with (our) utmost zeal that the commonwealth may be preserved. 5. We must not believe all men in everything. 6. We must set out immediately. 7. It is greatly to be desired that the war may be brought-to-an-end. 8. We must take great care (see No. 9 above) *that* we are *not* (ne) shut off from all help. 9. What must we do, citizens? Which-of-the-two (*dat.*) should we trust? 10. We ought so to learn as (ut) not immediately to forget,

EXERCISE LXII.

N.B. The Gerundive is employed more frequently than the Gerund. The Gerund is chiefly used where an ambiguity would be occasioned by the use of the Gerundive: as, studium plūra cognoscendī, *the desire of learning more*, rather than studium plūrium cognoscendōrum, which would leave it doubtful whether *things* or *men* were meant.

1. Bellum suscepit Catilina reipublicae delendae causa. 2. Timotheus erat civitatis regendae peritus. 3. Consilium iniit Catilina urbis incendendae. 4. Conservandae libertatis gratia initio creabantur consules. 5. Tiberius quasi ad firmandam valetudinem in Campaniam concessit. 6. Occupatus sum in litteris scribendis. 7. Studiosi solent esse juvenes equorum canumque alendorum. 8. Consilium inierunt Brutus et Cassius libertatis recuperandae. 9. Hostes in spem venerant potiendorum castrorum. 10. Oculus probe affectus est ad suum munus fungendum.

1. The Roman youth (*pl.*) were trained-up for (ad) managing the commonwealth. 2. Cicero formed a plan for crushing the conspiracy (*gen.*). 3. Nature has endowed (instruo) the mind with senses prepared for perceiving objects (res). 4. He burned with the desire of destroying his country. 5. Those wicked men formed a design of slaying the consul. 6. Virtue is especially (maxime) discerned in despising pleasure. 7. The first book is written (*perf.*) on-the-subject-of (de) despising death. 8. The utmost pleasure is derived (capio) from (ex) reading books. 9. A husbandman ought (oportet) to devote himself to cultivating his lands. 10. Cicero devoted himself with the utmost zeal to preserving the commonwealth.

A SHORT SYNTAX.

A Recapitulation of the Rules already given.

First, Concord.

§ 1. A Verb agrees with its Nominative case in Number and Person: as, pŭellă currĭt, *the girl runs;* pŭellae currunt, *the girls run.*

Second Concord.

§ 2. An Adjective agrees with its Substantive in Gender, Number, and Case: as, servŭs tĭmĭdŭs, *a timid slave;* parvum oppĭdum, *a small town.*

Third Concord.

§ 3. The Relative Pronoun agrees with the Antecedent in Gender, Number, and Person, but not in Case: as, Fēlix est rex quem omnēs cīvēs laudant, *Fortunate is the king whom all citizens praise.*

Apposition.

§ 4. When two Nouns refer to the same person or thing, they are put in the same case by *Apposition:* as, Rōmŭlŭs, rex Rōmānōrum, *Romulus, king of the Romans.*

Nominative Case.

§ 5. The Nominative case denotes the Subject.—When two Nouns in Latin are connected by sum, fīo, vĭdĕŏr, vŏcŏr, and similar Verbs, they are put in the same case: as, Brĭtannĭă est insŭlă, *Britain is an island.*

Accusative Case.

§ 6. The Accusative case denotes the Object.—Transitive Verbs govern the Accusative: as, ăquĭlă ālās hăbĕt, *the eagle has wings.*

§ 7. The answers to the questions, *How long? How far? How high? How deep? How broad? How old?* are put in the Accusative: as, sex ĕt vīgintī annōs regnāvĭt, *he reigned twenty-six years;* aggĕrem lātum pĕdēs trĕcentōs, altum pĕdēs quinquāgintā exstruxērunt, *they heaped up a mound 300 feet broad and 50 feet high.*—The Accusative, answering the question *How long?* is called the accusative of *duration of time.*

Genitive Case.

§ 8. The latter of two Nouns is put in the Genitive when one is dependent upon the other : as, Brĭtannĭă est insŭlă Eurōpae, *Britain is an island of Europe*

§ 9. Verbs signifying *to remember, to forget, to pity*, are commonly followed by the Genitive : as, mĭsĕrōrum hŏmĭnum mĭsĕrĕbĭmŭr, *we will pity the wretched men.*

Dative Case.

§ 10. The Dative indicates the person who gains or receives anything : as, Măgistĕr cŏlumbam pŭĕrō dăt, *the master gives a dove to the boy.*

Ablative Case.

§ 11. The Ablative indicates—(1) The instrument or means by which something is done: as, dŏmĭnŭs hastă servum occĭdĭt, *the lord kills the slave with a spear.*

(2) The time when something is done or takes place : as, noctēs hĭĕmĕ longae sunt, *the nights are long in winter.*

§ 12. But when the Ablative indicates the place *where*, it is used with the Preposition ĭn, *in :* as, hostēs ĭn plānĭtĭē ĕrant, *the enemies were in the plain.*

§ 13. Utŏr, frŭŏr, vescŏr, fungŏr, govern the Ablative : as, săpĭentĕr ūtĭmĭnī tempŏrĕ, *use time wisely.*

§ 14. When a subordinate clause has a different subject from the subject of the principal clause, the English Verb in the subordinate clause is in Latin expressed by a Substantive and Participle in the Ablative Case. This construction is called the ABLATIVE ABSOLUTE : as, sōlĕ ortō, Rōmānī hostēs vīdērunt, *when the sun had risen* [lit. *the sun having risen*], *the Romans saw the enemy.* (See also p. 89.)

Construction of the Names of Towns.

§ 15. In answer to the question *Whither?* names of towns and small islands are put in the Accusative without prepositions : as, Consŭl Rōmam prŏfectŭs est, *the Consul set out for Rome.*

§ 16. In answer to the question *Whence?* towns and small islands are put in the Ablative without prepositions : as, Consŭl Rōmā Athēnās prŏfectŭs est, *the Consul set out from Rome to Athens.*

§ 17. In answer to the question *Where?* names of towns and small islands are put in the Genitive, if the Substantive be of the First or Second Declension and Singular ; in all other cases in the Ablative without a preposition ; as, Rōmae Consŭlēs, Athēnīs Archontēs, Carthāgĭnĕ Suffētēs, sīvĕ jūdĭcēs, quŏtannis crĕābantŭr, *At Rome Consuls, at Athens Archons, at Carthage Suffetes, or judges, were elected annually ;* Diŏnȳsĭŭs Cŏrinthī puĕrōs dŏcēbăt, *Dionysius taught boys at Corinth.*

Comparative Degree.

§ 18. The English word *than* after the Comparative is translated by the Latin quam : as, Aestātĕ diēs longiōrēs sunt *quam* noctēs, *in summer the days are longer than the nights.*

§ 19. The Ablative is also used after the Comparative instead of *quam* with the Nominative or Accusative : as, vīlĭŭs argentum est aurō, *silver is more common than gold.*

Indicative Mood.

§ 20. The Indicative Mood speaks of a thing without any condition or doubt : as, aedĭfĭco dŏmum, *I am building a house ;* hăbĭtābo in ĕā, *I shall dwell in it.*

Subjunctive Mood.

§ 21. The Subjunctive Mood speaks of a thing with some condition or doubt : as, [aedĭfĭco dŏmum] ŭt ĭn ĕā *hăbĭtem,* [*I am building a house*] *in order that I may dwell in it.* Here there is no doubt about the act of *building ;* but whether the person building will *dwell* in the house or not is uncertain and depends upon circumstances.

§ 22. The Conjunctions ŭt, *that, in order that,* and nē, *that not,* are construed with the Subjunctive : as, ĕo ŭt spectem lūdōs, *I am going in order that I may look at the games ;* haec făcĭo nē mē ĭnĭmīcum tĭbi pŭtēs, *these things I do that you may not think me your enemy.*

§ 23. The Conjunction quĭn is used with the Subjunctive after *negative propositions and propositions expressing doubt :* as, diēs nullŭs est, quĭn littĕrās scrĭbam, *there is no day that I do not write a letter ;* nōn dŭbĭto quĭn vērum dixĕrĭs, *I do not doubt that you have spoken the truth.*

§ 24. The Conjunction quo is used for ŭt ēō with the

Subjunctive, and signifies *that thereby, in order that, so that:* haec lex dătă est, quō mălĕfĭcĭ dĕterrērentŭr, *this law was given (enacted) that thereby evil-doers might be deterred.*

§ 25. The Conjunction **quōmĭnŭs,** *that not,* is used with the Subjunctive after verbs of *hindering, preventing, resisting, &c.,* and must be frequently translated in English by *from* and a verbal substantive: as, aetās nōs non impĕdĭt quōmĭnŭs littĕrās tractēmŭs, *age does not prevent us from cultivating literature.*

§ 26. The Subjunctive is used in an Indirect Question; that is, a question quoted as having been asked, or one dependent upon some word expressing doubt, uncertainty, or wonder, in the former part of the sentence: as, Rŏgābŏ quĭd factum sĭt, *I will ask what has been done;* Mīrum est quae fŭĕrĭt causă, *It is strange what the reason may have been;* Vĭdēbo num rĕdĭĕrĭt, *I will see whether he has returned.*

Note.—The Rule for the sequence of tenses in the Subjunctive Mood is given on pp. 95, 96.

Infinitive Mood.

§ 27. The latter of two verbs is put in the Infinitive: as, Caesăr hostēs sŭpĕrārĕ pŏtest, *Caesar is able to overcome the enemy.*

§ 28. The Accusative Case and the Infinitive are used:

    I. After words of *saying, hearing, seeing, feeling, perceiving, thinking, knowing:* as, histŏrĭă narrăt Rōmam ā Rōmŭlō condĭtam essĕ, *history relates that Rome was founded by Romulus:* sentīmŭs călĕrĕ ignem, nĭvem essĕ albam, dulcĕ (essĕ) mĕl, *we perceive that fire is hot, that snow is white, that honey is sweet.*

    II. After such expressions as nōtum est, *it is known;* justum est, *it is just;* vērīsĭmĭlĕ est, *it is probable;* constăt, *it is agreed, it is certain,* etc.: as, constăt Rōmam ā Rōmŭlō condĭtam essĕ, *it is certain that Rome was founded by Romulus.*

The Supines.

§ 29. The Supine in **um** is used after verbs of motion: as Lăcĕdaemŏnĭĭ Ăgēsĭlāum *bellātum* ĭn Ăsĭam mīsērunt, *the Lacedaemonians sent Agesilaus into Asia to make war.*

The Supine in **ū** is used after many adjectives: as, făcĭlĭs, *easy*, difficilis, *difficult*, dulcis, *sweet*, &c., and with fas est, *it is lawful*, nĕfās est, *it is unlawful*, ŏpŭs est, *it is necessary ;* as, rēs difficilis factū est, *the thing is difficult to be done.*

The Gerund.

§ 30. The Gerund is a Neuter Verbal Substantive, governing the same case as the Verb from which it comes. It corresponds to the English Verbal Substantives in *ing ;* as *writing, walking.*

It is declined in the Singular only, and is not used in the Nominative case, the Present of the Infinitive mood taking the place of the Nominative : as,

Nom.	Lĕgĕre pulchra carmĭna suāve est,	*reading (to read) beautiful poems is delightful.*
Gen.	Ars puĕrōs ēdūcandī difficilis est,	*the art of educating boys is difficult.*
Dat.	Scrībendō ŏpĕram dăt,	*he devotes his care to writing.*
Acc.	Nătŭs ăd ăgendum,	*born for acting.*
Abl.	Littĕras tractandō mens ăcŭītŭr,	*the wits are sharpened by dealing with letters.*

Obs. The Accusative Case of the Gerund is used only with Prepositions; otherwise the Present Infinitive is used : as, disco nătăre, *I learn swimming.*

The Gerundive.

§ 31. The Gerundive is a Passive Verbal Adjective : as, scrībendus, a, um, *to be written, necessary* or *fit to be written.*

When the Verb from which the Gerundive comes governs an Accusative Case, the Gerundive agrees with the Nominative Case of its Substantive : as, scrībenda est mihi ēpistŏla, *a letter must be* or *ought to be written by me*, or *I must* or *ought to write a letter.*

The person by whom the thing is *to be done* is put in the Dative (see preceding example).

§ 32. But when the Verb from which the Gerundive comes is intransitive or governs any other case than the Accusative, the Gerundive is used impersonally in the Nominative Case Singular Neuter. The Object is put in the case which the Verb governs, and the Subject in the Dative Case : as, obtempĕrandum est nōbīs (*dative*) virtūtĭs praeceptīs (*dative*), *we must obey the lessons of virtue :* cuīque (*dative*) ūtendum est jūdĭciō suō (*ablative*), *each one must use his own judgment.*

N.B. The Dative of the Agent is not always expressed.

APPENDIX.

A. GREEK NOUNS.

First Declension.

Fem.	Masc.	Masc.
Nom. Ĕpĭtŏm-ē, *abridgment.*	Aenē-ās (proper name)	Anchīs-ēs (proper name)
Voc. Ĕpĭtŏm-ē	Aenē-ā	Anchīs-ē (ă, ā)
Acc. Ĕpĭtŏm-ēn	Aenē-ān (am)	Anchīs-ēn (am)
Gen. Ĕpĭtŏm-ēs	Aenē-ae	Anchīs-ae
Dat. Ĕpĭtŏm-ae	Aenē-ae	Anchīs-ae
Abl. Ĕpĭtŏm-ē.	Aenē-ā.	Anchīs-ē (ā).

Second Declension.

Nom. Orpheus	Orpheūs
Voc. Orpheū	Orpheū.
Acc. Orphĕum	Orphĕa
Gen. Orphĕī, Orpheî	Orphĕŏs
Dat. Orphĕŏ	Orpheî, Orphī
Abl. Orphĕŏ	

Nom. Dēlŏs	Andrŏgĕŏs
Voc. Dēlĕ	Andrŏgĕŏs
Acc. Dēlŏn, Dēlum	Andrŏgĕōn, Andrŏgĕō
Gen. Dēlī	Andrŏgĕī, Andrŏgĕō
Dat. Dēlō	Andrŏgĕō
Abl. Dēlō.	Andrŏgĕō.

Obs. Substantives in *ōs* sometimes form their Accusatives in *ōnă*: as, *Andrŏgeōnă*: so, *Nom.* Athōs, *Acc.* Athōnă.

Third Declension.

Sing.	Sing.
Nom. Pĕriclēs	Pallas
Voc. Pĕriclēs, Pĕriclĕs, Pĕricle	Pallas
Acc. Pĕriclem, Pĕriclĕă	Pallădem, Pallădă
Gen. Pĕriclĭs, Pĕriclī	Pallădĭs, Pallădos
Dat. Pĕriclī	Pallădi
Abl. Pĕricle.	Pallădĕ.

Nom. Părĭs	Sapphō
Voc. Parĭ	Sapphō
Acc. Părĭdem, Părĭdă, Părin	Sapphō, Sapphōnem
Gen. Părĭdĭs, Părĭdŏs	Sapphūs, Sapphōnĭs
Dat. Părĭdī	Sapphō, Sapphonī
Abl. Parĭde.	Sapphōnĕ.

Sing.	Plur.
Nom. chlămȳs, *a cloak.*	chlămȳdēs *or* -ĕs
Acc. chlămȳdem, chlămȳdă	chlămȳdēs, chlămȳdăs
Gen. chlămȳdĭs, chlămȳdŏs	chlămȳdum
Dat. chlămȳdī	chlămȳdĭbŭs
Abl. chlămȳdĕ	chlămȳdĭbŭs.

B. THE GENDERS OF NOUNS.

GENERAL RULES.

1. Males, Mountains, Months, Winds, and Rivers, are *Masculine.*

2. Females, Countries, Islands, Towns, and Trees, are *Feminine.*

3. Indeclinable Nouns, as, fās, *permitted by heaven,* nĕfas, *not permitted by heaven,* nĭhĭl, *nothing,* are *Neuter.*

4. Nouns denoting both the male and the female, as, conjux, *husband* or *wife,* are *Common.*

SPECIAL RULES RELATING TO THE DECLENSIONS.

I. FIRST DECLENSION.—All Nouns of the First Declension are Feminine, unless they designate males: as, nauta, *a sailor.*

II. SECOND DECLENSION.—Nouns in .us and er are Masculine; those in um are Neuter.

A few Nouns in us are Feminine: names of trees, as mălus, *an apple-tree:* also, alvus, *the belly;* cŏlus, *a distaff;* hŭmus, *the ground;* vannus, *a winnowing fan;* arctus, *the constellation Bear;* carbăsus, *fine flax.*

Three Nouns in us are Neuter: as, vīrus, *poison;* vulgus, *the multitude;* pĕlăgus, *the (open) sea.*

III. THIRD DECLENSION.—Nouns of the Third Declension are Masculine, Feminine, or Neuter. Their gender must be learned by practice. But the following terminations indicate genders :—

1. *Masculine.*—(*a*) Nouns in or derived from verbs: as, ăm-or, *love.* from ămo, *I love.*

(*b*) Nouns in tor derived from verbs: as, ămā-tor, *a lover,* from ămo, *I love;* vic-tor, *a conqueror,* from vinco, *I conquer.*

2. *Feminine.*—(a) Nouns in **io** and **tio** derived from verbs: as, audī-tio, *hearing*, from audio, *I hear*.

    (b) Nouns -in **tūs** derived from Substantives: as, vir-tus, *manliness*, from vir, *a man*.

    (c) Nouns in **tās** derived from Substantives and Adjectives: as, cīvī-tas, *citizenship*, from cīvis, *a citizen*; crūdēlī-tas, *cruelty*, from crūdēlis, *cruel*.

    (d) Nouns in **tūdo** derived from Adjectives: as, longĭ-tūdo, *length*, from longus, *long*.

    (e) Nouns in **trix** derived from Substantives in *tor*; as, vic-trix, *a female conqueror*, from vic-tor.

3. *Neuter.* — (a) Nouns in **e**: as, mărĕ, *the sea*.

    (b) Nouns in **měn** derived from Verbs: as, flū-men, *a river*, from flu-ere, *to flow*.

    (c) Nouns in **ŭs** and **ŭr**: as, ŏpus, *a work*; fulgur, *lightning*.

IV. Fourth Declension.—Nouns in **ŭs** are Masculine: those in **u** are Neuter.

A few Nouns in **us** are Feminine: namely, trĭbus, a *tribe* (a division of the Roman people); ăcus, *a needle*; portĭcus, *a portico*; dŏmus, *a house*; nŭrus, *a daughter-in-law*; ănus, *an old woman*; socrus, *a mother-in-law*; ĭdūs (*pl.*), *the Ides* (a division of the Roman month); mănus, *a hand*.

V. Fifth Declension.—All are Feminine except dies (*day*), which in the Plural is always Masculine, and in the Singular either Masculine or Feminine; and mērĭdies, *midday*, which is always Masculine.

C. PERFECTS AND SUPINES.

I. The First or A Conjugation.

The Perfects and the Supines of the First Conjugation end regularly in āvi, ātum: as, ămo, ămāvi, ămātum, ămāre, *to love*. The following are exceptions :—

Crĕpo,	crĕpui,	crĕpĭtum,	crĕpāre,	*to creak.*
Cŭbo,	cŭbui,	cŭbĭtum,	cŭbāre,	*to lie.*
Dŏmo,	dŏmui,	dŏmĭtum,	dŏmāre,	*to tame.*
Sŏno,¹	sŏnui,	sŏnĭtum,	sŏnāre,	*to sound.*
Vĕto,	vĕtui,	vĕtĭtum,	vĕtāre,	*to forbid.*
Tŏno,	tŏnui,	—	tŏnāre,	*to thunder.*
Mĭco,	mĭcui,		mĭcāre,	*to glitter.*
Plĭco,	plĭcui,	{plĭcĭtum, plĭcătum,	}plĭcāre,	*to fold.*
Frĭco,	frĭcui,	frictum,	frĭcāre,	*to rub.*
Sĕco,²	sĕcui,	sectum,	sĕcāre,	*to cut.*
Jŭvo,³	jūvi,	jūtum,	jŭvāre,	*to assist.*
Lăvo,	lāvi,	{lăvātum, lautum,	lăvāre,	*to wash.*
Do,	dĕdi,	dătum,	dăre,	*to give.*
Sto,	stĕti,	statum,	stāre,	*to stand.*

NOTE.—*Future Participles*, as a general rule, are formed from the Supines; but

1. Sŏno   *has*   sŏnātūrus.
2. Sĕco   „   sĕcātūrus.
3. Jŭvo   „   jŭvātūrus.

II. The Second or E Conjugation.

The Perfects and Supines of the Second Conjugation end regularly in uī and ĭtum: as, mŏneo, mŏnui, mŏnĭtum, mŏnēre, *to advise*. The following are exceptions :—

1. Perfect—ui. Supine—tum.

Dŏceo,	dŏcui,	doctum,	dŏcēre,	*to teach.*
Tĕneo,	tĕnui,	tentum,	tĕnēre,	*to hold.*
Misceo,	miscui,	{mixtum, mistum,	}miscēre,	*to mix.*
Torreo,	torrui,	tostum,	torrēre,	*to roast.*
Sorbeo,	{sorbui, sorpsi,	} —	sorbēre,	*to suck up.*
Censeo,	censui,	censum,	censēre,	*to assess, think.*

2. Perfect—ēvi. Supine—ētum.

Dēleo,	dēlēvi,	dēlētum,	dēlēre,	*to blot out, destroy*
Fleo,	flēvi,	flētum,	flēre,	*to weep.*
Neo,	nēvi,	nētum,	nēre,	*to spin.*
{Pleo only in composition.				
{Compleo,	complēvi,	complētum,	complēre,	*to fill up.*
Abŏleo,	ăbŏlēvi,	ăbŏlĭtum,	ăbŏlēre,	*to abolish.*

3. Perfect—i (di). Supine—sum.

Prandeo,	prandi,	pransum,	prandēre,	to breakfast.
Sĕdeo,	sēdi,	sessum,	sĕdēre,	to sit.
Vĭdeo,	vīdi,	vīsum,	vĭdēre,	to see.
Strĭdeo,	stridi,		strīdēre,	to creak.

With Reduplication in the Perfect Tenses.

Mordeo,	mŏmordi,	morsum,	mordēre,	to bite.
Pendeo,	pĕpendi,	pensum,	pendēre,	to hang.
Spondeo,	spŏpondi,	sponsum,	spondēre,	to promise.
Tondeo,	tŏtondi,	tonsum,	tondēre,	to shear.

4. Perfect—i (vi). Supine—tum.

Căveo,	cāvi.	cautum.	căvēre,	to guard one's self.
Făveo,	fāvi,	fautum,	făvēre,	to favour.
Fŏveo,	fōvi,	fōtum,	fŏvēre,	to cherish.
Mŏveo,	mōvi,	mōtum,	mŏvēre,	to move.
Vŏveo,	vōvi,	vōtum,	vŏvēre,	to vow.

Without Supine.

Păveo,	păvi,		păvēre,	to fear.
Ferveo,	{fervi, ferbui,}	—	fervēre,	to boil.
Conniveo,	{connīvi, connixi,}	—	connīvēre,	to wink.

5. Perfect—si. Supine—tum and sum.

Augeo,	auxi.	auctum,	augēre,	to increase.
Indulgeo,	indulsi,	indultum,	indulgēre,	to indulge.
Torqueo,	torsi,	tortum,	torquēre,	to twist.
Ardeo,	arsi,	arsum,	ardēre,	to blaze.
Haereo,	haesi,	haesum,	haerēre,	to stick.
Jŭbeo,	jussi,	jussum,	jŭbēre,	to order.
Măneo,	mansi,	mansum,	mănēre,	to remain.
Mulceo,	mulsi.	mulsum,	mulcēre,	to stroke.
Mulgeo,	mulsi,	mulctum,	mulgēre,	to milk.
Rīdeo,	rīsi,	rīsum,	rīdēre,	to laugh.
Suādeo,	suāsi,	suāsum,	suādēre,	to advise.
Tergeo,	tersi.	tersum,	tergēre,	to wipe.
Algeo,	alsi,	—	algēre,	}to be cold
Frĭgeo,	frixi,	—	frĭgēre,	
Fulgeo,	fulsi,	—	fulgēre,	to shine.
Lūceo,	luxi,	—	lūcēre,	to be light.
Lūgeo,	luxi,	—	lūgēre,	to grieve.
Turgeo,	(tursi),	—	turgēre,	to swell.
Urgeo,	ursi,	—	urgēre,	to press.

6. The Neuter-Passives.

Audeo,	ausus sum,		audēre,	to dare.
Gaudeo,	gāvīsus sum,		gaudēre,	to rejoice.
Sŏleo,	sŏlĭtus sum,	—	sŏlēre,	to be accustomed.

III. The Third (Consonant or U) Conjugation.

Verbs of the Third Conjugation are best classified according to the final consonants of the Stems.

1. *Verbs the Stems of which end in the Labials* B, P.

(a). *Perfect—si. Supine—tum.*

NOTE.—*B becomes p before s and t.*

Carpo,	carpsi,	carptum,	carpĕre,	to pluck.
Glūbo,	glupsi,	gluptum,	glūbĕre,	to peel.
Nūbo,	nupsi,	nuptum,	nūbĕre,	to marry.
Rēpo,	repsi,	reptum,	rēpĕre,	to creep.
Scalpo,	scalpsi,	scalptŭm,	scalpĕre,	to scratch.
Scrībo,	scripsi,	scriptum,	scrībĕre,	to write.
Serpo,	serpsi,	serptum,	serpĕre,	to crawl.

(b). *Perfect—ui. Supine—tum or Itum.*

{Cumbo,				
{Incumbo,	incŭbŭi,	incŭbĭtum,	incŭmbĕre,	to lie upon.
Strĕpo,	strĕpui,	strĕpĭtum,	strĕpĕre,	to make a noise.

(c). *Perfect—i. Supine—tum or wanting.*

Rumpo,	rūpi,	ruptum,	rumpĕre,	to burst.
Bĭbo,	bĭbi,		bĭbĕre,	to drink.
Lambo,	lambi,		lambĕre,	to lick.
Scăbo,	scăbi,		scăbĕre,	to scratch.

2. *Verbs the Stems of which end in the Gutturals* C, G, H, Q, X.

(a). *Perfect—si. Supine—tum.*

NOTE.—*Cs and gs become x. G becomes c before t.*

Dīco,	dixi,	dictum,	dīcĕre,	to say.
Dūco,	duxi,	ductum,	dūcĕre,	to lead.
Cŏquo,	coxi,	coctum,	cŏquĕre,	to cook.
Cingo,	cinxi,	cinctum,	cingĕre,	to surround.
{(Fligo, not used.				to strike.)
{Afflīgo,	afflixi,	afflictum,	afflīgĕre,	to strike to the ground.
Frīgo,	frixi,	{frictum, frixum,	}frīgĕre,	to parch, to fry.
Jungo,	junxi,	junctum,	jungĕre,	to join.
Lingo,	linxi,	linctum,	lingĕre,	to lick.
{(Mungo, not used.)				
{Ēmungo,	ēmunxi,	ēmunctum,	ēmungĕre,	to blow the nose.
Plango,	planxi,	planctum,	plangĕre,	to beat.

Rĕgo,	rexi,	rectum,	rĕgĕre,	to direct, rule.
Sūgo,	suxi,	suctum,	sūgĕrĕ,	to suck.
Tĕgo,	texi,	tectum,	tĕgĕre,	to cover.
Tingo, Tinguo,	} tinxi,	tinctum,	tingĕre, tinguĕre,	} to dip.
Ungo, Unguo,	} unxi,	unctum,	ungĕre, unguĕre,	} to anoint.
(Stinguo, not used.)				
Exstinguo,	exstinxi,	exstinctum,	exstinguĕre,	to extinguish.
Trăho,	traxi,	tractum,	trăhĕre,	to drag.
Vĕho,	vexi,	vectum,	vĕhĕre,	to carry, to draw.
Ango,	anxi,		angĕre,	to vex.
Ningit,	ninxit,		ningĕre,	to snow.
Fingo,	finxi,	fictum,	fingĕre,	to form, to invent.
Pingo,	pinxi,	pictum,	pingĕre,	to paint.
Stringo,	strinxi,	strictum,	stringĕre,	to grasp.

(b). Perfect—si. Supine—sum and xum.

Mergo,	mersi,	mersum,	mergĕre,	to sink.
Spargo,	sparsi,	sparsum,	spargĕre,	to scatter.
Tergo,	tersi,	tersum,	tergĕre,	to wipe.
Fīgo,	fixi,	fixum,	figĕre,	to fix.
Flecto,	flexi,	flexum,	flectĕre,	to bend.
Necto,	nexi,	nexum,	nectĕre,	to bind.
Pecto,	pexi,	pexum,	pectĕre,	to comb.
Plecto,	plexi,	plexum,	plectĕre,	to plait.

(c). Perfect—i (with Reduplication). Supine—sum and tum.

Pango,	pĕpĭgi,	pactum,	pangĕre,	to fix.
Parco,	pĕperci,	parsum,	parcĕre,	to spare.
Pungo,	pŭpŭgi,	punctum,	pungĕre,	to prick.
Tango,	tĕtĭgi,	tactum,	tangĕre,	to touch.
Disco,	dĭdĭci,		discĕre,	to learn.
Posco,	pŏposci,		poscĕre,	to demand.

(d). Perfect—i (with vowel of Stem lengthened).

Ăgo,	ēgi,	actum,	ăgĕre,	to do.
Frango,	frēgi,	fractum,	frangĕre,	to break.
Ĭco,	īci,	ictum,	īcĕre,	to strike (a treaty)
Lĕgo,	lēgi,	lectum,	lĕgĕre,	to read.
Linquo,	līqui,	(lictum),	linquĕre,	to leave.
Vinco,	vīci,	victum,	vincĕre,	to conquer.

(e). Perfect—ui. Supine—tum.

Texo,	texui,	textum,	texĕre,	to weave.

(f). Guttural Stem disguised.

Fluo,	fluxi,	fluctum,	fluĕre,	to flow.
Struo,	struxi,	structum,	struĕre,	to pile up.
Vīvo,	vixi,	victum,	vīvĕre,	to live.

3. *Verbs the Stems of which end in the Dentals* D, T.

(a). *Perfect—*si. *Supine—*tum.

NOTE.—*D* and *t* are generally dropped before *s*, but are sometimes changed into *s*.

Claudo,	clausi,	clausum,	claudĕre,	*to shut.*
Divĭdo,	divisi,	divisum,	divĭdĕre,	*to divide.*
Laedo,	laesi,	laesum,	laedĕre,	*to strike, to injure.*
Lūdo,	lūsi,	lūsum,	lūdĕre,	*to play.*
Plaudo,	plausi,	plausum,	plaudĕre,	*to clap the hands.*
Rādo,	rāsi,	rāsum,	rādĕre,	*to scrape.*
Rōdo,	rōsi,	rōsum,	rōdĕre,	*to gnaw.*
Trūdo,	trūsi,	trūsum,	trūdĕre,	*to thrust.*
{Vādo,	—		vādĕre,	*to go.*
{Invādo,	invāsi,	invāsum,	invādĕre,	*to go against.*
Cēdo,	cessi,	cessum,	cēdĕre,	*to yield.*
Mitto,	mīsi,	missum,	mittĕre,	*to send.*

(b). *Perfect with Reduplication.*

Cădo,	cĕcĭdi,	cāsum,	cădĕre,	*to fall.*
Caedo,	cĕcīdi,	caesum,	caedĕre,	*to strike, to cut.*
Pendo,	pĕpendi,	pensum,	pendĕre,	*to hang, to weigh.*
Tendo,	tĕtendi,	{tensum, tentum,	}tendĕre,	*to stretch.*
Tundo,	tŭtūdi,	{tunsum, tūsum,	}tundĕre,	*to beat.*
Do in compos.				*to put.*
Abdo,	abdĭdi,	abdĭtum,	abdĕre,	*to put away, to hide.*
Addo,	addĭdi,	addĭtum,	addĕre,	*to put to, to add.*
Condo,	condĭdi,	condĭtum,	condĕre,	*to put together, to build, conceal.*
Dēdo,	dēdĭdi,	dēdĭtum,	dēdĕre,	*to put down, to surrender.*
Edo,	ēdĭdi,	ĕdĭtum,	ēdĕre,	*to put forth, to publish.*
Indo,	indĭdi,	indĭtum,	indĕre,	*to put on.*
Perdo,	perdĭdi,	perdĭtum,	perdĕre,	*to ruin, to lose.*
Prōdo,	prōdĭdi,	prōdĭtum,	prōdĕre,	*to betray.*
Reddo,	reddĭdi,	reddĭtum,	reddĕre,	*to put back, to restore.*
Subdo,	subdĭdi,	subdĭtum,	subdĕre,	*to put under, to substitute.*
Trādo,	trādĭdi,	trādĭtum,	trādĕre,	*to put across, to deliver.*
Crēdo,	crēdĭdi,	crēdĭtum,	crēdĕre,	*to believe.*
Vendo,	vendĭdi,	vendĭtum,	vendĕre,	*to sell.*
Sisto,	stĭti,	stătum,	sistĕre,	*to cause to stand.*

(c). *Perfect—*i. *Supine—*sum.

Accendo,	accendi,	accensum,	accendĕre,	*to set on fire.*
Cūdo,	cūdi,	cūsum,	cūdĕre,	*to hammer.*

Ĕdo,	ēdi,	ēsum,	ĕdĕre,	to eat.
(Fendo, not used,				to strike.)
Dēfendo,	dēfendi,	dēfensum,	dēfendĕre,	to ward off, to defend.
Offendo,	offendi,	offensum,	offendĕre,	to strike against, to assault.
Fundo,	fūdi,	fūsum,	fundĕre,	to pour.
Incendo,	incendi,	incensum,	incendĕre,	to burn.
Mando,	mandi (rare),	mansum,	mandĕre,	to chew.
Pando,	pandi,	pansum or passum,	pandĕre,	to spread.
Prĕhendo,	prĕhendi,	prĕhensum,	prĕhendĕre,	to grasp.
Scando,	scandi,	scansum,	scandĕre,	to climb.
Strīdo, Strīdeo,	strīdi,		strīdĕre,	to creak.
Verto,	verti,	versum,	vertĕre,	to turn.
Findo,	fīdi,	fissum,	findĕre,	to cleave.
Scindo,	scĭdi,	scissum,	scindĕre,	to tear.
Frendo, Frendeo,		fressum, frēsum,	frendĕre,	to gnash the teeth.

(d). Other Forms.

Mĕto,	messui,	messum,	mĕtĕre,	to mow.
Pĕto,	pĕtīvi or pĕtĭi,	pĕtītum,	pĕtĕre,	to seek.
Sīdo,	sēdi (rarely sīdi),		sīdĕre,	to sit down.
Sterto,	stertui,		stertĕre,	to snore.
Fīdo,	fīsus sum,		fīdĕre,	to trust.

4. Verbs the Stems of which end in L, M, N.

*(a). Perfect—ui. Supine—ĭtum or tum.

Ălo,	ălui,	ălĭtum or altum,	ălĕre,	to nourish.
Cŏlo,	cŏlui,	cultum,	cŏlĕre,	to till.
Consŭlo,	consŭlui,	consultum,	consŭlĕre,	to consult.
Mŏlo,	mŏlui,	mŏlĭtum,	mŏlĕre,	to grind.
Occŭlo,	occŭlui,	occultum,	occŭlĕre,	to conceal.
Vŏlo,	vŏlui,		velle,	to wish.
Frĕmo,	frĕmui,	frĕmĭtum,	frĕmĕre,	to roar.
Gĕmo,	gĕmui,	gĕmĭtum,	gĕmĕre,	to groan.
Trĕmo,	trĕmui,		trĕmĕre,	to tremble.
Vŏmo,	vŏmui,	vŏmĭtum,	vŏmĕre,	to vomit.
Gigno,	gĕnui,	gĕnĭtum,	gignĕre,	to produce.

(b). Perfect with Reduplication.

Fallo,	fĕfelli,	falsum,	fallĕre,	to deceive.
Pello,	pĕpŭli,	pulsum,	pellĕre,	to drive.
Căno,	cĕcĭni,	cantum,	cănĕre,	to sing.

(c). Perfect—si. Supine—tum.

Cŏmo,	compsi,	comptum,	cōmĕre,	to adorn.
Dēmo,	dempsi,	demptum,	dēmĕre,	to take away.
Prŏmo,	prompsi,	promptum,	prŏmĕre,	to take forth.
Sūmo,	sumpsi,	sumptum,	sūmĕre,	to take up.
Tĕmno,	tempsi,	temptum,	temnĕre,	to despise.

(d). Other Forms.

Percello,	percŭlī,	perculsum,	percellĕre,	to strike down.
Psallo,	psallī,	—	psallĕre,	to play on a stringed instrument.
Vello,	velli,	vulsum,	vellĕre,	to pluck.
Tollo,	sustŭlī,	sublātum,	tollĕre,	to raise up.
Ĕmo,	ēmi,	emptum,	ĕmĕre,	to take or buy.
Prĕmo,	pressi,	pressum,	prĕmĕre,	to press.
Līno,	lēvi,	lĭtum,	līnĕre,	to smear.
Sīno,	sīvi,	sĭtum,	sĭnĕre,	to permit.

5. Verbs the Stems of which end in R.

Cerno,	crēvi,	crētum,	cernĕre,	to sift, to divide.
Sperno,	sprēvi,	sprētum,	spernĕre,	to despise.
Sterno,	strāvi,	strātum,	sternĕre,	to strew.
Gĕro,	gessi,	gestum,	gĕrĕre,	to carry.
Ūro,	ussi,	ustum,	ūrĕre,	to burn.
Curro,	cŭcurri,	cursum,	currĕre,	to run.
Fĕro,	tŭli,	lātum,	ferre,	to bear, carry.
Quaero,	quaesīvi,	quaesītum,	quaerĕre,	to seek.
Sĕro,	sĕrui,	sertum,	sĕrĕre,	to put in rows, to plait.
Sĕro,	sēvi,	sătum,	sĕrĕre,	to sow.
Tĕro,	trīvi,	trītum,	tĕrĕre,	to rub.
Verro,	verri,	versum,	verrĕre,	to sweep.

6. Verbs the Stems of which end in S, X.

Depso,	depsui,	depstum,	depsĕre,	to knead.
Pinso,	pinsui, pinsi,	pinsĭtum, pinsum,	pinsĕre,	to pound.
Pīso,		pistum,	pīsĕre,	to pound.
Vīso,	vīsi,		vīsĕre,	to visit.
Pōno,	pŏsui,	pŏsĭtum,	pōnĕre,	to place.
Arcesso,	arcessīvi,	arcessītum,	arcessĕre,	to send for.
Căpesso,	căpessīvi,	căpessītum,	căpessĕre,	to take in hand.
Făcesso,	făcessi,	făcessītum,	făcessĕre,	to make, to cause.
Lăcesso,	lăcessīvi,	lăcessītum,	lăcessĕre,	to provoke.

7. Verbs the Stems of which end in U, V.

Perfect—i. Supine—tum.

Ăcuo,	ăcui,	ăcūtum,	ăcuĕre,	to sharpen.
Arguo,	argui,	argūtum,	arguĕre,	to prove.

Imbuo,	imbui,	imbūtum,	imbuĕre,	*to soak.*
Induo,	indui,	indūtum,	induĕre,	*to put on.*
Exuo,	exui,	exūtum,	exuĕre,	*to put off.*
Mĭnuo,	mĭnui,	mĭnūtum,	mĭnuĕre,	*to lessen.*
Rŭo,*	rui,	rŭtum,	ruĕre,	*to rush.*
Spuo,	spui,	spūtum,	spuĕre,	*to spit.*
Stătuo,	stătui,	stătūtum,	stătuĕre,	*to set up.*
Suo,	sui,	sūtum,	suĕre,	*to sew.*
Trĭbuo,	trĭbui,	trĭbūtum,	trĭbuĕre,	*to distribute.*
Lăvo,	lăvi,	lautum, lōtum,	lăvĕre,	*to wash.*
Solvo,	solvi,	sŏlūtum,	solvĕre,	*to loosen.*
Volvo,	volvi,	vŏlūtum,	volvĕre,	*to roll.*
Congruo,	congrui,		congruĕre,	*to agree.*
Luo,†	lui,		luĕre,	*to atone.*
(Nuo,				*to nod.)*
Abnuo,	abnui,		abnuĕre,	*to refuse.*
Annuo,	annui,		annuĕre,	*to assent.*
Mĕtuo,	mĕtui,		mĕtuĕre,	*to fear.*
Pluit,	{ pluit *or* plūvit, }		pluĕre,	*to rain.*
Sternuo,	sternui,		sternuĕre,	*to sneeze.*

* rŭo, *Future Participle* ruĭtūrus.
† lŭo, „ „ luĭtūrus.

8. *Verbs the Present Tense of which ends in* sco.

Verbs ending in *sco* are *Inceptive;* that is, denote the beginning of an action. They are formed from Verbs, Nouns, and Adjectives. Inceptives formed from Verbs have the Perfects of the Verbs from which they are derived, but usually no Supines: as, incălesco, incălui, incălescĕre, *to grow warm,* from căleo, călui, călēre, *to be warm.* The following Inceptives are exceptions and have Supines:—

Ăbŏlesco,*	ăbŏlēvi,	ăbŏlĭtum,	ăbŏlescĕre,	*to grow out of use.*
Ădŏlesco,*	ădŏlēvi,	ădultum,	ădŏlescĕre,	*to grow up.*
Exŏlesco,*	exŏlēvi,	exŏlĭtum,	exŏlescĕre,	*to grow old.*
Cŏălesco, (ălo)	cŏălui,	cŏălĭtum,	cŏălescĕre,	*to grow together.*
Concŭpisco, (cŭpio)	concŭpīvi,	concŭpītum,	concŭpiscĕre,	*to desire.*
Convălesco, (văleo)	convălui,	convălĭtum,	convălescĕre,	*to grow strong.*
Exardesco, (ardeo)	exarsi,	exarsum,	exardescĕre,	*to take fire.*
Invĕtĕrasco, (invĕtĕro)	invĕtĕrāvi,	invĕtĕrātum,	invĕtĕrascĕre,	*to grow old.*
Rĕvīvisco, (vīvo)	rĕvixi,	rĕvictum,	rĕvīviscĕre,	*to come to life again.*
Scisco, (scio)	scīvi,	scītum,	sciscĕre,	*to seek to know, to enact.*

* Ăbŏlesco, ădŏlesco, exŏlesco are formed from an obsolete verb ŏleo, *to grow.*

Inceptives formed from Nouns and Adjectives have either Perfects in *ui* and no Supines, or they want both Perfects and Supines : as,

Consĕnesco, consĕnui, (sĕnex)	consĕnescĕre,	*to grow old.*
Ingrăvesco, (grăvis)	ingrăvescĕre,	*to grow heavy.*
Jŭvĕnesco, (jŭvĕnis)	jŭvĕnescĕre,	*to grow young.*
Mātŭresco, mātŭrui, (mātŭrus)	mātŭrescĕre,	*to grow ripe.*
Obmūtesco, obmūtui, (mūtus)	obmūtescĕre,	*to grow dumb.*

The following Verbs in *sco* are derived from forms no longer in use, and are therefore treated as underived Verbs :—

Cresco,	crēvi,	crētum,	crescĕre,	*to grow.*
Glisco,			gliscĕre,	*to swell.*
Hisco,			hiscĕre,	*to gape.*
Nosco,*	nōvi,	nōtum,	noscĕre,	*to learn, to know.*
Pasco,	păvi,	pastum,	pascĕre,	*to feed.*
Quiesco,	quiēvi,	quiētum,	quiescĕre,	*to become quiet.*
Suesco,	suēvi,	suētum,	suescĕre,	*to grow accustomed.*

* The Present signifies *I learn* ; the Perfect, *I know* ; the Pluperfect, *I knew*.

THIRD CONJUGATION WITH I IN CERTAIN TENSES.

Căpio,	cēpi,	captum,	căpĕre,	*to take.*
Făcio,	fēci,	factum,	făcĕre,	*to make.*
Jăcio,	jēci,	jactum,	jăcĕre,	*to throw.*
Fŭgio,	fūgi,	fŭgĭtum,	fŭgĕre,	*to flee.*
Fŏdio,	fōdi,	fossum,	fŏdĕre,	*to dig.*
Răpio,	răpui,	raptum,	răpĕre,	*to seize.*
Părio,*	pĕpĕri,	partum,	părĕre,	*to bring forth.*
Quătio,	(no perfect),	quassum,	quătĕre,	*to shake.*
Cŭpio,	cŭpīvi,	cŭpītum,	cŭpĕre,	*to desire.*
Săpio,	săpīvi,		săpĕre,	*to taste.*
Lăcio,			lăcĕre,	*to draw* ⎱ rare, except in
Spĕcio,			spĕcĕre,	*to look* ⎰ composition.

* părio, *Future Participle* părĭtūrus.

IV. THE FOURTH OR I CONJUGATION.

In the Fourth Conjugation the Perfect ends regularly in īvi, the Supine in ītum : as, audio, audīvi, audītum, audīre, *to hear*. The following are exceptions :—

Farcio,	farsi,	⎧fartum,⎫ ⎩(farctum)⎭	farcīre,	*to cram.*
Fulcio,	fulsi,	fultum,	fulcīre,	*to prop.*

Haurio,	hausi,	haustum,	haurīre,	to draw (water).
Sancio,	sanxi,	sancītum or sanctum,	sancīre,	to ratify.
Sarcio,	sarsi,	sartum,	sarcīre,	to patch.
Sentio,	sensi,	sensum,	sentīre,	to feel, to think.
Saepio,	saepsi,	saeptum,	saepīre,	to fence in.
Vincio,	vinxi,	vinctum,	vincīre,	to bind.
Eo,	īvi,	ītum,	īre,	to go.
Sălio,	sălui or sălii,	saltum,	sălīre,	to leap.
Sĕpĕlio,	sĕpĕlīvi,	sĕpultum,	sĕpĕlīre,	to bury.
Vĕnio,	vĕni,	ventum,	vĕnīre,	to come.
Ămĭcio,	ămĭcui or amixi,	ămictum,	ămĭcīre,	to clothe.
Ăpĕrio,	ăpĕrui,	ăpertum,	ăpĕrīre,	to open.
Ŏpĕrio,	ŏpĕrui,	ŏpertum,	ŏpĕrīre,	to cover.

V. Deponents.

1. In the First Conjugation the Perfects and Supines are all regular.

2. Second Conjugation:

Făteor,	fassus sum,	fătēri,	to confess.
Lĭceor,	lĭcĭtus sum,	lĭcēri,	to bid at a sale.
Mĕdeor,		mĕdēri,	to heal.
Mĕreor,	mĕrĭtus sum,	mĕrēri,	to earn, to deserve.
Mĭsĕreor,	mĭsĕrĭtus sum or misertus sum,	mĭsĕrēri,	to take pity on.
Pollĭceor	pollĭcĭtus sum,	pollĭcēri,	to promise.
Reor,	rătus sum,	rēri,	to think.
Tueor,	tuĭtus sum,	tuēri,	to protect.
Vĕreor,	vĕrĭtus sum,	vĕrēri,	to fear.

3. Third Conjugation:

Fruor,*	fruĭtus sum or fructus sum,	frui,	to enjoy.
Fungor,	functus sum,	fungi,	to perform.
Grădior,	gressus sum,	grădi,	to step.
Lābor,	lapsus sum,	lābi,	to slip.
Lĭquor,		lĭqui,	to melt.
Lŏquor,	lŏcūtus sum,	lŏqui,	to speak.
Mŏrior,†	mortuus sum,	mŏri,	to die.
Nītor,	nixus sum or nīsus sum,	nīti,	to strain.
Pătior,	passus sum,	păti,	to suffer.
Quĕror,	questus sum,	quĕri,	to complain.
Ringor,		ringi,	to show the teeth, to snarl.

Sĕquor,	sĕcūtus sum,	sĕqui,	to follow.
Ūtor,	ūsus sum,	ūti,	to use.
(Verto)			
Rĕvertor,	(rĕversus sum),	rĕverti,	to return.
(Plecto)			
Amplector,	amplexus sum,	amplecti,	to embrace.
Complector,	complexus sum,	complecti,	to embrace.
Ăpiscor,	aptus sum,	ăpisci,	to obtain.
Ădĭpiscor,	ădeptus sum,	ădĭpisci,	to obtain.
Commĭniscor	commentus sum,	commĭnisci,	to devise.
Rĕmĭniscor,		rĕmĭnisci,	to remember.
Dēfĕtiscor,	dēfessus sum,	dēfĕtisci,	to grow weary.
Expergiscor,	experrectus sum,	expergisci,	to wake up.
Irascor,		īrasci,	to be angry.
Nanciscor,	nactus sum,	nancisci,	to obtain by chance.
Nascor,	nātus sum,	nasci,	to be born.
Oblīviscor,	oblītus sum,	oblīvisci,	to forget.
Păciscor,	pactus sum,	păcisci,	to make an agreement.
Prŏfĭciscor,	prŏfectus sum,	prŏfĭcisci,	to set out.
Ulciscor,	ultus sum,	ulcisci,	to avenge.
Vescor,		vesci,	to eat.

* fruor, ⸤Future Participle fruĭtūrus.
† mŏrior, „ „ mŏrĭtūrus.

4. Fourth Conjugation :

Assentior,	assensus sum,	assentīri,	to agree to.
Blandior,	blandītus sum,	blandīri,	to flatter.
Expĕrior,	expertus sum,	expĕrīri,	to try.
Largior,	largītus sum,	largīri,	to give bountifully.
Mentior,	mentītus sum,	mentīri,	to lie.
Mĕtior,	mensus sum,	mētīri,	to measure.
Mōlior,	mōlītus sum,	mōlīri,	to labour.
Oppĕrior,	{oppertus sum, / oppĕrītus sum,	}oppĕrīri,	to wait for.
Ordior,	orsus sum,	ordīri,	to begin.
Orior,*	ortus sum,	ŏrīri,	to rise.
Partior,	partītus sum	partīri,	to divide.
Pŏtior,	pŏtītus sum,	pŏtīri,	to obtain possession of.
Sortior,	sortītus sum,	sortīri,	to take by lot.

* orior, *Future Participle* ŏrĭtūrus. The *Pres. Ind.* follows the 3rd Conjugation :
ŏrĕris, ŏrĭtur, ŏrĭmur. In the *Imperf. Subj.* both ŏrĕrer and ŏrīrer are found.

D. DEFECTIVE VERBS.

Defective Verbs are such as want many Tenses and Persons.

    I. Coepĭ,   *I began.*
    II. Mĕmĭnī, *I remember.*
    III. Odĭ,   *I hate.*

INDICATIVE.

Perfect.	Coepī	Mĕmĭnī	Odī.
Fut.-Perf.	Coepĕro	Mĕmĭnĕro	Odĕro.
Pluperf.	Coepĕram	Mĕmĭnĕram ·	Odĕram.

SUBJUNCTIVE.

Perfect.	Coepĕrim	Mĕmĭnĕrim	Odĕrim.
Pluperf.	Coepissem	Mĕmĭnissem,	Odissem.

IMPERATIVE.

Future.	(wanting.)	Mĕmento,	(wanting.)
		Mĕmentōte,	

INFINITIVE.

Perfect.	Coepissĕ	Mĕmĭnissĕ	Odissĕ.

PARTICIPLE.

Future.	Coeptūrŭs	(wanting.)	Osūrŭs.

IV. Aio, *I say :—*

INDICATIVE.	SUBJUNCTIVE.	INDICATIVE.	SUBJUNCTIVE.
Present.		*Imperfect.*	
S. Aio	—	*S.* Aiēbam	
Aĭs	Aiās	Aiēbās	
Aĭt	Aiăt	Aiēbăt	
P.		*P.* Aiēbămŭs	
		Aiēbătĭs	—
Aĭunt	Aiant	Aiēbant.	—

PRESENT PARTICIPLE.—Aiens.

V. Inquam, *say I :—*

INDICATIVE.		*Future.*	*Perfect.*
Present.	*Imperfect.*	—	—
Inquam	Inquiēbam	Inquiēs	Inquistī
Inquĭs	Inquiēbās	Inquiĕt	Inquĭt
Inquĭt	Inquiēbăt		
Inquĭmŭs	Inquiēbămŭs	IMPERATIVE.	
Inquĭtĭs	Inquiēbătĭs	*Present.*	*Future.*
Inquĭunt	Inquiēbant	Inquĕ	2 *Pers.* Inquĭto.

Obs. Inquam, like the English *say I*, *says he*, is always used after other words in a sentence.

VI. Fāri, *to speak*, a Deponent :—

INDICATIVE.	SUBJUNCTIVE.	IMPERATIVE.	INFINITIVE.
	Present.	*Present. S.* Fārĕ	Fārī
Fātur			
	Future.	**PARTICIPLES.**	
Fābŏr, fābĭtŭr		*Present.* Fantis, &c. (without a Nom.)	
	Perfect.	*Perfect.* Fātus (ă, um)	
Fātus sum, &c.	Fātus sim, &c.	*Gerundive.* Fandŭs (ă, um)	
	Pluperfect.	SUPINE—Fātū.	
Fātŭs ĕram	Fātŭs essem	GERUND—Fandī, &c.	

VOCABULARIES.

m. = masculine.
f. = feminine.
n. = neuter.
c. = common gender, that is, masculine and feminine.

Vocabulary 1.

āla, *f.*	*a wing.*
ăquĭla, *f.*	*an eagle.*
cŏlōnĭa, *f.*	*a colony.*
cŏlumba, *f.*	*a dove.*
cŏrōna, *f.*	*a crown.*
fēmĭna, *f.*	*a woman.*
fīlĭa, *f.*	*a daughter.*
insŭla, *f.*	*an island.*
mensa, *f.*	*a table.*
ōra, *f.*	*a coast.*
pĕcūnĭa, *f*	*money.*
porta, *f.*	*a gate.*
pŭella, *f.*	*a girl.*
rēgīna, *f*	*a queen.*
Rōma, *f*	*Rome* (the city).
rŏsa, *f.*	*a rose.*

Vocabulary 2.

agrĭcŏla, *m.*	*a husbandman.*
ămīcĭtĭa, *f.*	*friendship.*
Brĭtannĭa, *f.*	*Britain.*
causa, *f.*	*a cause.*
Eurōpa, *f.*	*Europe.*
Gallĭa, *f.*	*Gaul* (now France).
glōrĭa, *f.*	*glory.*
Graecĭa, *f.*	*Greece.*
incŏla, *c.*	*an inhabitant.*
ĭnĭmĭcĭtĭa, *f.*	*enmity.*
Ĭtălĭa, *f.*	*Italy.*
nauta, *m.*	*a sailor.*
patrĭa, *f.*	*a native land, country.*
pŏēta, *m.*	*a poet.*
pugna, *f.*	*a battle.*
Sĭcĭlĭa, *f.*	*Sicily.*
vīta, *f.*	*life.*

Vocabulary 3.

ămīcus, *m.*	*a friend.*
ăvus, *m.*	*a grandfather.*
dŏmĭnus, *m.*	*a lord, master.*
ĕquus, *m.*	*a horse.*
fīlĭus, *m.*	*a son.*
flŭvĭus, *m.*	*a river.*
glădĭus, *m.*	*a sword.*
hortus, *m.*	*a garden.*
ĭnĭmīcus, *m.*	*an enemy.*
Rhēnus, *m.*	*the Rhine.*
Rhŏdănus, *m.*	*the Rhone.*
rīpa, *f.*	*a bank.*
servus, *m.*	*a slave.*
taurus, *m.*	*a bull.*

Vocabulary 4.

ăger, *m.*	*a field.*
gĕner, *m.*	*a son-in-law.*
lĭber, *m.*	*a book.*
măgister, *m.*	*a master, teacher.*
mĭnister, *m.*	*a servant.*
pŭer, *m.*	*a boy.*
sŏcer, *m.*	*a father-in-law.*

Note. Mĭnister, lĭber, ăger are declined like măgister. Sŏcer, gĕner are declined like pŭer.

Vocabulary 5.

argentum, *n.*	*silver.*
aurum, *n.*	*gold.*
bellum, *n.*	*war.*
coelum, *n.*	*heaven.*
dīlĭgentĭa, *f.*	*diligence.*
dōnum, *n.*	*a gift.*
gaudĭum, *n.*	*joy.*
mĕtallum, *n.*	*a metal.*
oppĭdum, *n.*	*a town.*

praemium, *n.*	*a reward.*		pax, pācis, *f.*	*peace.*
regnum, *n.*	*a kingdom.*		jūdex, jūdĭcis, *m.*	*a judge.*
scūtum, *n.*	*a shield.*		lex, lēgis, *f.*	*a law.*
templum, *n*	*a temple.*		rex, rēgis, *m.*	*a king.*
*Dĕus, *m.*	*a god.*		bĕnignus, a, um,	*kind.*
discĭpŭlus, *m.*	*a pupil, scholar.*		firmus, a, um,	*strong.*
morbus, *m.*	*a disease.*		jūcundus, a, um,	*pleasant.*
mūrus, *m.*	*a wall.*		justus, a, um,	*just.*
Rōmānus, *m.*	*a Roman.*		Rōmŭlus, *m.*	*Romulus.*
terra, *f.*	*the earth, land.*		sĕvērus, a, um,	*severe.*

* Vocative Singular same as Nom.: Dĕus.

Vocabulary 6.

ăcūtus, a, um,	*sharp.*
albus, a, um,	*white.*
altus, a, um,	*high, deep.*
bellĭcōsus, a, um,	*warlike.*
bŏnus, a, um,	*good.*
grātus, a, um,	*pleasing.*
lātus, a, um,	*wide, broad.*
longus, a, um,	*long.*
magnus, a, um,	*great.*
mălus, a, um,	*bad, wicked.*
mŏlestus, a, um,	*troublesome.*
multus, a, um,	*much, many*
noxĭus, a, um,	*hurtful, injurious.*
parvus, a, um,	*small, little.*
răpĭdus, a, um,	*rapid.*
splendĭdus, a, um,	*splendid, bright.*
tĭmĭdus, a, um,	*timid.*
aeger, gra, rum,	*sick.*
mĭser, ĕra, ĕrum,	*wretched.*
nĭger, gra, grum,	*black.*
pulcher, cra, rum,	*beautiful.*
săcer, cra, rum,	*sacred.*
tĕner, ĕra, ĕrum,	*tender.*
exemplum, *n.*	*an example.*
hasta, *f.*	*a spear.*
nŭmĕrus, *m.*	*a number.*
pĕrīcŭlum, *n.*	*danger.*

Note. Grātus, mŏlestus, noxĭus are followed by the Dative case.

Vocabulary 7.

hĭems, hĭĕmis, *f.*	*winter.*
trabs, trăbis, *f.*	*a beam.*
urbs, urbis, *f.*	*a city.*
arx, arcis, *f.*	*a citadel.*
dux, dŭcis, *c.*	*a leader, general.*

Vocabulary 8.

cŏmes, cŏmĭtis, *c.*	*a companion.*
custos, custōdis, *c.*	*a guardian.*
ĕques, ĕquĭtis, *m.*	*a horse-soldier.*
lăpis, lăpĭdis, *m.*	*a stone.*
miles, mīlĭtis, *m.*	*a soldier.*
mors, mortis, *f.*	*death.*
obses, obsĭdis, *c.*	*a hostage.*
pĕdes, pĕdĭtis, *m.*	*a foot-soldier.*
aestas, tātis, *f.*	*a summer.*
cīvĭtas, tātis, *f.*	*a state, citizenship.*
tempestas, tātis, *f.*	*a tempest.*
vŏluntas, tātis, *f.*	*a wish, will.*
nox, noctis, *f.*	*night.*
auctumnus, i, *m.*	*autumn.*
nātūra, ae, *f.*	*nature.*
clārus, a, um,	*clear, renowned.*

Vocabulary 9

frāter, tris, *m.*	*a brother.*
māter, tris, *f.*	*a mother.*
păter, tris, *m.*	*a father.*
agger, ĕris, *m.*	*a mound.*
călor, ōris, *m.*	*heat.*
clāmor, ōris, *m.*	*a shout.*
cŏlor, ōris, *m.*	*colour.*
lăbor, ōris, *m.*	*labour, hardship.*
ŏdor, ōris, *m.*	*a smell, scent.*
sŏror, ōris, *f.*	*a sister.*
victor, ōris, *m.*	*a conqueror.*
flōs, ōris, *m.*	*a flower.*
sōl, sōlis, *m.*	*the sun.*
castra, ōrum, *n.pl.*	*a camp.*
tōtus, a, um,	*whole.*
fossa, ae, *f.*	*a ditch.*
mūnīmentum, i, *n.*	*a fortification.*
praeda, ae, *f.*	*booty.*
vărĭus, a, um,	*different, various.*

Vocabulary 10.

lĕo, ōnis, m.	a lion.
Jūno, ōnis, f.	Juno.
pāvo, ōnis, m.	a peacock.
sermo, ōnis, m.	a discourse.
consŭētūdo, ĭnis, f.	habit.
hŏmo, ĭnis, c.	{ a man, a woman.
multĭtūdo, ĭnis, f.	a multitude.
virgo, ĭnis, f.	a maiden.
ōrātor, ōris, m.	an orator.
*alter, ĕra, ĕrum,	second.
certus, a, um,	certain.
dĕa, ae, f.	a goddess.
doctus, a, um,	learned.
infīnītus, a, um,	unbounded, infinite.
Mĭnerva, ae, f.	Minerva.
vălĭdus, a, um,	strong.

* The Genitive Singular of *alter* is altĕr-
ius, Dat. alteri : see p. 23.

Vocabulary 11.

cīvis, is, c.	a citizen.
classis, is, f.	a fleet.
hostis, is, c.	an enemy (public enemy).
turris, is, f.	a tower.
vallis, is, f.	a valley.
vestis, is, f.	a garment
clādes, is, f.	slaughter.
nūbes, is, f.	a cloud.
rūpes, is, f.	a rock.
angustus, a, um,	narrow.
āter, atra, atrum,	black.
dūrus, a, um,	hard.
nix, nĭvis, f.	snow.
nōtus, a, um,	known.
pĕrītus, a, um,	skilful.
Rōmānus, a, um,	Roman.

Vocabulary 12.

grāmen, ĭnis, n.	grass.
nōmen, ĭnis, n.	a name.
gĕnus, ĕris, n.	a race, a class.
ŏpus, ĕris, n.	a work.
sīdus, ĕris, n.	a star, constellation.
scĕlus, ĕris, n.	a crime.
dĕcus, ŏris, n.	an ornament.
corpus, ŏris, n.	a body.

frīgus, ŏris, n.	cold.
lītus, ŏris, n.	a shore.
tempus, ŏris, n.	time.
căput, ĭtis, n.	a head.
crūs, crūris, n.	a leg.
fulgur, ŭris, n.	lightning.
ōs, ōris, n.	a mouth.
rēte, is, n.	a net.
măre, is, n.	the sea.
ănĭmăl, ālis, n.	an animal.
calcăr, āris, n.	a spur.
vectīgăl, ālis, n.	a tax.
annus, i, m.	a year.
antīquus, a, um,	ancient.
aurĕus, a, um,	golden.
bālaena, ae, f.	a whale.
Carthāgo, ĭnis, f.	Carthage (a city of Africa).
Cĭcĕro, ōnis, m.	Cicero (a celebrated Roman orator).
dŏmĭcĭlĭum, i, n.	abode.
ĕlĕphantus, i, m.	an elephant.
īra, ae, f.	anger.
nŏvus, a, um,	new.
ŏcŭlus, i, m.	an eye.
piscis, is, m.	a fish.
prŏfundus, a, um,	deep.

Vocabulary 13.

ācer, cris, cre,	keen, sharp.
cĕler, ĕris, ĕre,	swift.
brĕvis, e,	short.
dulcis, e,	sweet.
diffĭcĭlis, e,	difficult.
făcĭlis, e,	easy.
fĭdēlis, e,	faithful.
lĕvis, e,	light.
omnis, e,	all, every.
ūtĭlis, e,	useful.
audax, ācis,	bold.
răpax, ācis,	rapacious.
fēlix, īcis,	fortunate, successful.
vēlox, ōcis,	swift.
ingens, entis,	immense.
praesens, entis,	present.
praestans, antis,	excellent.
pŏtens, entis,	powerful.
prūdens, entis,	prudent.
arma, ōrum, n. pl.	arms.
carmĕn, ĭnis, n.	a song.

consĭlĭum, i, *n.* — *plan, counsel.*
fŭror, ōris, *m.* — *madness.*
hūmānus, a, um, — *human.*
ĭnĭtĭum, i, *n.* — *a beginning.*
nāvis, is, *f.* — *a ship.*
Persa, ae, *m.* — *a Persian.*
săgitta, ae, *f.* — *an arrow.*
vĭa, ae, *f.* — *a way, a road.*
vĕtus, vĕtĕris, — *old.*
vīnum, i, *n.* — *wine.*
vulnus, ĕris, *n.* — *a wound.*

Vocabulary 14.

ăcus, ūs, *f.* — *a needle.*
arcus, ūs, *m.* — *a bow.*
audītus, ūs, *m.* — *hearing.*
cursus, ūs, *m.* — *running.*
ĕquĭtātus, ūs, *m.* — *cavalry.*
exercĭtus, ūs, *m.* — *an army.*
fīcus, ūs, *f.* — *a fig.*
fructus, ūs, *m.* — *fruit.*
măgistrātus, ūs, *m.* — *a magistrate.*
mănus, ūs, *f.* — *a hand.*
pĕdĭtātus, ūs, *m.* — *infantry.*
portus, ūs, *m.* — *a harbour.*
quercus, ūs, *f.* — *an oak.*
sensus, ūs, *m.* — *a sense.*
vīsus, ūs, *m.* — *seeing.*
cornu, ūs, *n.* — *a horn.*
gĕnu, ūs, *n.* — *a knee.*
aurĭs, is, *f.* — *an ear.*
cervus, i, *m.* — *a stag.*
coelestis, e, — *belonging to the heavens:* hence
arcus coelestis, — *the rainbow.*
ĭnstrūmentum, i, *n.* — *an instrument.*
magnĭfĭcus, a, um, — *magnificent.*
tūtus, a, um, — *safe.*
Scўtha, ae, *m.* — *a Scythian.*
Scўthae, ārum, *m. pl.* — *the Scythians.*
sēdes, is, *f.* — *a seat.*
vŏluptas, tātis, *f.* — *pleasure.*

Vocabulary 15.

ăcĭes, ēĭ, *f.* — *a line of battle.*
dĭes, ēĭ, *m. & f.* — *a day.*
făcĭes, ēĭ, *f.* — *a countenance.*
fĭdes, ēĭ, *f.* — *faith, fidelity.*
plānĭtĭes, ēĭ, *f.* — *a plain.*
res, ēĭ, *f.* — *a thing.*

segnĭtĭes, ēĭ, *f.* — *slothfulness.*
spes, ēĭ, *f.* — *hope.*
crĕātor, ōris, *m.* — *a creator.*
dŏmĭna, ae, *f.* — *a mistress.*
fortūna, ae, *f.* — *a fortune.*
rārus, a, um, — *rare.*
sĕrēnus, a, um, — *clear.*
victōrĭa, ae, *f.* — *a victory.*

Vocabulary 16.

arbor, ōris, *f.* — *a tree.*
bestĭa, ae, *f.* — *a beast.*
cănis, is, *c.* — *a dog.*
conscĭentĭa, ae, *f.* — *conscience.*
dēbĭlis, e, — *feeble.*
dīvĭtĭae, ārum, *f.* — *riches.* (only pl.)
flūmen, ĭnis, *n.* — *a current, river.*
fortis, e, — *strong, brave.*
fulmen, ĭnis, *n.* — *lightning, a thunderbolt.*
fūnus, ĕris, *n.* — *a funeral.*
immortālis, e, — *immortal.*
jŭvĕnis, is, *c.* — *a young man or woman.*
mŏnŭmentum, i, *n.* — *a monument.*
mortālis, e, — *mortal.*
Neptūnus, i, *m.* — *Neptune.*
paucus, a, um, — *few.*
plēnus, a, um, *full.* (with *gen.*)
silva, ae, *f.* — *a wood.*

Vocabulary 17.

culpa, ae, *f.* — *blame, fault.*
Graecus, a, um, — *Grecian, Greek.*
hŏnor, ōris, *m.* — *an honour.*
indoctus, a, um, — *unlearned.*
ĭnĭmīcus, a, um, — *unfriendly.*
laus, laudis, *f.* — *praise.*
mĕmŏrābĭlis, e, — *to be remembered, memorable.*
vērus, a, um, — *true.*
virtūs, ūtis, *f.* — *valour, virtue.*

Vocabulary 18.

ădūlātĭo, ōnis, *f.* — *flattery.*
ămābĭlis, e, — *lovely.*
ămor, ōris, *m.* — *love.*

asper, ĕra, ĕrum,	rough, rugged.
Căto, ōnis, m.	Cato, a noble Roman.
ferrum, i, n.	iron.
Helvĕtĭa, ae, f.	the country of the Helvetii (in Switzerland).
hībernus, a, um,	wintry, of winter.
ĭmägo, ĭnis, f.	a likeness, portrait, image.
imprŏbus, a, um,	dishonest, wicked.
ĭter, ĭtĭnĕris, n.	journey.
lĕpus, ŏris, m.	a hare.
lŭna, ae, f.	the moon.
lux, lūcis, f.	light.
*mĕus, a, um,	my, mine.
mons, montis, m.	a mountain.
nĭhĭl, indec. n.	nothing.
nŏn, adv.	not.
ŏdĭum, ii, n.	hatred.
pernĭcĭōsus, a, um,	destructive.
quam, adv. & conj.	than, as.
rādix, īcis, f.	a root.
săpĭentĭa, ae, f.	wisdom.
semper, adv.	always, ever.
sĭmŭlātio, ōnis, f.	a pretence.
sŏnĭtus, ūs, m.	a sound.
spērātus, a, um,	hoped for.
suāvis, e,	sweet, delightful.
sŭus, a, um,	his, hers, its, their own.
tranquillus, a, um,	calm.
tŭus, a, um,	thy, thine.
vĕr, vēris, n.	the spring.
vultur, ŭris, m.	a vulture.

* The Vocative Sing. Masc. of *meus* is
:nĭ.

Vocabulary 19.

Ălexander, dri, m.	Alexander, a famous king of Macedonia.
†Augustus, i, m.	Augustus, the first emperor of Rome.
centŭrĭa, ae, f.	a century.
cĕrăsus, i, f.	a cherry-tree.
cĕrăsum, i, n.	a cherry.

† The month of August. previously
:alled Sextīlis, was named after the emperor Augustus.

cŏhors, rtis, f.	a cohort.
consul, ŭlis, m.	a consul.
injustus, a, um,	unjust.
lĕgĭo, ōnis, f.	a legion.
Măcĕdo, ōnis, m.	a Macedonian.
mālus, i, f.	an apple-tree.
mālum, i, n.	an apple.
mănĭpŭlus, i, m.	a maniple.
mensis, is, m.	a month.
mītis, e,	mild.
ŏs, ossis, n.	a bone.
pars, partis, f.	a part.
pĭrus, i, f.	a pear-tree.
pĭrum, i, n.	a pear.
prūnus, i, f.	a plum-tree.
prūnum, i, n.	a plum.
săpĭens, ntis, adj. and subs.	wise, a wise-man.
Xerxes, is, m.	Xerxes, a famous king of Persia.

Vocabulary 20.

attentus, a, um,	attentive.
bĕătus, a, um,	happy.
cārus, a, um,	dear.
contentus, a, um,	contented.
dīlĭgens, ntis,	diligent, careful.
dīves, ĭtis,	rich.
ignāvĭa, ae, f.	cowardice.
jŭs, jŭris, n.	right, law.
laetus, a, um,	joyful.
līber, ĕra, ĕrum,	free.
mĭmor, ŏris,	mindful.
noster, tra, trum,	our, ours.
nunc, adv.	now.
pauper, ĕris,	poor.
praeceptor, ōris, m.	a teacher.
prŏbus, a, um,	good, upright.
sălus, ūtis, f.	safety.
sors, rtis, f.	a lot.
Tĭtus, i (T.), m.	Titus, a common Roman forename.
tristis, e,	sad.
vester, tra, trum,	your, yours.
sī, conj.	if.

Vocabulary to Ex. 21, 22, 23.

ănĭmus, i, m.	mind, the soul, courage.
auctōrĭtas, ātis, f.	authority.

K

*autem, *conj.*   *but.*
auxĭlĭum, ii, *n.*   *help, aid.*
cŭpĭdĭtas, ātis, *f.*   *desire, passion.*
Dēmosthĕnēs, is,   *Demosthenes, the*
   m.   *famous Athe-*
       nian orator.
industrĭus, a, um,   *industrious,*
       busy.
ĭners, rtis,   *helpless, sluggish.*
lĭbĕri, orum, *m.*   *children.*
mĕmŏrĭa, ae, *f.*   *memory.*
părens, ntis, *c.*   *c parent.*
planta, ae, *f.*   *a sprout, plant.*
proelĭum, ii, *n.*   *a battle.*

   * The proper position of *autem* is *after*
th: first word of the clause to which it
belongs.

Vocabulary 24.

addictus, a, um,   *devoted.*
aeternus, a, um,   *eternal.*
bellŭa, ae, *f.*   *a great beast.*
Cimbri, ōrum, *m.*   *the Cimbrians,*
       a formidable
       Celtic tribe.
cŏr, cordis, *n.*   *a heart.*
ēlĕgans, ntis,   *elegant, exqui-*
       site.
fĭdēlis, e,   }
fīdus, a, um,   }   *faithful.*
fons, ntis, *m.*   *a fountain.*
*Līvius, ii, *m.*   *Livy, a Roman*
       historian.
luscĭnĭa, ae, *f.*   *a nightingale.*
mŭlĭer, ĕris, *f.*   *a woman, wife.*
*Sallustĭus, ii, *m.*   *Sallust, a Ro-*
       man historian.
salvus, a, um,   *safe.*
sanguis, ĭnis, *m.*   *blood.*
scriptor, ōris, *m.*   *a writer, author.*

   * Proper Names ending in *ius* make *i* in
the Vocative: *e.g.* Voc. *Livi, Sallusti.* So
also *filius* makes Voc. *fili,* and *genius,* a
guardian deity, *geni.*

Vocabulary 25 (a).

(A, B, C).

aedĭfĭco, āvi, ātum, 1. *I build.*
ambŭlo, etc.   *I walk.*
castīgo, etc.   *I chastise.*
crĕo, etc.   *I create, make.*
cŭro, etc.   *I take care, pains.*

do, dĕdi, dătum, *I give.*
   dăre,
ēmendo, āvi, etc.   *I improve.*
ēmigro, etc.   *I depart from.*
expugno, etc.   *I take by storm.*
firmo, etc.   *I strengthen.*
flo, etc.   *I blow.*
hăbĭto, etc.   *I dwell.*
intro, etc.   *I enter.*
jūdĭco, āvi, ātum, *I judge.*
laudo, etc.   *I praise.*
mŭto, etc.   *I change.*
oppugno, etc.   *I attack, assault.*
orno, etc.   *I adorn.*
păro, etc.   *I prepare, get,*
       gain.
pugno, etc.   *I fight.*
rĕcrĕo, etc.   *I refresh.*
vasto, etc.   *I lay waste.*
vĭgĭlo, etc.   *I watch, I am*
       awake.
vĭtŭpĕro, etc.   *I blame, find*
       fault with.

---

aedĭfĭcĭum, ii, *n.*   *a building.*
Cŏrinthus, i, *f.*   *Corinth.*
dīlĭgenter, *adv.*   *carefully.*
dum, *conj.*   *while.*
fraus, fraudis, *f.*   *dishonesty.*
jam, *adv.*   *now, already.*
lĭbertas, tātis, *f.*   *freedom, liberty.*
lĭtĕra, ae, *f.*   *a letter of the*
       alphabet.
lĭtĕrae, arum, *f.*   *letters, learn-*
       ing; also, an
       epistle, letter.
mōs, mōris, *m.*   *a manner, cus-*
nēmo, ĭnis, *c.*   *nobody.*   [*tom.*
ŏpŭlentus, a, um,   *wealthy.*
plăcĭdus, a, um,   *quiet.*
prŏbĭtas, ātis, *f.*   *honesty, integ-*
quum, *adv. & conj. when.*   [*rity.*
somnus, i, *m.*   *sleep.*
tĭmor, ōris,   *fear.*
vălētūdo, ĭnis, *f.*   *health.*
ventus, i, *m.*   *wind.*

(D, E, F.) (b).

advento, āvi, ātum, 1. *I am on the*
       point of ar-
       riving.

canto, āvi, ātum,		*I sing.*
dēlecto	„	*I delight, amuse.*
dīmīco	„	*I fight (a battle).*
dŭbīto	„	*I doubt.*
erro	„	*I err, make a mistake.*
exhīlăro	„	*I cheer.*
impĕro	„	*I command.*
(with *dat.*)		
lībĕro	„	*I free, deliver.*
occŭpo	„	*I seize upon.*
opto	„	*I wish, desire.*
porto	„	*I carry.*
rĕdămo	„	*I love in return.*
rĕnŏvo	„	*I make new again, restore.*
servo	„	*I preserve, save.*
sŭpĕro	„	*I overcome.*
tracto	„	*I handle, deal with.*

ăb (ā, abs), *prep.* (with *abl.*)		*from, by.*
dŭbĭus, a, um,		*doubtful.*
fortĭter, *adv.*		*bravely.*
fortissĭmē, *adv.*		*very bravely.*
Hannĭbal, ălis, *m.*		*Hannibal, the great Carthaginian general.*
hĕrī, *adv.*		*yesterday.*
intĕrĭtus, ūs, *m.*		*destruction.*
ĭtă, *adv.* (from *is, id*)		*in that way, thus.*
mājōres, um, *m.pl.*		*ancestors.*
rectus, a, um,		*straight, right.*
saepĕ, *adv.*		*often.*
stătĭo, ōnis, *f.*		*a post, station.*
terror, ōris, *m.*		*terror, alarm.*

Vocabulary 26.

cŏercĕo, ui, ĭtum, 2.	*I restrain, curb.*
dēbeo, ŭi, ĭtum, 2.	*I owe, ought.*
dēlĕo, ēvi, ētum, 2.	*I destroy.*
displĭcĕo, ui, ĭtum, 2. (with *dat.*)	*I displease.*
dŏcĕo, ui, ctum, 2.	*I teach.*
exercĕo, etc. 2.	*I exercise.*
flĕo, flēvi, flētum, 2.	*I weep.*
flŏrĕo, ŭi, 2.	*I bloom, flourish.*
*gaudĕo, gŭvīsus sum, 2.	*I rejoice.*

* The Verb *gaudeo* belongs to the class of Neuter-passives. (See Exercise xlvii.)

hăbĕo, ŭi, ĭtum, 2.		*I have.*
mĕrĕo	„	2. *I deserve.*
mŏnĕo	„	2. *I advise, warn.*
nŏcĕo	„	2. *I hurt, harm.*
(with *dat.*)		
pārĕo, ui, ĭtum,		2. *I obey.*
(with *dat.*)		
plăcĕo, ui, ĭtum,		2. *I please.*
(with *dat.*)		
praebĕo, ui, ĭtum,		2. *I furnish, afford, exhibit.*
terrĕo	„	2. *I terrify, frighten, alarm.*
vălĕo	„	2. *I am strong, in good health.*

ars, artis, *f.*	*art, handicraft.*
ăvis, is, *f.*	*a bird.*
Athēnĭensis, e,	*Athenian.*
bĕnĕ, *adv.*	*well.*
Caesar, ăris, *m.*	*Caesar, a famous Roman.*
cantus, ūs, *m.*	*a song.*
dĭū, *adv.*	*a long time.*
dīvĭnus, a, um,	*belonging to the gods, divine.*
Lătīnus, a, um,	*Latin.*
lingua, ae, *f.*	*tongue, language.*
praeceptum, i, *n.*	*precept, instruction, lesson.*
Pompēĭus, ēii, *m.*	*Pompey, the rival of Caesar.*
quĭă, quŏd, } *conjs.*	*because.*
saepissĭmē, *adv.*	*very often.*
sĕnectūs, ūtis, *f.*	*old age.*
Sŏlon, ōnis, *m.*	*Solon, the Athenian lawgiver.*
tĕmĕrĭtas, ātis, *f.*	*recklessness, rashness.*

Vocabulary 27.

absūmo, mpsi, mptum, 3.	*I consume, cut off.*
cingo, nxi, nctum, 3.	*I surround.*
contemno, mpsi, mptum, 3.	*I despise.*
contrăho, axi, actum, 3.	*I draw together.*

к 2

convŏlo, ăvi, ātum, *I fly or rush*
1. *together.*
corrĭgo, exi, ectum, *I correct.*
3.
dēfendo, di, sum, 3. *I defend.*
dēsĕro, rui, rtum, 3. *I abandon.*
dētĕgo, xi, ctum, 3. *I discover.*
dico, xi, ctum, 3. *I say, speak.*
disco, dĭdĭci, —, 3. *I learn.*
d̄ .co, xi, ctum, 3. *I lead.*
ĕmo, ēmi, emptum, *I buy.*
3.
excŏlo, cŏlŭi, cul- *I cultivate care-*
tum, 3. *fully.*
instĭtuo, ui, ūtum, *I appoint, in-*
3. *stitute.*
instrŭo, xi, ctum, *I arrange, draw*
3. *up in order.*
jungo, nxi, nctum, *I join.*
3.
lĕgo, lēgi, lectum, *I gather, read.*
3.
narro, āvi, etc. 1. *I relate.*
pingo, nxi, pictum, *I paint, em-*
3. *broider.*
rĕgo, xi, ctum, 3. *I rule.*
scribo, psi, ptum, 3. *I write.*
solvo, vi, utum, 3. *I loosen, pay.*
specto, etc. 1. *I look at, look*
on.
tĕgo, xi, ctum, 3. *I cover.*
trăho, axi, actum, *I draw, drag.*
3.
*triumpho, etc. 1. *I triumph.*
vŏlo, etc. 1. *I fly.*
Cămillus, i, *m.* *Camillus, a Ro-*
man general.
Căt.līna, ae, *m.* *Catiline, a con-*
spirator.
conjūrătĭo, ōnis, *f. a conspiracy.*
cŏpĭa, ae, *f.* *plenty.*
cŏpĭae, ārum(pl.).*f. forces.*
currus. ūs, *m.* *chariot.*
fĕrē, *adv.* *almost, com-*
monly.
Hellespontus, i, *m. the Hellespont*
(now the Dar-
danelles).
impĕrātor, ōris, *m. military com-*
mander.

* A triumph (*triumphus*) was a grand
procession of a Roman general through the
streets of Rome.

In, *prep.* (with *acc.*) *into.*
incendĭum, ii, *n.* *a fire, confla-*
gration.
innŭmĕrus, a, um, *innumerable.*
lŏcus, i, *m. pl.* -i *place.*
and -a,
mens, mentis, *f.* *mind.*
mundus, i, *m.* *the world.*
obsidĭo, ōnis, *f.* *a siege, blockade.*
ōrātĭo, ōnis, *f.* *oration, speech.*
pallĭum, ii, *n.* *a cloak.*
*pons, ntis, *m.* *a bridge.*
sĭmŭl ac (atque), *as soon as.*
or in one word,
sĭmŭlac, *conj.*
vix, *adv.* *scarcely.*

* Observe the phrase *jungere flumen
ponte, to throw a bridge over a river.*

Vocabulary 28.

custŏdĭo, īvi, ītum, *I guard, keep*
4. *guard.*
dormĭo, īvi, etc. 4. *I sleep.*
ĕrŭdĭo, etc. 4 *I train up, edu-*
cate.
finĭo, etc. 4. *I limit, put an*
end to.
mollĭo, īvi, etc. 4. *I soften, assuage.*
mūnĭo, etc. 4. *I fortify.*
nescĭo, īvi & ii, *I am ignorant*
etc. 4. *of.*
nūtrĭo, īvi, etc. 4. *I nourish, nur-*
ture.
ŏbēdĭo, etc. 4. *I obey.*
(with *dat.*)
pūnĭo, etc. 4. *I punish.*
rĕpĕrĭo, pĕrĭ, per- *I find.*
tum, 4.
scĭo, īvi, etc. 4. *I know.*
sĕpĕlĭo, īvi and ⎱ *I bury.*
ĭi. pultum, 4. ⎰
vĕnĭo, vēni, ven- *I come.*
tum, 4.
vestĭo, īvi, etc. 4. *I clothe.*
vincĭo, nxi, nctum, *I bind.*
4.

———

Alpēs, ium, *m.* *the Alps.*
Cornēlia, ae, *f.* *Cornelia, a Ro-*
man matron.
crūdēlis, e, *cruel.*

diligentissĭmē, adv. — most carefully.

dŏlor, ōris, m. — pain, grief.

ĕtíam, conj. — also, even.

fīnis, is, m. — end, limit, in pl. territories.

gnăvĭtĕr, adv. — actively, vigorously.

Lĭbўa, ae, f. — Africa.

lictor, ōris, m. — a lictor (attendant on a magistrate).

longinquus, a, um, — long, distant.

longinquĭtas,ātis,f. — length, distance.

membrāna, ae, f. — thin skin, membrane.

mollis, e, — soft, mellow.

mortŭus, a, um, — dead.

ōlim, adv. — formerly, once upon a time.

quŏquĕ, conj. — also, even.

tĕnŭis, e, — thin, delicate.

turpis, e, — base, disgraceful.

vestīmentum, i, n. — clothing.

vincŭlum, i, n. — a chain, bond.

vox, vōcis, f. — a voice.

Vocabulary 29.

ēdŭco, āvi, ātum, 1. — I educate.

ēdŭco, xi, ctum, 3. — I lead out.

fŭgo, āvi, ātum, 1. — I put to flight.

vulnero, āvi, ātum, — I wound.

Antĭŏchus, i, m. — Antiochus, a name of several kings of Syria.

ĕgrĕgĭus, a, um, — excellent, eminent.

grăvĭtĕr, adv. — heavily, severely.

Lўcurgus, i, m. — Lycurgus, the Spartan legislator.

Trōja, ae, f. — Troy, the city.

Vesta, ae, f. — Vesta, the goddess of fire and the hearth.

Vocabulary 30.

mănĕo, nsi, nsum, 2. — I remain.

mŏvĕo, ōvi, ōtum, 2. — I move, disturb.

tĭmeo, ui, 2. — I fear.

---

adventus, ūs, m. — arrival.

Nĕro, ōnis, m. — Nero, a Roman emperor.

strēnŭus, a, um, — vigorous.

strēnuē, adv. — vigorously.

stŭdium, ii, n. — zeal, pursuit, study

sŭbĭtus, a, um, — sudden.

Vocabulary 31.

afflīgo, xi, ctum, 3. — I cast down, prostrate.

cŏlo, cŏlŭi, cultum, 3. — I cultivate, cherish, &c.

dilĭgo, exi, ectum. 3. — I esteem, love.

fingo, finxi, fictum, 3. — I frame, feign, invent.

stŭdĕo, ŭi, 2. — I am eager, zealous.

vĕho, exi, ectum, 3. — I carry, in Pass. I ride.

vinco, vīci, victum, 3. — I conquer.

vīvo, vixi, victum, 3. — I live.

---

clādes, is, f. — disaster, defeat.

făbŭla, ae, f. — a fable, story.

nōbĭlis, e, — distinguished.

perversus, a, um, — wilful, perverse.

Phăĕthon, ōntis, m. — Phaëthon, a son of Apollo.

prŏbē, adv. — rightly, properly.

quĭdem, adv. — indeed.

rătĭo, ōnis, f — reason.

Scīpio, ōnis, m. — Scipio, a noble Roman.

vĕhĕmentĕr, adv. — vehemently, warmly.

Vocabulary 32.

cădo, cĕcĭdi, căsum, 3. — I fall.

āĕr, āĕris, m. — the air.

Afrĭcănus, i, *m.*   *Africanus, a sur-name of the Scipios.*

cognĭtio, ōnis, *f.*   *inquiry, know-ledge.*

ērŭdītus, a, um,   *trained, edu-cated.*

Gracchus, i, *m.*   *Gracchus, a no-ble Roman.*

injustē, *adv.*   *unjustly.*

justē, *adv.*   *justly.*

lăpĭdĕus, a, um,   *of stone.*

nĕgōtium, ii, *n.*   *business.*

pellis, is, *f.*   *skin* (of an ani-mal).

prĭus, *adv.*   *sooner, before.*

Pŭnĭcus, a, um,   *Punic, -Cartha-ginian.*

Sŏcrătēs, is, *m.*   *Socrates, the sage of Athens.*

sōlum, *adv.*   *only.*

summus, a, um,   *highest, utmost, greatest.*

Tĭbĕrĭus, ĭi, *m.* (Ti.)   *Tiberius, a com-mon Roman fore-name.*

Vocabulary 33.

absurdus, a, um,   *absurd.*

bŏna, ōrum, *n.* (pl.) *goods.*

celsus, a, um,   *lofty, tall.*

margărīta, ae, *f.*   *a pearl.*

nĕcessărĭus, a, um, *necessary, need-ful.*

nīdus, i, *m.*   *a nest.*

versus, ūs, *m.*   *a line, a verse.*

Vocabulary 34.

admīror, ātus, 1.   *I wonder at, I admire.*

aspernor, etc. 1.   *I reject, despise.*

cŏnor, 1.   *I attempt.*

contemplor, 1.   *I observe care-fully, contem-plate.*

hortor, 1.   *I urge, exhort, encourage.*

mĕdĭtor, 1.   *I meditate on, study.*

mīror, 1.   *I wonder at, admire.*

vĕnĕror, 1.   *I reverence, wor-ship.*

---

dēmum, *adv.*   *indeed.**

pŏtestas, ātis, *f.*   }*power.†*

pŏtentia, ae, *f.*   }

quīdam, quaedam, quoddam *or* quid-dam,   }*a certain, cer-tain one.*

tum, *adv.*   *then.*

* As, tum demum, *then indeed; then and not till then.*

† *Potestas* is the regular power of a ma-gistrate; *Potentia,* the power which arises out of personal weight and influence.

Vocabulary 35.

*accĭpĭo, cēpi, cep-tum, 3.   *I receive.*

*confĭtĕor, fessus, 2.   *I confess.*

*dēcĭpĭo, cēpi, etc. 3.   *I deceive.*

*ējĭcio, ēci, ectum, 3.   *I cast forth.*

fătĕor, fassus, 2.   *I confess.*

ĭmĭtor, 1.   *I imitate.*

intŭeor, ĭtus, 2.   *I look upon, into.*

mĭsĕrĕor, rtus, 2.   *I pity, have pity on.*

pollĭceor, ĭtus, 2.   *I promise.*

rĕcordor, ātus, 1.   *I call to mind.*

tŭeor, ĭtus, 2.   *I gaze, guard, protect.*

vĕreor, ĭtus, 2.   *I fear, reverence.*

* Observe the change of ă to ĭ when a preposition is prefixed in composition: as, accĭpĭo = ad + căpĭo; confĭteor = con + făteor, etc.

Ăsĭa, ae, *f.*   *Asia.*

Dārĭus, ĭi, *m.*   *Darius, a king of Persia.*

ex, ē, *prep.* (with abl.)   *out of.*

făcĭnus, ŏris, *n.*   *bold or daring deed, crime.*

Plīnius, ii, *m.*   *Pliny, the name of two Roman authors.*

VOCABULARIES. 135

praetĕrĭtus, a, um, *past.*
rĕus, i, *m.*   *an accused man, defendant.*

Vocabulary 36.

ăbūtor, ūsus, 3.   *I abuse.*
ădhortor, ātus, 1.   *I urge, exhort.*
ădĭpiscor, ădeptus, 3.   *I acquire, attain to.*
allŏquor, lŏcūtus, 3.   *I speak to.*
committo, īsi, issum, 3.   *I send together, join (fight) battle.*
dēflăgro, 1.   *to be burnt down.*
fruor, fruĭtus *and* fructus, 3.   *I enjoy.*
fungor, functus, 3. *I discharge.*
gĕro, gessi, gĕstum, 3.   *I carry on war, wage war.*
incūso, 1.   *I accuse, find fault with.*
jŭbĕo, jussi, jussum, 2.   *I order, bid.*
lŏquor, lŏcūtus, 3. *I speak.*
mŏrĭor, mortŭus, (fut. part. mŏrĭturus, about to die), 3.   *I die.*
nascor, nātus, 3.   *I am born.*
oblīviscor, lītus, 3. *I forget.*
pătior, passus, 3. *I endure, suffer.*
prŏfĭciscor, fectus, 3.   *I set out.*
rĕmĭniscor, 3.   *I remember*
sĕquor, cūtus, 3. *I follow.*
ūtor, ūsus, 3.   *I use.*
vescor, —, 3.   *I feed, live on.*

ăd, *prep.* (with *acc.*) *to, at, near.*
ălĭquando, *adv.* *sometimes.*
ăpŭd, *prep.* (with *acc.*) *at, near.*
bĕnignē, *adv.* *kindly.*
căro, carnis, *f.* *flesh.*
cāsĕus, i, *m.* *cheese.*
consŭlātus, ūs, *m.* *office of consul, consulate.*
crŭcĭātus, ūs, *m.* *torture.*

Eurĭpĭdes, is, *m.*   *Euripides, an Athenian tragic poet.*
immortālĭtas, ātis, *f.* *immortality.*
Lăbĭēnus, i, *m.*   *Labienus, one of Caesar's lieutenants.*
lac, lactis, *n.* *milk.*
lăcus, ūs, *m.* *a lake.*
laetĭtĭa, ae, *f.* *joy.*
Mĕnăpĭi, ōrum, *m. Menapii, a Gallic tribe.*
mox, *adv.* *soon, shortly.*
mūnus, ĕris, *n.*   *a gift, duty, function.*
nēvĕ, *conj.* (with *subj.*) *nor, and lest.*
nĭmĭs, *adv.* *too, too much*
pĕr, *prep.* (with *acc.*) *through.*
poena, ae, *f.* *punishment.*
Poeni, ōrum, *m.* *the Carthaginians.*
pristĭnus, a, um, *former, olden.*
rārŏ, *adv.* *seldom.*
Rēgŭlus, i, *m.*   *Regulus, a famous Roman.*
Sălămis, is, *f.*   *Salamis, an island near Athens.*
tantum, *adv.* *only.*
Trăsĭmēnus, i, *m. Lake Trasimene in Italy.*

Vocabulary 37.

blandĭor, ītus (with *dat.*), 4.   *I flatter, win upon.*
expĕrĭor, rtus, 4. *I try, experience.*
mētĭor, mensus, 4. *I measure.*
mentĭor, ītus, 4. *I lie, tell a lie.*
ordĭor, orsus, 4. *I begin.*
partĭor, ītus, 4. *I share, divide.*
pŏtĭor, ītus, 4. (with *abl.*) *I obtain possession of.*

cīvĭlis, e,   *belonging to a citizen, civil.*
Ĕpămĭnondas, ae, *m.* *Epaminondas, a famous Theban.*

frous, ntis, *f*.   the   forehead, brow.
nunquam, *adv*.   *never*.
vultus, ūs, *m*.   *a countenance, looks*.

Vocabulary 38.

fluo, uxi, uxum, 3. *I flow*.
migro, etc. 1.   *I migrate, depart*.

---

mᵉtus, ūs, *m*.   *fear*.
occidens, ntis, *m*. *the west (the setting sun)*.
permulti, ae, a,   *very many*.
primo, *adv*.   *at first*.

Vocabulary 39.

divĭdo, īsi, īsum, 3. *I divide, separate*.
mitto, mīsi, missum, 3.   *I send*.

---

cᵉter (caet.), ĕra, *the rest*.
ĕrum,
Germāni, ōrum, *m. the Germans*.
Helvētĭus, a, um,   *Helvetian*.
lēgātus, i, *m*.   *ambassador, lieutenant*.
ōcĕānus, i, *m*.   *the ocean*.

Vocabulary 40.

fulgĕo, lsi, lsum, 2. *I shine*.
prŏfĕro, tūli, lātum, *I extend*.
   ferre, *irr. v*.

Aegyptus, i, *f*.   *Egypt*.
impĕrĭum, ii, *n*.   *empire*.
Indi, ōrum, *m. pl. Indians, the people of India*.
marmor, ŏris, *n*.   *marble*.
servĭtūs, ūtis, *f*.   *slavery*.
tăbernācŭlum, i, *n. a tent*.
uxor, ōris, *f*.   *a wife*.

Vocabulary 41.

accēdo, essi, essum, *I approach*.
   3.

āgo, ēgi, actum, 3. *I lead, act, do*.
excēdo, essi, essum, *I depart from*.
   3.
incĭpĭo, ēpi, eptum, *I begin*.
   3.
perdo, dĭdi, dĭtum, *I destroy*.
   3.
rĕsisto, stĭti, stĭtum, 3. (with dat.) *I resist*.

---

atque, ac, *conj*.   *and*.
attentē, *adv*.   *attentively*.
audactĕr, *adv*.   *boldly, daringly*.
Hasdrŭbal, ălis, *m. Hasdrubal, the brother of Hannibal*.
jŭventūs, ūtis, *f. youth*.
lātē, *adv*.   *widely, wide*.
longē, *adv*.   *far*.
Roscĭus, ii, *m*.   *Roscius, a Roman name*.
sătis, *adv*.   *enough, sufficiently*.
tigris, is *or* ĭdi, *c. a tiger, tigress*.

Vocabulary 42.

infringo, frēgi,   *I break, impair*.
   fractum, 3.
obscūro, āvi, ātum, *I darken, obscure*.
   1.
rĕlinquo, īqui,   *I leave, quit*.
   ictum, 3.

---

aequus, a, um,   *level, even, just*.
cur, *adv*.   *why?*
impĕtus, ūs, *m*.   *an onset, attack*.
invĭdia, ae, *f*.   *envy, ill-will*.
splendor, ōris, *m*. *brightness, brilliancy*.
tўrannus, I, *m*.   *a despot, tyrant*.

Vocabulary 43.

cŏmĭtor, ātus, 1. *I accompany*.
immŏlo, āvi, 1.   *I sacrifice*.
indulgĕo, lsi, ltum, *I indulge*.
   2 (with *dat*.).
lūdo, si, sum, 3.   *I play*.
mĕtŭo, ŭi, ūtum, 3. *I fear*.

ōro, āvi, 1.   I entreat, pray.
salto, āvi, 1.   I dance.
sĭdĕo, sēdi, sessum, I sit.
   2.
vĭdĕor, vīsus, 2.   I seem, appear.

Ăpollo, ĭnis, m.   Apollo, a Roman
                     divinity.
hostĭa, ae, f.   a victim.
nōbĭlis, e,   distinguished,
                     noble.
Pȳthăgŏras, ae, m. Pythagoras, a
                     famous Greek
                     philosopher.

Vocabulary 44.

sĕro, sēvi, sătum, 3. I plant, sow.

aerumna, ae, f.   trouble, afflic-
                     tion.
frūges, um (pl.), f. fruits, a crop.
ĭnops, ŏpis,   destitute.
ŏnus, ĕris, n.   a load, burden.
pătĭentĕr, adv.   patiently.
paupertas, ātis, f. poverty.
prūdentia, ae, f.   knowledge, pru-
                     dence.

Phrase:—
Auxilium ferre, to render assistance.

Vocabulary 45.

occīdo, īdi, īsum, 3. I kill, slay.
stătuo, ŭi, ūtum, 3. I fix, determine.

ătrox, ōcis,   stern, sangui-
                     nary, cruel.
făcĭlĭ, adv.   easily.
fămēs, is, f.   hunger.
hĭlăris, e,   cheerful.
ignāvē, adv.   indolently.
ōrācŭlum, i, n.   an oracle.
sĭlentĭum, ii, n.   silence.
suprēmus, a, um, last.
unquam, adv.   at any time, ever.

Vocabulary 46.

adjŭvo, jūvi, jūtum, I assist.
  1.

nĕquĕo, quīvi and I am unable,
  ĭi, ĭtum, nĕquīre   cannot.
  (like eo), 4.

---

cāsus, ūs, m.   chance, accident.
infectus, a, um,   undone.
grăvis, e,   heavy, severe.
noxĭus, a, um,   guilty.
sŏcĭus, ii, m.   a partner, ally,
                     companion.
Thĕmistocles, is, m. Themistocles, a
                     famous Athe-
                     nian.

Vocabulary 47.

addisco, addĭdĭci, I learn in ad-
  3.   dition.
bĭbo, bĭbi, bĭbĭtum, I drink.
  3.
conservo, āvi, etc. 1. I preserve,
                maintain.
curro, cŭcurri, cur- I run.
  sum, 3.
interfĭcĭo, fēci,   I put to death,
  fectum, 3.   kill.

ălĭquis, quĭd, pron. some one, some-
                     thing.
Carthāgĭniensis, e, Carthaginian.

nāvŭlis, e,   naval.
Nĭlus, i, m.   the river Nile.
nonnullus, a, um, some.
quŏtĭdĭē, adv.   every day.
tam, adv.   so, to such a de-
                     gree.

Phrase:—
In legem jurare, to swear to a law.

Vocabulary 48.

dēplōro, āvi, 1.   I lament over,
                   deplore.
īrascor, īrātus, 3,   I am angry.
  dep.
tăceo, ui, 2.   I am silent.
trĭbŭo, ŭi, ūtum, 3. I give, assign.

Arĭovistus, i, m.   Ariovistus, a
                     German king.

fortĕ, *adv.* — *by chance.*
iufāmīa, ae, *f.* — *infamy.*
mĭnĭmē, *adv.* — *in the least degree.*

nec, nĕquĕ, *conj.* — *neither, nor.*
stultītīa, ae, *f.* — *folly.*

Vocabulary 49.

cunctus, a, um, — *all, all together.*
dissīmīlis, e, — *unlike.*
fērox, ōcis, — *fierce, spirited.*
ignōrätio, ōnis, *f.* — *ignorance.*
infĕrīor, īus (*comp.*) — *lower, inferior.*
mălum, i, *n.* — *an evil.*
perfectus, a, um, — *finished, perfect.*
Phīdīas, ae, *m.* — *Phidias, a famous Athenian sculptor.*

praestābīlis, e, — *excellent.*
proxīmus, a, um, — *nearest, next.*
scīentīa, ae, *f.* — *knowledge.*
sĕd, *conj.* — *but.*
sīmīlis, e, — *like.*
sīmŭlācrum, i, *n.* — *an image, statue.*
vīlis, e, — *cheap, common.*

Vocabulary 50.

cognosco, nōvi, nī- tum, 3. — *I learn, ascertain.*
comprĕhendo, di, sum, 3. — *I seize.*
conf Icĭo, fēci, fec- tum, 3. — *I finish, accomplish.*
conscendo, di, sum, 3. — *I mount, go on board (ship).*
contendo, di, sum and tum, 3. — *I strain, hasten.*
convŏco, ävi, ä‡um, 1. — *I call together.*
efflōresco, flōrui, 3. — *to blossom forth.*
expōno, pŏsui, pŭ- sītum, 3. — *I put forth, disembark (troops).*
intŭmesco, tŭmui, 3. — *I swell.*
lăbor, lapsus, 3, *dep.* — *I glide, pass away, fall.*
ŏrĭor, ortus, ŏrīri, 3, *dep.* : see p. 69. — *I rise.*
perlĕgo, lēgi, lec- tum, 3. — *I read through.*

perrumpo, ūpi, ptum, 3. — *I burst through.*
praemitto, īsi, is- sum, 3. — *I send on before.*
rĕcĭto, ävi, ätum, 1. — *I read aloud.*
rĕcŭpĕro, ävi, ätum, 1. — *I recover, get back.*
regno, ävi, ätum, 1. — *I reign, am king.*
sentĭo, nsi, nsum, 4. — *I feel, perceive.*
subsĕquor, scŏŭtus, 3, *dep.* — *I follow up.*
suscĭpio, ēpi, ep- tum, 3. — *I undertake.*
vexo, ävi, ätum, 1. — *I vex, harass.*

---

aetas, ätis, *f.* — *age, time of life.*
Arbēla, ae, *f.* — *Arbela, a town in Assyria.*
Cassivelaunus, i, *m.* — *Cassivelaunus, a British chief.*
dēlectus, ūs, *m.* — *a levy.*
hīberna, orum, *n. pl.* — *winter-quarters.*
infirmus, a, um, — *infirm, feeble.*
Pīsistrātus, i, *m.* — *Pisistratus, a despot of Athens.*
sĕnätus, ūs, *m.* — *the senate.*
stätim, *adv.* — *immediately.*

Phrases:—

Delectum habēre, — *to hold a levy.*
Maxima itīnĕra, — *forced marches.*
Navem (naves) conscendĕre, *to embark.*

Vocabulary 51.

exstrŭo. xi, ctum, 3. — *I heap up.*
obsĭdĕo, ēdi, es- sum, — *I blockade, lay siege to.*
pōno, pŏsui, pŏsī- tum, 3. — *I place.*

Ăthēnae, ärum, *f.* — *Athens.*
bestīŏla, ae, *f.* — *a small animal, insect.*
campus, i, *m.* — *a plain.*
dŏmĭnätus, ūs, *m.* — *rule, sovereignty.*
hōra, ae, *f.* — *an or the hour.*

Hanno, ōnis, m.   *Hanno, a Carthaginian.*

Mărăthon, ōnis, m. *Marathon, a plain near Athens.*

nātus, a, um, *part.* *born, aged.* and *adj.*

passus, ūs, m.   *a pace* (about five feet).

Plăto, ōnis, m.   *Plato, a famous Greek philosopher.*

Săguntīni, ōrum, *Saguntines, the* m.   *people of Saguntum, in Spain.*

Phrases :—

Castra ponĕre,   *to pitch a camp.*
Murum, aggerem, ducere, *to carry a wall or mound along, i.e. construct.*

Vocabulary 52.

cēdo, ssi, ssum, 3. *I yield, retire.*

confĕro, tŭli, etc. *I bring together,* 3. *(irr.)*   *betake.*

oppōno, ŏsŭi, ĭtum, *I set against,* 3.   *oppose.*

parvĕnĭo, ēni, *I arrive at.* ntum, 4.

pĕto, īvi *and* ĭi, *I seek.* ītum, 3.

reverto, ti, sum, *I turn back, re* rĕvertor, versus, *3.* *turn.* dep.

Alcĭbĭădes, is, m. *Alcibiades, a celebrated Athenian.*

Aeschĭnes, is, m. *Aeschines, an orator.*

Oŭrius, ii, m. *Curius, a Roman general.*

Cănŭsĭum, ii, n. *Canusium, a town in Apulia.*

0ăpŭa, ae, f. *Capua, a city of Campania.*

Crēta, ae, f. *Crete, an island of Greece.*

exĭlĭum, ii, n. *banishment, exile.*

Ĭbi, *adv. (fr.* is, id),*there.*

Lăcĕdaemon, ōnis,*Lacedaemon or* f.   *Sparta.*

Leŏnĭdas, ae, m. *Leonidas, a king of Sparta.*

Lūcĕrĭa, ae, f. *Luceria, a town in Apulia.*

Lūcius, ii (L.), m. *Lucius, a Roman fore-name.*

mandātum, i, n. *a charge, commission.*

perpĕtŭus, a, um, *continual.*

Rhŏdus, i, f. *Rhodes, an island of Greece.*

Sparta, ae, f. *Sparta.*

Phrase :—

Exilium agere, *to live in exile.*

Vocabulary 53.

constĭtŭo, ŭi, *I settle, de* ūtum, 3.   *termine.*

consūmo, mpsi, *I consume,* mptum, 3.   *waste away.*

expello, pŭlī, pul- *I drive out.* sum, 3.

hĭĕmo, 1.   *I winter.*

jăcĕo, etc. 2. *I lie.*

Ăpollōnĭa, ae, f. *Apollonia, a town in Epirus.*

Ărĭstīdes, is, m. *Aristides, a noble Athenian.*

Arpīnum, i, n. *Arpinum, a town in Latium.*

Băbўlŏn, ōnis, f. *Babylon, a city of Assyria.*

Oannae, ārum, f. *Cannae, a village in Apulia.*

Cŏnōn, ōnis, m. *Conon, an Athenian general.*

Cūmae, ārum, f. *Cumae, a city in Campania.*

Cyprus, i, f. *Cyprus, an island off Cilicia.*

Delphi, ōrum, m. *Delphi, a city in Greece.*

Diŏnўsĭus, ii, m. *Dionysius, a tyrant of Syracuse.*

Dyrrachium, ii, n.	Dyrrachium, a town in Epirus.
Fabricius, ii, m.	Fabricius, a noble Roman.
Hŏrātius, ii, m.	Horace, a Roman poet.
Lesbus, i, f.	Lesbus, an island off Asia Minor.
Mărius, ii, m.	Marius, a Roman general.
quālis, e,	of what sort, as.
Sȳrācūsæ, arum, f.	Syracuse.
tālis, e,	of that sort, such.
Tĭmŏthěus, i, m.	Timotheus, a famous Greek.
Vĕnūsĭa, ae, f.	Venusia, a town in Italy.

Phrase:—

Morbo-consūmi,	to be carried off by illness.

Vocabulary 54.

advĕnĭo, vēni, ventum, 4.	I arrive.
ănĭmadverto, ti, sum, 3.	I observe.
confŭgĭo, ūgi, etc. 3.	I flee to.
constat, stĭtit, imp. 1.	it is evident, it is agreed, &c.
contĭnĕo, ŭi, entum, 2.	I hold together.
nĕgo, āvi, 1.	I deny.
părĭo, pĕpĕri, partum, 3.	I bring forth.
prŏdo, dĭdi, dĭtum, 3.	I hand down, betray.
pŭto, āvi, ātum, 1.	I think.
trādo, dĭdī, dĭtum, 3.	I hand down, deliver.
vĭdĕo, vīdi, vīsum, 2.	I see.

caecus, a, um,	blind.
causā (abl.),	for the sake of.
crēdĭbĭlis, e,	credible.
Delŏs, i, f.	Delos, an island of Greece.

Diāna, ae, f.	Diana, a goddess.
flōrens, ntis,	flourishing.
Hŏmērus, i, m.	Homer.
imprūdentĭa, ae, f.	ignorance, imprudence.
Lātōna, ae, f.	Latona, mother of Apollo and Diana.
mănĭfestus, a, um,	evident, manifest.
nĭsi, conj.	unless, except.
quondam, adv.	sometime, formerly.
stella, ae, f.	a star.
Thales, ētis, m.	Thales, the philosopher.
Trōjānus, a, um,	Trojan, of Troy.
vĕrĭsĭmĭlis, e,	likely, probable.

Vocabulary 55.

consentĭo, nsi, nsum, 4.	I agree.
crēdo, dĭdi, dĭtum, 3.	I believe.
dīrĭpio, rĭpŭi, reptum, 3.	I plunder pillage.
intellĭgo, exi, ectum, 3.	I understand.
respondĕo, di, sum,	I answer.

bĕnĕvŏlus, a, um,	well-wishing, benevolent.
bŏnum, i, n.	a good, a blessing.
dīvīnus, a, um,	of the gods, divine.
ēlŏquens, ntis,	eloquent.
ignĕus, a, um,	fiery, made of fire.
Lūcrētĭus, ii, m.	Lucretius, a Roman poet.
mălĕvŏlus, a, um,	ill-wishing, malevolent.
mendax, ācis,	lying, a liar.
prīmārĭus, a, um,	first-rate, eminent.
stultus, a, um,	foolish.
sŭpĕrus, a, um, (see p. 25)	upper.
turpĭtūdo, ĭnis, f.	disgrace.

Vocabulary 56.

abjĭcĭo, jēci, jec- *I cast away.*
tum, 3.
antĕpōno, pŏsui, *I prefer.*
pŏsĭtum, 3.
conjĭcĭo, jēci, jec- *I fling (together).*
tum, 3.
ēvĕnĭo, vēni, ven- *to happen.*
tum, 4.
nŭmĕro, āvi, ātum, *I count.*
1.
quaero, quaesīvi, *I seek, enquire.*
sītum, 3.
rŏgo, āvi, ātum, 1. *I ask.*
spĕcŭlor, ātus, 1. *I spy out.*
viso, si, sum, 3. *I go to see, visit.*
Blaesus, i, m. *Blaesus, a Roman name.*
Chaerĕphon, on- *Chaerephon, a disciple of Socrates.*
tis, m.
Croesus, i, m. *Croesus, a king of Lydia.*
cur, adv. *why? to what end?*
fēlīcĭtĕr, adv. *luckily.*
incertus, a, um, *uncertain.*
infāmis, e, *infamous.*
injustus, a, um, *unjust.*
Laeca, ae, m. *Laeca, a Roman.*
mórtuus, a, um, *dead.*
nŏvus, a, um, *new.*
phĭlŏsŏphus, i, m. *a philosopher.*
plānē, adv. *altogether.*
quaestĭo, ōnis, f. *a question.*
quantus, a, um, *how great.*
quārē, adv. *why, on what account.*
quŏt, indec. adj. *how many.*
saepĕnŭmĕro, adv. *oftentimes.*
subdiffĭcĭlis, e, *somewhat difficult.*
tēlum, i, n. *a dart, weapon, missile.*
ŭbi, adv. *where.*
Xĕnŏphon, ontis, *Xenophon, an Athenian.*
m.

Vocabulary 57.

accĭdo, ĭdi, —, 3. *to happen.*
cerno, crēvi, crē- *I see, discern.*
tum, 3.

cŏhortor, ātus, 1. *I encourage.*
*confīdo, īsus, *I trust.*
sum, 3.
dĕterreo, ŭi, ĭtum, *I frighten, deter.*
2.
*diffīdo, īsus, sum, *I distrust.*
3.
dīmitto, īsi, issum, *I let go, dismiss.*
3.
ēnarro, āvi, ātum, 1. *I relate.*
ēnītor, īsus & ixus, *I strive hard.*
3.
exclāmo, āvi, ātum, *I cry out.*
1.
intrěeo, īvi & ĭi, *I enter.*
etc., 4.
nītor, īsus & ixus, *I strive.*
3.
*obsto, stĭti, stĭ- *I oppose, prevent.*
tum, 1.
opprĭmo, essi, es- *I press upon, overwhelm, crush.*
sum, 3.
*persuādĕc, ǎsi, *I persuade.*
āsum, 2.
praevĕnio, vēni, *I anticipate.*
ventum, 4.
prĕmo, essi, essum, *I press.*
3.
prŏhĭbĕo, ui, ĭtum, *I keep off, prohibit.*
2.
rĕcūso, āvi, ātum, 1. *I object, refuse.*
spēro, āvi, ātum, 1. *I hope.*
sto, stĕti, stătum, 1. *I stand.*
*suādeo, ǎsi, asum, *I advise.*
2.
tĕneo, ui, ntum, 2. *I hold, retain.*
transdūco, uxi, *I lead across.*
uctum, 3.
ventĭto, āvi, ātum, *I come frequently.*
1.

* With Dative.

Bĭbŭlus, i, m. *Bibulus, a Roman.*
fŏrum, i, n. *market-place, forum.*
impĕrītus, a, um, *unskilful.*
impransus, a, um, *unbreakfasted.*
infirmĭtas, ătis, f. *weakness.*
latro, ōnis, m. *a robber.*
lŭdus, i, m. *play, game, school.*

magnŏpĕrĕ, adv.   *greatly, earnestly.*

mīrus, a, um,   *wonderful.*

mŏdus, i, m.   *a measure, manner.*

moenĭa, ĭum, n.   *fortifications.*

Nervĭi, ōrum, m.   *the Nervii, a Gallic tribe.*

praealtus, a, um,   *very high.*

Satrĭus, ii, m.   *Satrius, a Roman.*

signum, i, n.   *a sign, signal.*

Trĕbōnĭus, ii, m.   *Trebonius, one of Caesar's lieutenants.*

Phrases:—

Sĕquĭtur (with *acc.* and *inf.* or *ut* and *subj.*), *it follows.* Făcĕrĕ nōn possum quīn, *I cannot but.* Per me (te) stĕtit (quomĭnus), *it was owing to me or you (that something did not happen).* Mĭnĭmum ăbest quĭn sim, *very little is wanting that I should be; I am very near being.*

Vocabulary 58.

ăquor, ātus, 1.   *I fetch water.*

bello, āvi, ātum, 1.   *I wage war.*

consŭlo, lŭi, ltum, 3.   *I consult.*

convĕnĭo, vēni, ventum, 4.   *I assemble.*

gusto, āvi, 1.   *I taste.*

pābŭlor, ātus, 1.   *I forage.*

postŭlo, āvi, ātum, 1.   *I demand.*

progrĕdĭor, gressus, 3.   *I advance.*

Aeduĭ, ōrum, m.   *the Aedui, a Gallic tribe.*

Ăgēsĭlāus, i, m.   *Agesilaus, a king of Sparta.*

Divitĭăcus, i, m.   *Divitiacus, a Gaul.*

Fābĭus, ii, m.   *Fabius, a Roman name.*

Lăcĕdaemōnĭi, ōrum, m.   *the Lacedaemonians.*

longius, adv. (comp.)   *farther, too far.*

lūdi, ōrum, m. pl.   *games.*

Maxĭmus, i, m.   *Maximus, the greater, a surname of Fabius.*

nĕfas, indec. n.   *wickedness, impiety.*

ŏpus, indec. n.   *need, necessity.*

pūblĭcus, a, um,   *public.*

Vēientes, um, m. pl.   *the people of Veii, near Rome.*

quisnam, quaenam, etc., like quis   *who, what?*

Phrases:—

Nĕfas est, *it is or would be an impiety.* Ŏpus est, *there is need of* (with *abl.*).

Vocabulary 59.

ăcŭo, ŭi, ūtum, 3.   *I sharpen.*

ălo, ŭi, ĭtum *and* altum, 3.   *I nourish.*

ardĕo, arsi, sum, 2.   *I burn, am on fire.*

cōgĭto, āvi, ātum, 1.   *I think, meditate.*

collŏquor, cūtus, 3.   *I converse.*

compăro, āvi, 1.   *I get together.*

ĕdo, ēdi, ēsum, 3.   *I eat.*

vēnor, ātus, 1.   *I hunt.*

---

bĕˌtē, adv.   *happily.*

grātĭa, ae, f.   *favour.*

grātĭā, abl.   *for the sake of.*

haud, adv.   *not.*

lībĕrē, adv.   *freely.*

mărīnus, a, um,   *of the sea.*

ŏpĕra, ae, f.   *pains, labour.*

plūs, ūris, adj. n. in sing.; in pl. plūres, -a   *more.*

stŭdĭōsus, a, um,   *zealous, eager after.*

Phrases:—

Ŏpĕram dărĕ, *to give one's whole energies to anything; to devote oneself to it.* Intĕr bĭbendum, &c., *whilst drinking, &c.*

Vocabulary 60.

ădhĭbĕo, ŭi, Ĭtum, *I employ.*
2.
observo, āvi, ātum, *I observe, re-*
1. *spect.*
prŏvĭdĕo, vīdi, *I foresee, pro-*
vīsum, 2. *vide.*

---

ardŭus, a, um, *lofty, steep,*
difficult.

Phrase:—
gĕrĕ aetātem, *to spend one's life.*

Vocabulary 61.

ingrĕdĭor, gressus, *I enter.*
3.
interclūdo, si, sum, *I shut off, inter-*
3. *cept*
obtempĕro, āvi, *I obey, comply*
ātum, 1. *with*

---

commĕātus, ūs, *m. provisions, sup-*
plies.
commīlĭto, ōnis, *m. fellow - soldier,*
comrade.
istīc, *adv.* (from *thither, where*
iste) *you are.*

jūdĭcĭum, ii, *n.* *judgment.*
părātus, a, um, *prepared, ready.*
quisque, quaeque,
quodque & quid- }*every one.*
que, *pron.*
quŏ, *adv.* *whither.*

Phrase:—
Fĭĕri de ălĭquo, *to become of one;* as,
quid factum est de illo, *what has become of
that man?*

Vocabulary 62.

concēdo, essi, es- *I yield, retire.*
sum, 3.
incendo, di, sum, *I burn* (trans.)
3.
percĭpio, cēpi, *I perceive.*
ceptum, 3.

---

affectus, a, um, *made, disposed.*
Brūtus, i, *m.* *Brutus, a Ro-*
man.
Cassĭus, ii, *m.* *Cassius, a Ro-*
man.
Campānĭa, ae, *f.* *Campania, a*
part of Italy.
occŭpātus, a, um, *engaged, busy*
quăsĭ, *adv.* *as if, just as.*

Phrases:—
Consĭlĭum Inĭre, *to enter on, form, a
design.* In spem vĕnĭre, *to conceive a hope.*

INDEX I. TO VOCABULARIES.

LATIN WORDS.

LIST OF ABBREVIATIONS.

abl.	—	ablative.	*gen.*	—	genitive.	*pl.*	= plural.
acc.	=	accusative.	*indec.*	=	indeclinable.	*prep.*	= preposition.
adj.	=	adjective.	*indef.*	=	indefinite.	*pron.*	= pronoun,
adv.	=	adverb.	*interj.*	=	interjection.		pronominal.
c. or *com.*	=	common gender.	*inter.*	=	interrogative.	*rel.*	= relative.
comp.	=	comparative.	*m.*	=	masculine.	*sing.*	= singular.
conj.	=	conjunction.	*n.*	=	neuter.	*sup.*	= superlative.
dat.	=	dative.	*p.*	=	page.		
f.	=	feminine.	*part.*	=	participle.		

1, 2, 3, 4, indicate the conjugation of a verb.

AB.

Ab (ā, abs), *prep.* with *abl., from, by.*
ăbĕo, ĭi or īvi, ĭtum, ire, 4, *to go away.*
abjĭcĭo, jēci, jectum, *I cast away.*
absum, abfui, abesse, *I am absent.*
absūmo, mpsi, mptum, 3, *I consume, cut* [*off.*
absurdus, a, um, *adj., absurd.* [*off.*
ăbūtor, ūsus, 3, *v. dep., I abuse.*
accēdo, essi, essum, 3, *I approach.*
accĭdo, ĭdi (no *perf. part.*), 3, *n. v., to* *happen.*
accĭpĭo, cēpi, ceptum, 3, *I receive.*
ācer, cris, cre, *adj., keen, sharp.*
ăcĭes, ēi, *f., a line of battle.*
ăcŭo, ui, ūtum, 3, *I sharpen.*
ăcus, ūs, *f., a needle.*
ăcūtus, a, um, *adj., sharp.*
ăd, *prep.* with *acc., to, at, near.*
addictus, a, um, *devoted.*
addisco, addĭdĭci (no *perf. part.*), 3, *I* *learn in addition to.*
ădĕo, īvi or ĭi, ĭtum, 4, *to go to.*
ădhĭbĕo, ŭi, ĭtum, 2, *I employ.*
ădhortor, ātus, 1, *v. dep., I urge, exhort.*
ădĭpiscor, eptus, 3, *v. dep., I acquire,* *attain to.*
adjŭvo, jūvi, jŭtum, 1, *I assist.*
admīror, ātus, 1, *v. dep., I wonder at, I* *admire.*
adsum, affui, adesse, *I am present,* *stand by, side with.*

ALA.

ădūlātĭo, ōnis, *f., flattery.*
advĕnĭo, vēni, ventum, 4, *I arrive.*
advento, āvi, ātum, 1, *v. freq., I am on* *the point of arriving.*
adventus, ūs, *m., arrival.*
adversŭs or um, *prep.* with *acc., towards,* *against.*
aedĭfĭcĭum, ii, *n., a building.* [*against.*
aedĭfĭco, āvi, ātum, 1, *I build.*
Aedŭi, ōrum, *m. pl., the Aedui, a* *Gallic tribe.*
aeger, gra, grum, *adj., sick.*
Aegyptus, i, *f., Egypt.*
aequus, a, um, *adj., level, even, just.*
āēr, āĕris, *m., the air.*
aerumna, ae, *f., trouble, affliction.*
Aeschĭnes, is, *m., Aeschines, an orator.*
aestas, ātis, *f., summer.*
aetas, ātis, *f., age, time of life.*
aeternus, a, um, *adj., eternal.*
affectus, a, um, *part., made, disposed.*
affĕro, attŭli, allātum, afferre, *I bring to.*
afflīgo, ixi, ictum, 3, *I cast down, pro-* *strate.*
Afrĭcānus, i, *m., Africanus, a surname* *of the Scipios.*
ăger, gri, *m., a field.* [*of the Scipios.*
Agēsĭlāus, i, *m., Agesilaus, a king of* *Sparta.*
agger, ĕris, *m., a mound.* [*Sparta.*
ăgo, ēgi, actum, 3, *I lead, act, do.*
agrĭcŏla, ae, *m., a husbandman.*
āla, ae, *f., a wing.*

BONUM.

bŏnum, i, n., a good.
bŏnus, a, um, adj., good.
brĕvis, e, adj., short.
Brĭtannĭa, ae, f., Britain.
Brūtus, i, m., Brutus, a Roman

Cădo, cĕcĭdi, casum. 3, I fall.
caecus, a, um, adj., blind.
Caesar, ăris, m., Caesar, a famous Roman.
Cāĭus (C.), Caius, a Roman praenomen.
calcăr, āris, n., a spur.
călor, ōris, m., heat.
Cămillus, i, m., Camillus, a Roman general.
Campānĭa, ae, f., Campania, a part of campus, i, m., a plain.   [Italy.
cănis, is, c., a dog.
Cannae, ārum, f. pl., Cannae, a village canto, āvi, atum, 1, I sing. [in Apulia.
cantus, ūs, m., a song.
Cănūsĭum, ii, n., Canusium, a town in Apulia.
Căpŭa, ae, f., Capua, a city of Campania.
căpŭt, ĭtis, n., a head.
carmĕn, ĭnis, n., a song.
căro, carnis, f., flesh.
Carthāgĭnĭensis, e, adj., Carthaginian.
Carthāgo, ĭnis, f., Carthage, a city of cārus, a, um, adj., dear.   [Africa.
cāsĕus, i, m., cheese.
Cassĭus, ii, m., Cassius, a Roman.
Cassivelaunus, i, m., Cassivelaunus, a British chief.
castĭgo, āvi, ātum, 1, I chastise.
castră, ōrum, n. pl., a camp.
cāsus, ūs, m., chance, accident.
Cătĭlīna, ae, m., Catiline, a conspirator.
Căto, ōnis, m., Cato, a noble Roman.
causa, ae, f., a cause. In abl. with gen. of subs., on account of.
cautus, a, um, part., secured.
cēdo, cessi, cessum, 3, I yield, retire.
cĕler, ĕris, ĕre, adj., swift.
celsus, a, um, adj., lofty, tall.
centūrĭa, ae, f., a century.
cĕrăsum, i, n., a cherry.
cĕrăsus, i, f., the cherry-tree.
cerno, crēvi, crētum, 3, I see, discern.
certus, a, um, adj., certain.
cervus, i, m., a stag.

CONFIDO.

cĕter (caet.), ĕra, ĕrum, adj., the rest.
Chaerĕphōn, ontis, m., Chaerephon, disciple of Socrates.
Cĭcĕro, ōnis, m., Cicero, a celebrated Roman orator.
Cimbri, ōrum, m. pl., the Cimbrians, a formidable Celtic tribe.
cingo, nxi, nctum, 3, I surround.
circā, circum, prep. with acc., around.
circĭtĕr, prep. with acc., about.
cis, citrā, prep. with acc., on this side of.
cīvīlis, e, adj., belonging to a citizen.
cīvis, is, com., a citizen.   [civil.
cīvĭtas, tātis, f., the state, citizenship.
clādes, is, f., slaughter.
clam, prep. with acc. or abl., secretly, without the knowledge of.
clămor, ōris, m., a shout.
clārus, a, um, adj., clear, renowned.
classis, is, f., a fleet.
coelestis, e, adj., belonging to the heavens.
coelum, i, n., heaven.
coeno, āvi, ātum, 1, and coenatus sum. neut. pass. v., to sup, dine.
cŏĕo, īvi or ĭi, ĭtum, 4, I join together.
cŏercĕo, ŭi, ĭtum, 2, I restrain, curb.
cōgĭto, āvi, ātum, 1, I think, meditate.
cognĭtĭo, ōnis, f., knowledge.
cognosco, nōvi, nĭtum, 3, I learn, ascer-cŏhors, rtis, f., a cohort.   [tain
cŏhortor, ātus, 1, v. dep., I encourage.
collŏquor, cūtus, 3, v. dep., I converse.
cŏlo, cŏlŭi, cultum, 3, I cultivate, cherish
cŏlōnĭa, ae, f., a colony.   [&c
cŏlor, ōris, m., colour.
cŏlumba, ae, f., a dove.
cŏmes, ĭtis, com., a companion.
cŏmĭtor, ātus, 1, v. dep., I accompany.
commĕātus, ūs, m., provisions, supplies.
commīlĭto, ōnis, m., fellow-soldier, com-rade.
committo, īsi, issum, 3, I send together, join (fight) battle.
compăro, āvi, ātum, 1, I get together.
comprĕhendo, di, sum, 3, I seize.
concēdo, essi, essum, 3, I yield, retire.
confĕro, tŭli, collātum, conferre, 3, irr. I bring together, betake.
confĭcĭo, fēci, fectum, 3, I finish, ac-complish.
confīdo, īsus, sum, 3, with dat., I trust.

CONFITEOR.

confĭtĕor, fessus, 2, v. dep., I confess.
confŭgĭo, fūgi, 3, I flee to.
conjĭcĭo, jēci, jectum, 3, I fling (together).
conjūrātĭo, ōnis, f., a conspiracy.
Cŏnōn, ōnis, m., Conon, an Athenian general.
cōnor, ātus, 1, v. dep., I attempt.
conscendo, di, sum, 3, I mount, go on board (ship).
conscĭentĭa, ae, f., conscience.
consentĭo, nsi, nsum, 4, I agree.
conservo, āvi, ātum, 1, I preserve, main-consĭlĭum, i, n., plan, counsel. [tain.
constat, stĭtit, 1, impers. v., it is evident, it is agreed, &c.
constĭtŭo, ŭi, ūtum, 3, I settle, determine.
consŭētūdo, ĭnis, f., habit.
consul, ŭlis, m., a consul.
consŭlātus, ūs, m., office of consul, con-sulate.
consŭlo, lŭi, ltum, 3, I consult.
consumo, mpsi, mptum, 3, I consume, waste away.
contemno, mpsi, mptum, 3, I despise.
contemplor, ātus, 1, v. dep., I observe carefully, contemplate.
contendo, di, sum and tum, 3, I strain, hasten.
contentus, a, um, adj., contented.
contĭnĕo, ŭi, entum, 2, I hold together.
contrā, prep. with acc., against, con-trary to.
contrăho, axi, actum, 3, I draw together.
convĕnĭo, vēni, ventum, 4, I assemble.
convŏco, āvi, ātum, 1, I call together.
cōpĭa, ae, f., plenty.
cōpĭae, ārum, f. pl., forces.
cŏr, cordis, n., the heart.
cōram, prep. with abl., in the presence of.
Cŏrinthus, i, f., Corinth.
Cornēlĭa, ae, f., Cornelia, a Roman cornu, ūs, n., a horn. [matron.
cŏrōna, ae, f., a crown.
corpus, ŏris, n., a body.
corrĭgo, exi, ectum, 3, I correct.
crĕātor, ōris, m., a creator.
crēdĭbĭlis, e, adj., credible.
crēdo, dĭdi, dĭtum, 3, I believe.
crĕo, āvi, ātum, 1, I create, make.
Crēta, ae. f., Crete, an island of Greece.
Croesus, i, m., Croesus, a king of Lydia.

DICO.

crŭcĭātus, ūs, m., torture.
crūdēlis, e, adj., cruel.
crūs, crūris, n., a leg.
culpa, ae, f., blame, fault.
cum, prep. with abl., with.
Cūmae, ārum, f., Cumae, a city in Campania.
cunctus, a, um, adj., all, all together
cŭpĭdĭtas, ātis, f., desire, passion.
cŭpĭo, īvi or ĭi, ītum, 3, I desire.
cur, adv., why.
cūro, āvi, ātum, 1, I take care, pains.
curro, cŭcurri, cursum, 3, I run.
currus, ūs, m., a chariot.
cursus, ūs, m., running.
custōdĭo, īvi or ĭi, ītum, 4, I guard, keep guard.
custos, custōdis, c., a guardian.
Cyprus, i, f., Cyprus, an island off Cilicia.

Dārīus, i, m., Darius, a king of Persia.
dē, prep. with abl., down from, from, [concerning.
dĕa, ae, f., a goddess.
dēbĕo, ŭi, ĭtum, 2, I owe, ought.
dēbĭlis, e, adj., feeble.
dĕcĕt, dĕcŭit, dĕcērĕ, 2, impers. v., it is seemly.
dēcĭpĭo, cēpi, ceptum, 3, I receive.
dĕcus, ŏris, n., an ornament.
dēdĕcĕt, dĕcŭit, dĕcērĕ, 2, impers. v., it is unseemly.
dēfendo, di, sum, 3, I defend.
dēflăgro, āvi, ātum, 1, to be burnt down.
dēlecto, āvi, ātum, 1, I delight, amuse.
dēlectus, ūs, m., a levy.
dēlĕo, ēvi, ētum, 2, I destroy.
Dēlŏs, i, f., Delos, an island of Greece.
Delphi, ōrum, m. pl., Delphi, a city in Greece.
Dēmosthĕnēs, is, m., Demosthenes, the famous Athenian orator.
dēmum, adv., indeed. [deplore.
dēplōro, āvi, ātum, 1, I lament over,
dēsĕro, rui, rtum, 3, I abandon.
dēsum, fŭi, esse, with dat., I am want-dētĕgo, xi, ctum, 3, I discover. [ing.
dēterrĕo, ŭi, ĭtum, 2, I frighten, deter.
Dĕus, i, m., God.
Dĭāna, ae, f., Diana, a goddess.
dīco, xi, ctum, 3, I say, speak.

hŏnor, ōris, *m.*, *an honour.*
hōra, ae, *f.*, *an or the hour.*
Hŏrātĭus, ii, *Horatius, a Roman poet.*
hortor, ātus, 1, *v. dep.*, *I urge, exhort,*
hortus, i, *m.*, *a garden.*   [*encourage.*
hostĭa, ae, *f.*, *a victim.*
hostis, is, *com.*, *an enemy, public enemy.*
hūmānus, a, um, *adj.*, *human.*
hŭmĭlis, e, *adj.*, *low.* See p. 25.

Ĭbi, *adv.*, *there.*
ignāvē, *adv.*, *indolently.*
ignāvĭa, ae, *f.*, *cowardice.*
ignĕus, a, um, *adj.*, *fiery, made of fire.*
ignŏrātĭo, ōnis, *f.*, *ignorance.*
Ĭmāgo, Ĭnis, *f.*, *a likeness, portrait,*
    image.
Ĭmĭtor, atus, 1, *v. dep.*, *I imitate.*
immŏlo, āvi, ātum, 1, *I sacrifice.*
immortālis, e, *adj.*, *immortal.*
immortālĭtas, ātis, *f.*, *immortality.*
impĕrātor, ōris, *m.*, *military commander.*
impĕrītus, a, um, *adj.*, *unskilful.*
impĕrĭum, ĭi, *n.*, *empire.*   [*mand.*
impĕro, āvi, ātum, 1, with *dat.*, *I com-*
impĕtus, ūs, *m.*, *an attack, onset.*
impransus, a, um, *adj.*, *unbreakfasted.*
imprŏbus, a, um, *adj.*, *dishonest, wicked.*
imprūdentĭa, ae, *f.*, *ignorance, impru-*
    dence.
in, *prep.* with *acc.*, *into*, with *abl.*, *in.*
incendĭum, ĭi, *n.*, *a fire, conflagration.*
incendo, di, sum, 3, *I set fire to, burn.*
incertus, a, um, *adj.*, *uncertain.*
incĭpĭo, cēpi, ceptum, 3, *I begin.*
incŏla, ae, *com.*, *an inhabitant.*
incūso, āvi, ātum, 1, *I accuse, find fault*
    with.   [*India.*
Indi, ōrum, *m. pl.*, *Indians, people of*
indoctus, a, um, *adj.*, *unlearned.*
indulgĕo, si, tum, 2, with *dat.*, *I indulge.*
industrĭus, a, um, *adj.*, *industrious, busy.*
Ĭnĕo, ivi or ĭi, ĭtum, 4, *I go into, enter.*
Ĭners, tis, *adj.*, *helpless, sluggish.*
infāmĭa, ae, *f.*, *infamy.*
infāmis, e, *adj.*, *infamous.*
iufectus, a, um, *adj.*, *undone.*
infĕrĭor, ĭus, *comp.* of infĕrus, *adj.*, *lower,*
    inferior.   [*I carry into.*
infĕro, intŭli, illātum, inferrĕ, 3, *v. irr.*,

infīnītus, a, um, *adj.*, *unbounded, in-*
infirmĭtas, ātis, *f.*, *weakness.*   [*finite.*
infirmus, a, um, *adj.*, *infirm, feeble.*
infrā, *prep.* with *acc.*, *below.*
infringo, frēgi, fractum, 3, *I break, im-*
ingens, entis, *adj.*, *immense.*   [*pair.*
ingrĕdĭor, gressus sum, 3, *v. dep.*, *I*
Ĭnĭmĭcĭtĭa, ae, *f.*, *enmity.*   [*enter.*
Ĭnĭmīcus, a, um, *adj.*, *unfriendly.*
Ĭnĭtĭum, ĭi, *n.*, *a beginning.*
injustē, *adv.*, *unjustly.*
injustus, a, um, *adj.*, *unjust.*
innŭmĕrus, a, um, *adj.*, *innumerable.*
Ĭnops, ŏpis, *adj.*, *destitute.*
instĭtŭo, ui, ūtum, 3, *I appoint, institute.*
instrūmentum, i, *n.*, *an instrument.*
instrŭo, xi, ctum, 3, *I arrange, draw up*
insŭla, ae, *f.*, *an island.*   [*in order.*
insum, fui, esse, *v. irr.*, with *dat.*, *I am*
    in or upon.
intellĭgo, lexi, lectum, 3, *I understand.*
intĕr, *prep.* with *acc.*, *between, among.*
interclūdo, ūsi, ūsum, 3, *I shut off,*
    intercept.
intĕrĕo, īvi or ĭi, ĭtum, 4, *I perish.*
interfĭcĭo, fēci, fectum, 3, *I put to death,*
intĕrĭtus, ūs, *m.*, *destruction.*   [*kill.*
intersum, fŭi, esse, *v. irreg.*, with *dat.*,
    I am among.
intrā, *prep.* with *acc.*, *inside of, within.*
intro, āvi, ātum, 1, *I enter.*
intrŏĕo, īvi or ĭi, ĭtum, 4, *I go into, enter.*
intŭĕor, ĭtus sum, 2, *v. dep.*, *I look*
    upon, into.
intŭmesco, ŭi, 3, *v. incep.*, *I swell.*
invĭdĭa, ae, *f.*, *envy, ill-will.*
īra, ae, *f.*, *anger.*
īrascor, īrātus, 3, *v. dep.*, *I am angry.*
istūc, *adv.*, *thither, where you are.*
Ĭtă, *adv.*, *in that way, thus.*
Ĭtālĭa, ae, *f.*, *Italy.*
Ĭter, Ĭtĭnĕris, *n.*, *a journey.*

Jăcĕo, ŭi, Ĭtum, 2, *I lie.*
jăcĭo, jēci, jactum, 3, *I throw.*
jam, *adv.*, *now, already.*
jŭbĕo, jussi, jussum, 2, *I order, bid.*
jūcundus, a, um, *adj.*, *pleasant.*
jūdex, Ĭcis, *com.*, *a judge.*
jūdĭcĭum, ii, *n.*, *judgment.*
jūdĭco, āvi, ātum, 1, *I judge.*

JUNGO.

jungo, nxi, nctum, 3, *I join.*
Jūno, ōnis, *f.*, *Juno, a goddess.*
jūro, āvi, ātum or jurātus sum, 1, *I*
jūs, jūris, **n.**, *right, law.* [*swear.*
jusjūrandum, jūrisjūrandi, *n.*, *an oath.*
justē, *adv.*, *justly.*
justus, a, um, *adj.*, *just.*
jŭvĕnis, is, *com.*, *a young man or woman.*
jŭventūs, ūtis, *f.*, *youth.*
juxtā, *prep.* with *acc.*, *near, hard by,*
next to.

Lăbĭēnus, i, *m.*, *Labienus, one of Caesar's*
lieutenants.
lăbor, ōris, *m.*, *labour, hardship.*
lābor, lapsus, 3, *v. dep.*, *I glide, pass*
lac, lactis, *n.*, *milk.* [*away, fall.*
Lăcĕdaemon, ŏnis, *f.*, *Lacedaemon or*
Sparta.
Lăcĕdaemŏnii, ōrum, *m.*, *the Lacedae-*
lăcĭo, lăcĕre, 3, *I draw.* [*monians.*
lăcus, ūs, *m.*, *a lake.*
Laeca, ae, *m.*, *Laeca, a Roman.*
laetĭtĭa, ae, *f.*, *joy.*
laetus, a, um, *adj.*, *joyful.*
lăpis, ĭdis, *m.*, *a stone.*
lăpĭdĕus, a, um, *adj.*, *of stone.*
lātē, *adv.*; *widely, wide.*
Lătīnus, a, um, *adj.*, *Latin.*
Lātōna, ae, *f.*, *Latona, mother of Apollo*
and Diana.
latro, ōnis, *m.*, *a robber.*
lātus, a, um, *adj.*, *wide, broad.*
laudo, āvi, ātum, 1, *I praise.*
laus, laudis, *f.*, *praise.*
lēgātus, i, *m.*, *ambassador, lieutenant.*
lĕgĭo, onis, *f.*, *a legion.*
lĕgo, lēgi, lectum, 3, *I gather, read.*
lĕo, ōnis, *m.*, *a lion.*
Lĕōnĭdas, ae, *m.*, *Leonidas, a king of*
lĕpus, ŏris, *m.*, *a hare* [*Sparta.*
Lesbus, i, *f.*, *Lesbus, an island off Asia*
lēvis, e, *adj.*, *light.* [*Minor.*
lex, lēgis, *f.*, *a law.*
lĭber, bri, *m.*, *a book.*
līber, ĕra, ĕrum, *adj.*, *free.* See p. 24.
lĭbĕrĕ, *adv.*, *freely.*
lĭbĕri, ōrum, *m. pl.*, *children.*
lĭbĕro, āvi, ātum, 1, *I free, deliver.*
lībertas, ātis, *f.*, *freedom, liberty.*

MALEVOLUS.

lĭbet, lĭbŭit and lĭbitum est, lĭcēre, 2, *v.*
impers., with *dat.*, *it pleases.*
Lĭbўa, ae, *f.*, *Africa.*
lĭcet, lĭcŭit and lĭcĭtum est, lĭcēre, 2,
v. impers., with *dat.*, *it is lawful,*
allowed.
lictor, ōris, *m.*, *a lictor.*
lingua, ae, *f.*, *tongue, language.*
lĭquet, lĭquēre, 2, *v. impers.*, with *dat.*,
it is clear, evident.
lĭtĕra, ae, *f.*, *a letter of the alphabet.*
lĭtĕrae, ārum, *f. pl.*, *letters, learning,*
also an epistle, letter.
lītus, ōris, *n.*, *a shore.*
Līvĭus, ii, *m.*, *Livy, a Roman historian.*
lŏcus, i, *m.*, *a place* (*in pl.* loci. *single*
places; loca, *places connected with one*
another, regions).
longē, *adv.*, *far, far off.*
longinquĭtas, ātis, *f.*, *length, distance.*
longinquus, a, um, *adj.*, *long, distant.*
longĭus, *adv. comp.*, *farther, too far.*
longus, a, um, *adj.*, *long.*
lŏquor, lŏcūtus, 3, *v. dep.*, *I speak.*
Lūcĕrĭa, ae, *f.*, *Luceria, a town in*
Apulia.
lūcescit (illuxit), lūcescĕre, 3, *v. impers.*,
it becomes light. [*name.*
Lūcĭus, ii, *m.*, *Lucius, a Roman fore-*
Lūcrētĭus, ii, *m.*, *Lucretius, a Roman*
lūdi, ōrum, *m. pl.*, *games.* [*poet.*
lūdo, si, sum, 3, *I play.*
lūdus, i, *m.*, *play, game, school.*
lūna, ae, *f.*, *the moon.*
luscĭnĭa, ae, *f.*, *nightingale.*
lux, lūcis, *f.*, *light.* [*legislator.*
Lўcurgus, i, *m.*, *Lycurgus, the Spartan*

Măcĕdo, ŏnis, *m.*, *a Macedonian.*
măgis, *adv.* (*sup.* maxĭmē), *rather, in a*
higher degree.
măgister, tri, *m.*, *a master, teacher.*
măgistrātus, ūs, *m.*, *a magistrate.*
magnĭfĭcus, a, um, *adj.*, *magnificent.*
magnŏpĕrĕ, *adv.*, *greatly, earnestly.*
magnus, a, um, *adj.*, *great.*
mājōres, um, *m. pl.*, *ancestors.*
mălĕ, *adv.*, *comp.* pējus, *sup.* pessĭmē,
badly, ill. [*levolent.*
mălĕvŏlus, **a**, um, *adj.*, *ill-wishing, ma-*

MALO.

mălo, mălui, mallĕ, *irr. v., I am more
willing, I prefer, to have rather.*
mălum, i, *n., an apple.*
mălum, i, *n., an evil.*
mălus, i, *f., an apple-tree.*
mălus, a, um, *adj., bad, wicked.*
mandătum, i, *n., a charge, commission.*
mănĕo, nsi, nsum, 2, *I remain.*
mănĭfestus, a, um, *adj., evident, mani-*
mănĭpŭlus, i, *m., a maniple.* [*fest.*
mănus, ūs, *f., a hand.*
Mărăthon, ōnis, *f., Marathon, a plain*
măre, is, *n., the sea.* [*near Athens.*
margărĭta, ae, *f., a pearl.*
mărīnus, a, um, *adj., of the sea.*
Mărĭus, ii, *m., Marius, a Roman general.*
marmor, ŏris, *n., marble.*
măter, tris, *f., a mother.*
Maxĭmus, i, *m., Maximus, the greater, a
surname of Fabius.* [*study.*
mĕdĭtor, ātus, 1, *v. dep., I meditate on,*
membrāna, ae, *f., thin skin, membrane.*
mĕmor, ŏris, *adj., mindful.*
mĕmŏrābĭlis, e, *adj., to be remembered,*
mĕmŏrĭa, ae, *f., memory.* [*memorable.*
Mĕnăpĭi, ōrum, *m. pl., Menapii, a Gallic
tribe.*
mendax, ācis, *adj. and subs., lying, a*
mens, mentis, *f., mind.* [*liar, false.*
mensis, is, *m., a month.*
mentior, ītus, 4, *v. dep., I lie, tell a lie.*
mĕrĕo, ŭi, ĭtum, 2, *I deserve.*
mĕtallum, i, *n., a metal.*
mētĭor, mensus, 4, *v. dep., I measure.*
mĕtŭo, ŭi, ūtum, 3, *I fear.*
mĕtus, ūs, *m., fear.*
mĕus, a, um,* *pronom. adj., my, mine.*
migro, āvi, ātum, 1, *I migrate, depart.*
mĭles, mīlĭtis, *m., a soldier.*
Mĭnerva, ae, *f., Minerva.*
mĭnĭmē, *adv., in the least degree.*
mĭnister, tri, *m., a servant.* [*admire.*
mīror, ātus, 1, *v. dep., I wonder at,*
mīrus, a, um, *adj., wonderful.*
mĭser, era, erum, *adj., wretched.*
mĭsĕrĕor, rtus or ĭtus, 2, *v. dep., I pity,
have pity on.*
mĭsĕret, mĭsĕrĭtum est, mĭsĕrērĕ, *v.
impers., it excites pity.*

* Voc. sing. masc. mi.

NERVII.

mītis, e, *adj., mild.*
mitto, mīsi, missum, 3, *I send.*
mŏdus, i, *m., a measure, manner.*
moenĭa, ium, *n. pl., fortifications.*
mŏlestus, a, um, *adj., troublesome.*
mollĭo, īvi or ĭi, ītum, 4, *I soften,*
mollis, e, *adj., soft, mellow.* [*assuage.*
mŏneo, ŭi, ĭtum, 2, *I advise, warn.*
mons, ntis, *m., a mountain.*
mŏnŭmentum, i, *n., a monument.*
morbus, i, *m., a disease.*
mŏrĭor, mortŭus, 3, *v. dep., I die (fut.
part. mŏrĭtūrus, about to die).*
mors, tis, *f., death.*
mortălis, e, *adj., mortal.*
mortŭus, a, um, *adj., dead.*
mōs, mōris, *m., manner, custom.*
mŏvĕo, mōvi, mōtum, 2, *I move, disturb.*
mox, *adv., soon, shortly.*
mŭlĭer, ĕris, *f., a woman, wife.*
multĭtūdo, ĭnis, *f., a multitude.*
multus, a, um, *adj., much, many*
mundus, i, *m., the world.*
mūnĭmentum, i, *n., a fortification.*
mūnĭo, īvi or ĭi, ītum, 4, *I fortify.*
mūnus, ĕris, *n., a gift, duty, function.*
mūrus, i, *m., a wall.*
mūto, āvi, ātum, 1, *I change.*

Narro, āvi, ātum, 1, *I relate.*
nascor, nātus, 3, *v. dep., I am born.*
nātūra, ae, *f., nature.*
nātus, a, um, *part. and adj., born, aged.*
nauta, ae, *m., a sailor.*
nāvālis, e, *adj., naval.*
nāvis, is, *f., a ship.* [p. 97.)
nē, *adv. and conj., no, that not.* (See
nec, nĕquĕ, *conj., neither, nor.* [*ful.*
nĕcessărĭus, a, um, *adj., necessary, need-*
nĕfas, *n., indecl., wickedness, impiety.*
nĕgo, āvi, ātum, 1, *I deny.*
nĕgōtĭum, ii, *n., business.*
nēmo, ĭnis, com., *nobody.* [*sea.*
Neptūnus, i, *m., Neptune, the god of the*
nēquam, *indecl. adj., comp. nēquĭor,
sup. nēquissĭmus, worthless.*
nĕquĕo, īvi or ĭi, ĭtum, īre, 4, *I am unable, cannot.*
Nĕro, ōnis, *m., Nero, a Roman emperor.*
Nervĭi, ōrum, *m. pl., the Nervii, a Gallic
tribe.*

NESCIO.

nescĭo, īvī or ĭi, ītum, 4, *I am ignorant of.*

neuter, tra, trum, *adj.* (*gen. sing.* īŭs, *dat.* ī), *neither of two.* (See p. 23.)

nēve, *adv., and not, nor.*

nīdus, i, *m., a nest.*

nīger, gra, grum, *adj., black.*

nĭhil, *n., indecl., nothing.*

Nīlus, i, *m., the Nile, a river in Egypt.*

nĭmis, *adv., too, too much.*

ningit, ninxit, ningĕre, 3, *v. impers., it snows.*

nĭsi, *conj., unless, except.*

nītor, nīsus and nixus, 3, *v. dep., I strive.*

nix, nĭvis, *f., snow.*

nōbĭlis, e, *adj., distinguished, noble.*

nŏcĕo, ŭi, ĭtum, 2, with *dat., I hurt, harm.*

nōlo, nōlŭi, nolle, *v. irreg., I am unwilling, I do not wish.*

nōmen, ĭnis, *n., a name.*

nōn, *adv., not.*

nonnullus, a, um, *adj., some.*

noster, stra, strum, *pronom. adj., our, ours.*

nōtus, a, um, *adj., known.*

nŏvus, a, um, *adj., new.*

nox, noctis, *f., night.*

noxĭus, a, um, *adj., hurtful, injurious.*

nūbes, is, *f., a cloud.*

nullus, a, um, *adj., none; gen. s.* īŭs,

nŭmĕro, āvi, ātum, 1, *I count.* [*dat.* ī.

nŭmĕrus, i, *m., a number.*

nunc, *adv., now.*

nunquam, *adv., never.* [*nurture.*

nūtrĭo, īvi and ĭi, ītum, 4, *I nourish,*

Ŏb, *prep.* with *acc., on account of.*

ŏbēdĭo, īvi or ĭi, ītum, 4, with *dat., I obey.*

ŏbĕo, īvi or ĭi, ĭtum, 4, *I meet, esp. meet death, I die.*

oblīviscor, lītus, 3, *v. dep., I forget.*

obscūro, āvi, ātum, 1, *I darken, obscure.*

observo, āvi, ātum, 1, *I observe, respect.*

obses, ĭdis, *com., a hostage.* [*siege to.*

obsĭdĕo, sēdi, sessum, 2, *I blockade, lay*

obsĭdĭo, ōnis, *f., a siege, blockade.*

obsto, stĭti, stĭtum, 1, *I oppose, prevent.*

obsum, obfui or offui, obesse, *v. irreg.,* with *dat., I am in the way, am hurtful to, injure.* [*with.*

obtempĕro, āvi, ātum, 1, *I obey, comply*

PATRIA.

occĭdens, tis, *m., the west, the setting sun.*

occīdo, īdi, īsum, 3, *I slay, kill.*

occŭpātus, a, um, *adj., engaged, busy.*

occŭpo, āvi, ātum, 1, *I seize upon.*

ōcĕānus, i, *m., the ocean.*

ŏcŭlus, i, *m., an eye.*

ŏdĭum, ii, *n., hatred.*

ŏdor, ōris, *m., a smell, scent.* [*I present.*

offĕro, obtŭlī, oblātum, offerre, 3, *v. irr.;*

ōlim, *adv., formerly, once upon a time.*

omnis, e, *adj., all, every.*

ŏnus, ĕris, *n., a load, burden.*

ŏpĕra, ae, *f., pains, labour.*

ŏportet, ŭit, 2, *v. impers., it behoves, is* [*necessary.*

oppĭdum, i, *n., a town.*

oppōno, ŏsŭi, ĭtum, 3, *I set against, oppose.* [*upon, overwhelm.*

opprīmo, pressi, pressum, 3, *I press*

oppugno, āvi, ātum, 1, *I attack, assault.*

opto, āvi, ātum, 1, *I wish, desire.*

ŏpŭlentus, a, um, *adj., wealthy.*

ŏpus, ĕris, *n., a work.*

ŏpus, *n., indecl., need, necessity.*

ōra, ae, *f., the coast.*

ōrācŭlum, i, *n., an oracle.*

ōrātĭo, ōnis, *f., an oration, speech.*

ōrātor, ōris, *m., an orator.*

ordĭor, orsus, 4, *v. dep., I begin.*

ŏrĭor, ortus, ōriri, 3, *v. dep., I rise.*

orno, āvi, ātum, 1, *I adorn.*

ōro, āvi, ātum, 1, *I entreat, pray.*

ōs, ōris, *n., a mouth.*

ŏs, ossis, *n., a bone.*

Pābŭlor, ātus, 1, *v. dep., I forage.*

pallium, ii, *n., a cloak.*

părātus, a, um, *adj., prepared, ready.*

părens, ntis, *c., a parent.*

părĕo, ŭi, ĭtum, 2, with *dat., I obey.*

părĭo, pĕpĕri, părĭtum and partum, 3, *I bring forth.*

păro, āvi, ātum, 1, *I prepare, get gain.*

pars, tis, *f., a part.*

partĭor, ītus, 4, *v. dep., I share, divide.*

parvus, a, um, *adj., small, little.*

passus, ūs, *m., a pace* (about 5 *feet*).

păter, tris, *m., a father.*

pătĭenter, *adv., patiently.*

pătĭor, passus, 3, *v. dep., I endure, suffer.*

patrĭa, ae, *f., a native land, country.*

PAUCUS.

paucus, a, um, *adj.*, *few.*
pauper, ĕris, *adj.*, *poor.*
paupertas, ātis, *f.*, *poverty.*
pāvo, ōnis, *m.*, *a peacock.*
pax, pācis, *f.*, *peace.*
pĕcūnĭa, ae, *f.*, *money.*
pĕdes, ĭtis, *m.*, *a foot-soldier.*
pĕdĭtātus, ūs, *m.*, *infantry.*
pellis, is, *f.*, *a skin, hide (of an animal).*
pĕnĕs, *prep.* with acc., *in the power of.*
per, *prep.* with acc., *through.*
percĭpĭo, cēpi, ceptum, 3, *I perceive*
perdo, dĭdi, dĭtum, 3, *I destroy.*
pĕrĕo, ĭi or īvi, ĭtum, 4, *I perish*
perfectus, a, um, *adj.*, *finished, perfect.*
perfĕro, tŭli, lātum, ferre, *v. irr.*, *I bear through, endure.*
pĕrīcŭlum, i, *n.*, *danger.*
pĕrītus, a, um, *adj.*, *skilful.*
perlĕgo, lēgi, lectum, 3, *I read through.*
permulti, ae, a, *adj.* (pl.), *very many.*
pernĭcĭōsus, a, um, *adj.*, *destructive*
perpĕtŭus, a, um, *adj.*, *continual.*
perrumpo, rūpi, ruptum, 3, *I burst through.*
Persă, ae, *m.*, *a Persian.*
persŭādĕo, āsi, āsum, 2, with *dat.*, *I persuade.*
pervĕnĭo, vēni, ventum, 4, *I arrive at.*
perversus, a, um, *adj.*, *wilful, perverse.*
pĕto, īvi and ĭi, ĭtum, 3, *I seek.*
Phăĕthon, ontis, *m.*, *Phaëthon, a son of Apollo.*
Phīdĭas, ae, *m.*, *Phidias, a famous Athenian sculptor.*
phĭlŏsŏphus, i, *m.*, *a philosopher.*
pĭgĕt, pĭgŭit and pĭgĭtum est, pĭgēre, 2, *v. impers.*, *it vexes.*
pingo, nxi, pictum, 3, *I paint, embroider.*
pĭrum, i, *n.*, *a pear.*
pĭrus, i, *f.*, *a pear-tre*
piscis, is, *m.*, *a fish.*
Pĭsistrātus, i, *m.*, *Pisistratus, a despot of Athens.*
plăcĕo, ŭi, ĭtum, 2, with *dat.*, *I obey.*
plăcet, ŭit or ĭtum est, ēre, 2, *v. impers.*, *it pleases.*
plăcĭdus, a, um, *adj.*, *quiet.*
plānē, *adv.*, *altogether.*
plānĭtĭes, ēi, *f.*, *a plain.*
planta, ae, *f.*, *a sprout, plant.*
Plăto, ōnis, *m.*, *Plato, a famous Greek philosopher.*
plēnus, a, um, *adj.* with gen., *full.*

PREMO.

Plīnĭus, ii, *m.*, *Pliny, the name of two Roman authors.* [pers., it rains.
plŭit, plŭit or plŭvit, plŭĕre, 3, *v. impers.*
plūs, ūris, *adj.* (in pl. plūres, plūra), [more.
poena, ae, *f.*, *punishment.*
Poeni, ōrum, *m.* pl., *the Carthaginians.*
poenitet, ĭtŭit, ĭtēre, 2, *v. impers.*, *it causes sorrow, repents.*
pŏēta, ae, *m.*, *a poet.*
pollĭcĕor, ĭtus, 2, *v. dep.*, *I promise.*
Pompēius, ēii, *m.*, *Pompey, the rival of Caesar.*
pōnĕ, *prep.* with acc., *behind.*
pōno, pŏsŭi, pŏsĭtum, 3, *I place.*
pons, ntis, *m.*, *a bridge.*
porta, ae, *f.*, *a gate.*
porto, āvi, ātum, 1, *I carry.*
portus, ūs, *m.*, *a harbour.*
possum, pŏtŭi, posse, *v. irreg.*, *I am able, can.* (See p. 76.)
post, *prep.* with acc., *after.*
postŭlo, āvi, ātum, 1, *I demand*
pŏtens, entis, *adj.*, *powerful.*
pŏtentĭa, ae, *f.*, *power, i.e. power from personal weight, influence.*
pŏtestas, ātis, *f.*, *power, i.e. magisterial power.*
pŏtĭor, ĭtus, 4, *v. dep.*, with *abl.*, *I take possession of, obtain.*
prae, *prep.* with *abl.*, *before, in comparison with.*
praealtus, a, um, *adj.*, *very high.*
praebĕo, ŭi, ĭtum, 2, *I furnish, afford, exhibit.*
praeceptor, ōris, *m.*, *a teacher.*
praeceptum, i, *n.*, *precept, instruction, lesson.*
praeda, ae, *f.*, *booty.*
praeĕo, īvi or ĭi, ĭtum, 4, *I go before.*
praefero, tŭli, lātum, *v. irreg.*, *I prefer.*
praemitto, mīsi, missum, 3, *I send on before.*
praemĭum, ii, *n.*, *a reward.*
praesens, entis, *adj.*, *present.*
praestābĭlis, e, *adj.*, *excellent.*
praestans, antis, *adj.*, *excellent.*
praesum, fŭi, esse, *v. irreg.*, with *dat.*, *I am before, at the head of.*
praetĕr, *prep.* with acc., *beside.*
praetĕrĕo, īvi or ĭi, ĭtum, 4, *v. irreg.*, *I pass by.*
praetĕrĭtus, a, um, *adj.*, *past.*
praevĕnĭo, vēni, ventum, 4, *I anticipate.*
prĕmo, essi, essum, 3, *I press.*

PRIMARIUS.

prīmārĭus, a, um, *adj.*, *first-rate*, *emi-*
prīmo, *adv.*, *at first.* [*nent.*
pristĭnus, a, um, *adj.*, *former, olden.*
prĭus, *adv.*, *sooner, before.*
pro, *prep.* with *abl.*, *before, for, on be-*
probē, *adv.*, *rightly, properly.* [*half of.*
prŏbĭtas, ātis, *f.*, *honesty, integrity.*
prŏbus, a, um, *adj.*, *good, upright.*
prōdo, dĭdi, dĭtum, 3, *I hand down,*
proelĭum, ii, *n.*, *a battle.* [*betray.*
prōfĕro, tŭli, lātum, ferre, *v. irreg.*, *I*
extend.
prōfĭciscor, fectus, 3, *v. dep.*, *I set out.*
prŏfundus, a, um, *adj.*, *deep.*
progrĕdior, gressus, 3, *v. dep.*, *I ad-*
vance.
prŏhĭbĕo, ŭi, ĭtum, 2, *I keep off, prohibit.*
prŏpĕ, *prep.* with *acc.*, *near.*
prŏpĕ, *adv.*, *nearly.*
prŏpinquus, a, um, *adj.*, *near.*
proptĕr, *prep.* with *acc.*, *on account of.*
prōsum, fŭi, prōdesse, *v. irreg.*, *I am*
wanting. [*provide.*
prōvĭdĕo, vīdi, vīsum, 2, *I foresee,*
proxĭmus, a, um, *sup. adj.*, *nearest,*
prudens, ntis, *adj.*, *prudent.* [*next.*
prūdentĭa, ae, *f.*, *knowledge, prudence.*
prūnum, i, *n.*, *a plum.*
prunus, i, *f.*, *a plum-tree.*
pūblĭcus, a, um, *adj.*, *public.*
pŭdet, ŭit or pŭdĭtum, ĕre, 2, *v. impers.*,
pŭella, ae, *f.*, *a girl.* [*it shames.*
pŭer, ĕri, *m.*, *a boy.*
pugna, ae, *f.*, *a battle.*
pugno, āvi, ātum, 1, *I fight.*
pulcher, cra, crum, *adj.*, *beautiful.*
Pūnĭcus, a, um, *adj.*, *Punic, Cartha-*
ginian.
pūnĭo, īvi or ĭi, ītum, 4, *I punish.*
pŭto, āvi, ātum, 1, *I think.*
Pȳthăgŏras, ae, *m.*, *Pythagoras, a fa-*
mous Greek philosopher.

Quaero, quaesīvi, sītum, 3, *I seek,*
quaestĭo, ōnis, *f.*, *a question.* [*enquire.*
quālis, e, *pron. adj.*, *of what sort, as.*
quam, *adv.* and *conj.*, *than, as.*
quantus, a, um, *adj.*, *how great.*
quārē, *adv.*, *why, on what account.*
quăsi, *adv.*, *as if, just as.*
quătĭo, *no perf.*, quassum, 3, *I shake.*

RESISTO.

quercus, ūs, *f.*, *an oak.*
quĭa, *conj.*, *because.*
quīdam, quaedam, quoddam and quid-
dam, *pron. indef.*, *a certain, certain*
quĭdem, *adv.*, *indeed.* [*one, somebody.*
quĭn, *conj.*, *that not* (with *subj.*). (See
p. 97.) [*which, what ?*
quis, quae, quid, *pron. interr.*, *who,*
quisnam, quaenam, quidnam, *interrog.*
pron., *who, which, what ?*
quisquĕ, quaeque, quodque (and *subst.*
quidque or quicque), *ind. pron.*, *every*
quō, *adv.*, *whither.* [*one, whoever.*
quo, *conj.* with *subj.*, *that.* (See p. 98.)
quŏd, *conj.*, *because.* [p. 98.)
quōmĭnus, *conj.* with *subj.*, *that not.* (See
quondam, *adv.*, *some time, formerly.*
quŏquĕ, *conj.*, *also, even, too.*
quŏt, *indecl. adj.*, *how many*
quŏtĭdĭē, *adv.*, *every day.*
quum, *adv.* and *conj.*, *when*

Rādix, īcis, *f.*, *a root.*
răpax, ācis, *adj.*, *rapacious.*
răpĭdus, a, um, *adj.*, *rapid.*
răpĭo, ŭi, raptum, ĕre, 3, *I seize.*
rārō, *adv.*, *seldom, rarely.*
rārus, a, um, *adj.*, *rare.*
rătĭo, ōnis, *f.*, *reason.*
rĕcĭto, āvi, ātum, 1, *I read aloud.*
rĕcordor, ātus, 1, *v. dep.*, *I call to mind.*
rĕcrĕo, āvi, ātum, 1, *I refresh.*
rectus, a, um, *adj.*, *straight, right.*
rĕcŭpĕro, āvi, ātum, 1, *I recover, get*
back.
rĕcūso, āvi, ātum, 1, *I object, refuse.*
rĕdămo, āvi, ātum, 1, *I love in return.*
rĕdĕo, ĭi, ĭtum, 4, *I return.*
rĕfĕro, rĕtŭlī or rettŭlī, rĕlātum, 3,
v. irreg., *I bring back.*
rēgīna, ae, *f.*, *a queen.*
regno, āvi, ātum, 1, *I reign, am king.*
regnum, i, *n.*, *a kingdom.*
rĕgo, xi, ctum, 6, *I rule.* [*Roman.*
Rĕgŭlus, i, *m.*, *Regulus, a famous*
rĕlinquo, līqui, lictum, 3, *I leave, quit.*
rĕmĭniscor, 3, *I remember.* [*restore.*
rĕnŏvo, āvi, ātum, 1, *I make new again,*
rĕpĕrĭo, pĕri, pertum, 4, *I find.*
rēs, rĕi, *f.*, *a thing.* [*sist.*
resisto, stĭti, stĭtum, 3, with *dat.*, *I re-*

respondĕo, di, sum, 2, *I answer.*
rēte, is, *n.*, *a net.*
rĕus, i, *m.*, *an accused man, defendant.*
rĕverto, ti, sum, 3, *I turn back, return.*
rĕvertor, versus, 3, *v. dep.*, *I turn back,*
rex, rēgis, *m.*, *a king.*   [*return.*
Rhēnus, i, *m.*, *the Rhine.*
Rhŏdănus, i, *m.*, *the Rhone.*
Rhŏdus, i, *f.*, *Rhodes, an island of*
rīpa, ae, *f.*, *a bank, shore.*   [*Greece.*
rŏgo, āvi, ātum, 1, *I ask.*
Rōma, ae, *f.*, *Rome (the city).*
Rōmānus, *m.*, *a Roman.*
rōmānus, a, um, *adj.*, *Roman.*
Rōmŭlus, i, *m.*, *Romulus.*
rŏsa, ae, *f.*, *a rose.*
Roscīus, ii, *m.*, *Roscius, a Roman name.*
rūpes, is, *f.*, *a rock.*

Săcer, cra, crum, *adj.*, *sacred.*
saepĕ, *adv.*, *often.*
saepĕnŭmĕro, *adv.*, *oftentimes.*
saepissĭmē, *adv.*, *very often.*
săgitta, ae, *f.*, *an arrow.*
Săguntīni, ōrum, *m. pl.*, *Saguntines, the*
    people of Saguntum in Spain.
Sălămis, is, *f.*, *Salamis, an island near*
    Athens.
Sallustīus, ii, *m.*, *Sallust, a Roman his-*
salto, āvi, ātum, 1, *I dance.*   [*torian.*
sălus, ūtis, *f.*, *safety.*
salvus, a, um, *adj.*, *safe.*
sanguis, ĭnis, *m.*, *blood.*
săpĭens, ntis, *adj.* and *subs.*, *wise, wise-*
săpĭentia, ae, *f.*, *wisdom.*   [*man.*
săpĭo, īvi or ĭi, 3, *I savour of, taste, am*
sătis, *adv.*, *enough, sufficiently.*   [*wise.*
Satrīus, ii, *m.*, *Satrius, a Roman.*
scĕlus, ĕris, *n.*, *a crime.*
scĭentia, ae, *f.*, *knowledge.*
scĭo, ii or īvi, ītum, 4, *I know.*
Scīpĭo, ōnis, *m.*, *Scipio, a noble Roman.*
scrībo, psi, ptum, 3, *I write.*
scriptor, ōris, *m.*, *a writer, author.*
scūtum, i, *n.*, *a shield.*
Scўthae, arum, *m. pl.*, *the Scythians.*
sĕcundum, *prep.* with *acc.*, *following, in*
sĕd, *conj.*, *but.*   [*accordance with.*
sĕdĕo, sēdi, sessum, 2, *I sit.*
sōdes, is, *f.*, *a seat.*
segnĭtĭes, ēi, *f.*, *slothfulness.*

semper, *adv.*, *always, ever.*
sĕnātus, ūs, *m.*, *the senate.*
sĕnectus, ūtis, *f.*, *old age.*
sensus, ūs, *m.*, *a sense.*
sentĭo, si, sum, 4, *I feel, perceive.*
sĕpĕlĭo, īvi or ĭi, pultum, 4, *I bury.*
sĕquor, sĕcūtus, 3, *v. dep.*, *I follow.*
sĕrēnus, a, um, *adj.*, *clear.*
sermo, ōnis, *m.*, *a discourse.*
sĕro, sēvi, sătum, 3, *I plant, sow.*
servĭtūs, ūtis, *f.*, *slavery.*
servo, āvi, ātum, 1, *I preserve, save.*
servus, i, *m.*, *a slave.*
sĕvērus, a, um, *adj.*, *severe.*
sī, *conj.*, *if.*
Sĭcĭlĭa, ae, *f.*, *Sicily.*
sīdus, ĕris, *n.*, *a star, constellation.*
signum, i, *n.*, *a sign, signal.*
sĭlentĭum, ii, *n.*, *silence.*
silva, ae, *f.*, *a wood.*
sĭmĭlis, e, *adj.*, *like.* (See p. 25.)
sĭmŭl, *adv.*, *at the same time.*
sĭmŭlăc, *adv.*, *as soon as.*
sĭmŭlăcrum, i, *n.*, *an image, statue.*
sĭmŭlātĭo, ōnis, *f.*, *a pretence.*
sĭne, *prep.* with *abl.*, *without.*
sŏcer, ĕri, *m.*, *a father-in-law.*
sŏcĭus, ii, *m.*, *a partner, ally, companion.*
Sōcrătēs, is, *m.*, *Socrates, the sage of*
sōl, sōlis, *m.*, *the sun.*   [*Athens.*
sŏlĕo, ĭtus sum, ēre, 2, *v. n.*, *I am accus-*
    tomed.
Sŏlon, ōnis, *m.*, *Solon, the Athenian law-*
sōlum, *adv.*, *only.*   [*giver.*
sōlus, a, um, *adj.*, *gen. sing.* īus, *dat.* i,
    alone.
solvo, solvi, sŏlūtum, 3, *I loosen, pay.*
somnus, i, *m.*, *sleep.*
sŏnĭtus, ūs, *m.*, *a sound, noise.*
sŏror, ōris, *f.*, *a sister.*
sors, tis, *f.*, *a lot.*
Sparta, ae, *f.*, *Sparta.*
spĕcĭo, spexi, ĕre, 3, *to look.*   [*behold.*
specto, āvi, ātum, 1, *I look at, look on,*
spĕcŭlor, ātus, 1, *v. dep.*, *I spy out.*
spērātus, a, um, *adj.*, *hoped for.*
spēro, āvi, ātum, 1, *I hope.*
spes, ĕi, *f.*, *hope.*   [*bright.*
splendĭdus, a, um, *adj.*, *splendid,*
splendor, ōris, *m.*, *brightness, brilliancy.*
stătim, *adv.*, *immediately.*

STATIO.

státĭo, onis, *f.*, *a post, station.*
státuo, ŭi, ūtum, 3, *I fix, determine.*
stella, ae, *f.*, *a star.*
sto, stĕti, stătum, 1, *I stand.*
strēnŭē, *adv.*, *vigorously.*
strēnŭus, a, um, *adj.*, *vigorous.*
stŭdĕo, ŭi, 2, *I am eager, zealous.*
stŭdĭōsus, a, um, *adj.*, *zealous, eager after.*
stŭdĭum, ii, *n.*, *zeal, a pursuit, study.*
stultĭtĭa, ae, *f.*, *folly.*
stultus, a, um, *adj.*, *foolish.*
suādĕo, āsi, āsum, 2, with *dat.*, *I advise.*
suāvis, e, *adj.*, *sweet, delightful.*
sŭb, *prep.* with *abl.* or *acc.*, *up to, under; of time, about.*
subdiffĭcĭlis, e, *adj.*, *somewhat difficult.*
subĕo, ĭi, ĭtum, 3, *I go up to, under.*
sŭbĭtus, a, um, *adj.*, *sudden.*
subsĕquor, cūtus, 3, *v. dep.*, *I follow up.*
subsaum, *no perf.*, *v. irreg.*, *I am under, amongst.*
subter, *prep.* with *acc.* or *abl.*, *under.*
summus, a, um, *sup. adj.*, *highest, utmost, greatest.*
sŭper, *prep.* with *acc.* or *abl.*, *over.*
sŭpĕro, āvi, ātum, 1, *I overcome.*
sŭpersum, fui, esse, *v. irreg.*, *I remain over, survive.*
sŭpĕrus, a, um, *adj.* (comp. sŭpĕrĭor, superl. sŭperrĭmus, or suprēmus),
suprā, *prep.* with *acc.*, *above.* [*upper.*
suprēmus, a, um, *adj.*, *superl.* of sŭpĕrus, *highest; relat.* to time, *last.*
suscĭpĭo, ēpi, eptum, 3, *I undertake.*
sŭus, a, um, *reflec. pron. poss.*, *his, hers, its, their own.*

Tăbernācŭlum, i, *n.*, *a tent.*
tăcĕo, ŭi, ĭtum, 2, *I am silent.*
taedĕt, dŭ't or sum est, *v. impers.*, *it disgusts, wearies.*
tālis, e, *adj.*, *of that sort, such.*
tam, *adv.*, *so, to such a degree.*
tantum, *adv.*, *only.*
taurus, i, *m.*, *a bull.*
tĕgo, xi, ctum, 3, *I cover.*
tēlum, i, *n.*, *a dart, weapon, missile.*
tĕmĕrĭtas, ātis, *f.*, *recklessness, rashness.*
tempestas, ātis, *f.*, *a tempest.*
templum, i, *n.*, *a temple.*

UBI.

tempus, ŏris, *n.*, *time.*
tĕnĕo, ŭi, tentum, 2, *I hold, retain.*
tĕner, ĕra, ĕrum, *adj.*, *tender, soft.*
tĕnŭis, e, *adj.*, *thin, delicate.*
tĕnŭs, *prep.* with *abl.*, *reaching to, as terra, ae, f., the earth, land.* [*far as.*
terrĕo, ŭi, ĭtum, 2, *I terrify, frighten,*
terror, ōris, *m.*, *terror, alarm.* [*alarm.*
Thales, ētis, *m.*, *Thales, the philosopher.*
Thĕmistocles, is, *m.*, *Themistocles, a famous Athenian.*
Tĭbĕrĭus, ii, *m.*, *Tiberius* (a common Roman fore-name).
tigris, is or ĭdis, *com.*, *a tiger, tigress.*
tĭmĕo, ŭi, 2, *I fear.*
tĭmĭdus, a, um, *adj.*, *timid.*
tĭmor, ōris, *m.*, *fear.* [*Greek.*
Tĭmŏthĕu-, ĕi, *m.*, *Timotheus, a famous*
Tĭtus (T.), i, *m.*, *Titus* (a common Roman fore-name).
tŏnat, ŭit, āre, 1, *v. impers.*, *it thunders.*
tōtus, a, um, *adj.*, *whole, all.*
trabs, trăbis, *f.*, *a beam.*
tracto, āvi, ātum, 1, *I handle, deal with.*
trădo, dĭdi, dĭtum, 3, *I hand down, deliver.*
trăho, axi, actum, 3, *I draw, drag.*
tranquillus, a, um, *adj.*, *calm.*
trans, *prep.* with *acc.*, *across.*
transdūco, xi, ctum, 3, *I lead across.*
transĕo, ii, ĭtum, 4, *v. irreg.*, *I cross over.*
Trăsĭmēnus, i, *m.*, *the lake Trasimene in Italy.* [*Caesar's lieutenants.*
Trĕbōnĭus, ĭi, *m.*, *Trebonius, one of*
trĭbŭo, ŭi, ūtum, 3, *I give, assign.*
tristis, e, *adj.*, *sad.*
trĭumpho, āvi, ātum, 1, *I triumph.* (See Voc. 27.) [*Minor.*
Trōja, ae, *f.*, *Troy, the city in Asia*
Trōjānus, a, um, *adj.*, *Trojan, of Troy.*
tŭĕor, tŭĭtus, 2, *v. dep.*, *I gaze, guard,*
tum, *adv* and *conj.*, *then.* [*protect.*
turpis, e, *adj.*, *base, disgraceful.*
turpĭtŭdo, ĭnis, *f.*, *disgrace.*
turris, is, *f.*, *a tower.*
tūtus, a, um, *adj.*, *safe.*
tŭus, a, um, *pron. adj.*, *thy, thine.*
tўrannus, i, *m.*, *a despot, tyrant.*

Ŭbi, *adv.*, *where.*

ULLUS.

XERXES.

ullus, a, um, *adj.* (*gen. sing.* īŭs, *dat. sing.* ī), *any.*   [*side of, beyond.*

ultrā, *prep.* with acc., *on the farther*

unquam, *adv., at any time, ever.*

ūnus, a, um, *adj.* (*gen. sing.* īŭs, *dat. sing.* ī), *one.*

urbs, urbis, *f., a city.*

ŭt, *adv.* and *conj., that, in order that.* (See p. 97.)

ūter, rā, rum, *adj.* (*gen. sing.* īus, *dat. sing.* ī), *which of two.*

ūtĭlis, e, *adj., useful.*

ūtor, ūsus, 3, *v.* dep., *I use.*

uxor, ōris, *f., a wife.*

Vălĕo, ŭi, ĭtum, 2, *I am strong, in good*

vălēt ido, ĭnis, *f., health.*   [*health.*

vălĭdus, a, um, *adj., strong.*

vallis, is, *f., a valley.*

vărĭus, a, um, *adj., different, various.*

vasto, āvi, ātum, 1, *I lay waste.*

vectīgăl, ālis, *n., a tax.*

vĕhĕmenter, *adv., vehemently, warmly.*

vĕho, exi, ectum, 4, *I carry* (in pass., *I ride*).

Vēientes, um, *m. pl., the Veientes, the people of Veii, near Rome.*

vĕlox, ōcis, *adj., swift.*   [*worship.*

vĕnĕror, ātus, 1, *v. dep., I reverence,*

vĕnĭo, vēni, ventum, 4, *I come.*

vēnor, atus, 1, *v. dep., I hunt.*

ventĭto, āvi, 1, *v. freq., I come frequently.* [*quently.*

ventus, i, *m., the wind.*

Vĕnūsĭa, ae, *f., Venusia, a town in*

vēr, vēris, *n., the spring.*   [*Italy.*

vĕrĕor, ĭtus, 2, *v. dep., I fear, reverence.*

vērĭsĭmilis, e, *adj., likely, probable.*

versus, ūs, *m., a line, verse.*

versŭs, *prep.* with acc., *towards* (*only of place or direction*).

vērus, a, um, *adj., true.*

vescor, 3, *v. dep., I feed, live on.*

vespĕrascit, āvit, ascĕre, *v. impers., evening approaches.*

Vesta, ae, *f., Vesta, the goddess of fire and the hearth.*   [*yours.*

vestĕr, tra, trum, *pronom. adj., your,*

vestĭmentum, i, *n., clothing.*

vestĭo, īvi or ĭi, ĭtum, 4, *I clothe*

vestis, is, *f., clothing, a garment.*

vĕtus, vĕtĕris, *adj., old.*

vexo, āvi, ātum, 1, *I vex, harass.*

vĭa, ae, *f., a way, road.*

victor, ōris, *m., a conqueror.*

victōrĭa, ae, *f., victory.*

vĭdĕo, vīdi, visum, 2, *I see.*

vĭdĕor, vīsus, 2, *I seem, appear.*

vĭgĭlo, āvi, ātum, 1, *I watch, I am* [*awake.*

vīlis, e, *adj., cheap, common.*

vincĭo, nxi, nctum, 4, *I bind.*

vinco, vīci, victum, 3, *I conquer.*

vincŭlum, i, *n., a chain, bond.*

vīnum, i, *n., wine.*

virgo, ĭnis, *f., a maiden.*

vir, vĭri, *m., a man.*

virtus, ūtis, *f., valour, virtue.*   [*view.*

vīso, si, sum, 3, *v. freq., I look at often,*

vīsus, ūs, *m., a seeing, looking, look.*

vīta, ae, *f., life.*

vītŭpĕro, āvi, ātum, 1, *I blame, find fault with.*

vīvo, vixi, victum, 3, *I live.*

vix, *adv., scarcely.*

vŏlo, āvi, ātum, 1, *I fly.*

vŏlo, vŏlŭi, vellĕ, *v. irreg., I wish, am*

vŏluntas, ātis, *f., a wish, will.* [*willing.*

vŏluptas, tātis, *f., pleasure.*

vox, vōcis, *f., a voice.*

vulnĕro, āvi, ātum, 1, *I wound*

vulnus, ĕris, *n., a wound.*

vultur, ŭris, *m., a vulture.*

vultus, ūs, *m., countenance, looks.*

Xĕnŏphōn, ontis, *m., Xenophon, an Athenian.*

Xerxes, is, *m., Xerxes, a famous king of Persia.*

INDEX II. TO VOCABULARIES.

ENGLISH WORDS.

———◆———

as far as, tĕnŭs, *prep.* with *abl.* and *gen.*
as soon as, sĭmŭl atque (ac).
ascertain, cognosco, ōvi, ĭtum, 3.
ask, rŏgo, avi, atum, 1.
assault, oppugno, avi, atum, 1.
assign, trĭbuo, ŭi, ūtum, 3.
assist, adjŭvo, jūvi, jūtum, 1.
assistance, auxĭlium, ii, *n.*
assuage, mollio, īvi, ītum, 4.
at, ăd, *prep.* with *acc.*
Athenian, Athēnĭensis, e, *adj.*
Athens, Athēnae, arum, *f.*
attack (*subs.*), impĕtus, us, *m.*
attack (*verb*), oppugno, avi, atum, 1.
attain to, ădĭpiscor, eptus, 3.
attempt, cōnor, atus, 1.
attentive, attentus, a, um, *adj.*
attentively, attentē, *adv.*
author, scriptor, ōris, *m.*
authority, auctōrĭtas, ātis, *f.*
autumn, auctumnus, i, *m.*
awake, to be, vĭgĭlo, avi, atum. 1.

Bad, mălus, a, um, *adj.*
bank, rīpa, ae, *f.*
base, turpis, e, *adj.*
battle, pugna, ae, *f.*; proelĭum, ii, *n.*
be, to, sum, fui, esse, p. 29.
— in, among, &c. see compounds of sum,
beam, trabs, trăbis, *f.*   [p. 31.
bear, fĕro, tŭli, lātum, p. 80.
— through, perfĕro, etc.
beast, bestia, ae, *f.*
beast, great, bellua, ae, *f.*
beast, small, bestiola, ae, *f.*
beautiful, pulcher, ra, rum, *adj.*
because, quĭă, quŏd, *conj.*
because of, ŏb, propter, *prepp.* with *acc.*
become, fĭo, p. 84.
becomes, it, dĕcet, p. 86.
before, antĕ, *prep.* with *acc.*; prae, *prep.*
beg, pĕto, īvi and ĭi, ītum, 3. [with *abl.*
begin, incĭpĭo, cēpi, ceptum, 3.
beginning, ĭnĭtium, ii, *n.*
behalf of, on, prō, *prep.* with *abl.*
behind, pōnĕ, *prep.* with *acc.*
behoves, it, ŏportet, p. 86.
believe, crēdo, dĭdi, dĭtum, 3.   [*abl.*
beneath, sŭb, subtĕr, *prep.* with *acc* and
beside, praetĕr, *prep.* with *acc.*
besiege, obsĭdeo, sēdi, sessum, 2.

between, inter, *prep.* with *acc.*
beyond, ultrā, *prep.* with *acc.*
bind, vincio, xi, nctum, 4.
bird, ăvis, is, *f.*
black, nĭger, gra, grum; āter, tra, trum.
blame, culpo, avi, atum, 1
—, subs., culpa, ae, *f.*
blockade, obsĭdio, ōnis, *f*
blood, sanguis, ĭnis, *m.*
bloom, flōreo, ui, —, 2.
blossom forth, efflōresco, flŏrui, 3.
blow, flo, avi, atum, 1.
body, corpus, ŏris, *n.*
bold, audax, ācis, *adj.*
bond, vincŭlum, i, *n.*
bone, ŏs, ossis, *n.*
book, lĭber, bri, *m.*
booty, praeda, ae, *f.*
born, be, nascor, nātus, 3.
boundary, fīnis, is, *m*
boy, pŭer, ĕri, *m.*
bow, arcus, us, *m.*
brave, fortis, e, *adj.*
bravely, fortĭtĕr, *adv*
bridge, pons, tis, *m.*
bright, splendĭdus, a, um, *adj.*
bring, fĕro, p. 80.
— in, &c. see compounds of fero, p. 81.
— to an end, fĭnio, ivi, ĭtum, 4; confĭcio, fēci, fectum, 3.
bring forth, părio, pĕpĕri, partum, 3.
Britain, Brĭtannia, ae, *f.*
Briton, Brĭtannus, i, *m.*
broad, lātus, a, um, *adj.*
brother, frāter, tris, *m.*
build, aedĭfĭco, avi, atum, 1.
building, aedĭfĭcium, ii, *n.*
bull, taurus, i, *m.*
bury, sĕpĕlio, īvi, pultum, 4.
burden, ŏnus, ĕris, *n.*
burn, intrans., ardeo, si, sum, 2.
burnt down, to be, dēflagro, avi, atum, 1.
business, nĕgōtium, ii, *n.*
busy, occŭpātus, a, um, *adj.*
but, sĕd, autem; see *Vocab.* 21.
buy, ĕmo, ēmi, emptum, 3.
by, ā, ăb, *prep.* with *abl.*

Call, vŏco, avi, atum, 1.
— together, convŏco, avi, atum, 1.
— to mind, rĕcordor, atus, 1.

CALM.

calm, tranquillus, a, um, *adj.*
camp, castra, orum, *pl. n.*
can, possum, p. 76.
cannot, nĕqueo, īvi, ĭi, ĭtum, 4.
cannot but, I, făcĕrĕ nōn possum quīn.
care, take, cūro, avi, atum, 1.
careful, dilĭgens, ntis, *adj.*
carefully, dīlĭgenter, *adv.*
carry, perto, avi, atum, 1.
carry on, gĕro, essi, estum, 3.
carry a wall, mūrum dūco, xi, ctum, 3.
Carthage, Carthāgo, ĭnis, *f.*
Carthaginian, *subs.*, Poenus, i, *m.*
—— *adj.*, Carthāgĭniensis, e.
cast away, abjĭcio, ēci, ectum, 3.
cast forth, out, ējĭcio, ēci, ectum, 3.
cast down, dējĭcio, ēci, ectum ; affligo,
  xi, ctum, 3.
catch, căpio, cēpi, captum, 3.
Catiline, Cătĭlīna, ae, *m.*
cause, causa, ae, *f.*
cavalry, ĕquĭtātus, us, *m.*
celebrated, clārus, a, um, *adj.*
century, centūria, ae, *f.*
certain, certus, a, um, *adj.*
chain, vincŭlum, i, *n.*
chance, cāsus, us, *m.*
chance, by, fortĕ cāsū.
change, mūto, avi, atum, 1.
charge, mando, avi, atum, 1.
chariot, currus, us, *m.*
chastise, castīgo, avi, atum, 1.
cheap, vīlis, e, *adj.*
cheer, exhĭlăro, avi, atum,
cheerful, hĭlăris, e, *adj.*
cheese, cāseus, i, *m.*
cherish, cŏlo, ui, cultum, 3.
cherry, cĕrăsum, i, *n.*
cherry-tree, cĕrăsus, i, *f.*
children, lībĕri, orum, *m.*
Cimbrians, Cimbri, orum, *m.*
citadel, arx, arcis, *f.*
citizen, cīvis, is, *c.*
citizenship, cīvĭtas, ātis, *f.*
city, urbs, bis, *f.*
civil, belonging to a citizen, cīvilis, e,
clear, clārus, a, um, *adj.*   [*adj.*
cloak, pallium, ii, *n.*
clothe, vestio, īvi, ītum, 4.
clothing, vestis, is, *f.* ; vestīmentum, i, *n.*
cloud, nūbes, is, *f.*

CRUSH.

coast, ōra, ae, *f.*
cohort, cŏhors, rtis, *f.*
cold, frīgus, ŏris, *n.*
colony, cŏlōnia, ae, *f.*
colour, cŏlor, ōris, *m.*
come, vĕnio, vēni, ventum, 4.
—— frequently, ventĭto, avi, atum, 1.
—— to pass, fīo, factus, fĭĕri.
commander, impĕrātor, ōris, *m*
commission, mandātum, i, *n.*
common, commūnis, e ; vīlis, e, *adj.*
commonly, fĕrĕ, *adv.*
commonwealth, respublĭca ; see p. 22.
companion, cŏmes, ĭtis, *c.*
comparison, in, prae, *prep.* with acc.
comrade, sŏcius, ii, *m.*
concerning, dē, *prep.* with *abl.*
confess, făteor, fassus ; confĭteor, fessus,
conflagration, incendium, ii, *n.*   [2.
conquer, vinco, vīci, victum, 3.
conqueror, victor, ōris, *m.*
conscience, conscientia, ae, *f.*
conspiracy, conjūrātio, ōnis, *f.*
constellation, sīdus, ĕris, *n.*
consul, consul, ŭlis, *m.*
——, office of, consŭlātus, us, *m.*
consult, consŭlo, lui, ltum, 3.
consume, absūmo, sumpsi, sumptum, 3.
contemplate, contemplor, atus, 1.
contented, contentus, a, um, *adj.*
continual, perpĕtuus, a, um, *adj.*
contrary to, contrā, *prep.* with *acc.*
converse, collŏquor, lŏcūtus, 3.
Corinth, Cŏrinthus, i, *f.*
correct, corrĭgo, exi, ectum, 3.
counsel, consĭlium, ii, *n.*
count, nŭmĕro, avi, atum, 1.
countenance, vultus, us, *m.*
country, one's, patria, ae, *f.*
cover, tĕgo, xi, ctum, 3.
cowardice, ignāvia, ae, *f.*
create, crĕo, avi, atum, 1.
creator, crĕātor, ōris, *m.*
credible, crēdĭbĭlis, e, *adj.*
Crete, Crēta, ae, *f.*
crime, scĕlus, ĕris, *n.*
crop, messis, is, *f.*
cross over, transeo, p. 83.
crown, cŏrōna, ae, *f.*
cruel, crūdēlis, e, *adj.*
crush, opprĭmo, essi, essum, 3.

M

CRY OUT.

cry out, clāmo, exclāmo, avi, atum, 1.
cultivate, cŏlo, cŏlui, cultum, 3.
—— carefully, excŏlo, etc.
curb, cŏŏrceo, ui, ĭtum, 2.
current, flūmen, ĭnis, n.
custom, consuētūdo, ĭnis, f.
out off, interclūdo, si, sum, 3.

Dance, salto, avi, atum, 1.
danger, pĕrīcŭlum, i, n.
dangerous, perīcŭlōsus, a, um, adj.
dare, audeo, p. 85.
daring, audax, ācis, adj.
daringly, audactĕr, adv.
darken, obscūro, avi, atum, 1.
dart, tēlum, i, n.
daughter, fīlia, ae, f.
day, dĭes, ēi, m. and f.
dead, mortuus, a, um, adj.
deal with, tracto, avi, atum, 1.
dear, cārus, a, um, adj.
death, mors, rtis, f.
deceive, dēcĭpio, cēpi, ceptum, 3.
deed, bold, daring, fácĭnus, ŏris, n.
deep, altus, a, um, adj.
defeat, clādes, is, f.
defend, dēfendo, i, sum, 3.
defendant, rēus, i, m.
delicate, tĕnuis, e, adj.
delight, dēlecto, avi, atum, 1.
delightful, dulcis, suāvis, e, adj.
delightfully, jūcundē, adv.
deliver, lībĕro, avi, atum, 1.
demand, postŭlo, avi, atum, 1.
deny, nĕgo, avi, atum, 1.
depart, excēdo, cessi, cessum, 3; migro,
    ēmigro, avi, atum, 1.
deplore, dēplōro, avi, atum, 1.
deserve, mĕreor, ĭtus, 2.
desire, cŭpio, īvi and ĭi, ĭtum, 3. [ātis, f.
——, subs., stŭdium, ii, n.; căpĭdĭtas,
despise, contemno, mpsi, mptum, 3;
    aspernor, atus, 1.
despot, tȳrannus, i, m.
destitute, ĭnops, ŏpis, adj.
destroy, perdo, dĭdi, dĭtum, 3.
destruction, exĭtium, ii, n.
destructive, pernĭcĭōsus, a, um, adj.
deter, dēterreo, ui, itum, 2.
determine, constĭtuo, ŭi, ūtum, 3.

EAR.

devote one's self, ŏpĕram do, dĕdi, dăt
    dăre, 1.
devoted to, addictus, a, um, adj.
die, mŏrior, mortuus, 3.
difficult, diffĭcĭlis, e, adj.
difficult, somewhat, subdiffĭcĭlis, e, adj.
dig, fŏdio, fōdi, fossum, 3.
diligence, dĭlĭgentia, ae, f.
diligent, dĭlĭgens, ntis, adj.
dine, coeno, avi, atum.
disaster, clādes, is, f.
discern, cerno, crēvi, crētum, 3.
discharge, fungor, nctus, 3, p. 71.
discourse, sermo, ōnis, m.
discover, dĕtĕgo, xi, ctum, 3.
disease, morbus, i, m.
disembark, trans., expōno, pŏsui,
disgrace, turpĭtūdo, ĭnis, f.   [tum,
disgraceful, turpis, e, adj.
disgusts, it, taedet, p. 86.
dishonest, imprŏbus, a, um, adj.
dishonesty, fraus, dis, f.
dismiss, dīmitto, mīsi, missum, 3.
displease, displĭceo, ui, ĭtum, 2, with
disposed, affectus, a, um, adj.   [dat
distance, longinquĭtas, ātis, f.
distant, longinquus, a, um, adj.
——, to be, absum, p. 31.
distinguished, insignis, e; ēgrĕgius, s,
distrust, diffīdo, īsus, 3, p. 85. [um, adj.
disturb, turbo, avi, atum, 1; mŏveo,
ditch, fossa, ae, f.   [mōvi, mōtum, 2.
divide, sēpăro, avi, atum, 1; dīvĭdo, ĭsi,
divine, dīvīnus, a, um, adj.   [īsum, 3.
do, fácio, fēci, factum, 3.
dog, cănis, is, c.
doubt, dŭbĭto, avi, atum, 1.
doubtful, dŭbius, a, um, adj.
dove, cŏlumba, ae, f.
drag, draw, trăho, xi, ctum, 3.
draw together, contrăho, xi, ctum, 3.
draw up in order, instruo, xi, ctum, 3.
drink, bĭbo, i, ĭtum, 3.
drive out, expello, pŭli, pulsum, 3.
duty, mūnus, ĕris, n.
dwell, hăbĭto, avi, atum, 1.

Eager after, stŭdiōsus, a, um, adj. with
eager, be, stŭdeo, uī, —, 2.   [gen
eagle, ăquĭla, ae, f
ear, auris, is, f.

EARNESTLY.

arnestly, věhěmentěr, magnŏpěrě, *adv.*
arth, terra, ae, *f.*
asily, făcĭlě, *adv.*
asy, făcĭlis, e, *adj.*
at, ědo, ēdi, ēsum, 3.
educate, ēdŭco, avi, atum, 1.
legant, ēlěgans, ntis, *adj.*
lephant, ělěphantus, i, *m.*
loquent, ēlŏquens, ntis, *adj.* [sum, 3.
mbark, nāvem (naves) conscendo, di,
mbroider, pingo, nxi, ctum, 3.
minent, exĭmius, ēgrěgius, a, um, *adj.*
v pire, impěrium, ii, *n.*
 ploy, ădhĭbeo, ui, ĭtum, 2.
 ourage, hortor, atus, 1.
 l, fĭnis, is, *m.*
 l, put to, finio, ivi, ĭtum, 4.
 dure, pătior, passus, 3; fěro, p. 80.
 emy (public), hostis, is, *c*
 —, *personal*, ĭnĭmīcus, i, *m.*
ngaged, occŭpātus, a, um, *adj.*
njoy, fruor, ĭtus and ctus, 3, with *abl.*
mmity, ĭnĭmīcĭtia, ae, *f.*
mough, sătĭs, *adv.*
nquire, quaero, quaesīvi, quaesītum, 3.
nter, intro, avi, atum, 1.
ntice, lăcio (*obs.*).
ntreat, ōro, avi, atum, 1.
nvy, invĭdia, ae, *f.*
pistle, ěpistŏla, ae, *f.*
steem, dilĭgo, exi, ectum, 3.
sternal, aeternus, a, um, *adj.*
Europe, Eurōpa, ae, *f.*
ven, adj., aequus, a, um.
—, *conj.*, ětiam.
vening comes on, vespěrascit, p. 87.
ver = at any time, unquam, *adv.*
— *= at all times*, semper, *adv.*
very, omnis, e, *adj.*
every day, quŏtīdĭě, *adv.*
very one, quisque, quaeque, quodque,
 and *subst.* quicque (quidque), *pron.*
vident, it is, constat, stĭtit, 1.
vil, an, mălum, i, *n.*
xample, exemplum, i, *n.* [e, *adj.*
xcellent, praestans, antis; prestăbĭlis,
xcept, praeter, *prep.* with *acc.*
xercise, to, exerceo, ui, ĭtum, 2.
xhibit, prăebeo, ui, ĭtum, 2.
xhort, hortor, ădhortor, atus, 1.
ile, exĭlium, ii, *n.*

FLEET.

exile, live in, exĭlium ăgo, ēgi, actum, 3.
experienced, pěrītus, a, um, *adj.*
extend, prŏfěro, tŭli, lătum, ferre, 3.
eye, ŏcŭlus, i, *m.*

Fable, fābŭla, ae, *f.*
fall, cădo, cěcĭdi, cāsum, 3.
faith, fĭdes, ěi, *f.*
faithful, fĭdēlis, e; fĭdus, a, um, *adj.*
far, longē, *adv.*
—— *and wide*, longē lātēquě.
farther, too far, longius, *adv. comp.*
father, păter, tris, *m.*
father-in-law, sŏcer, ěri, *m.*
fault, culpa, ae, *f.*
fault find, vĭtŭpěro, culpo, avi, atum, 1.
favour, grātia, ae, *f.*
fear, mětus, us; tĭmor, ōris, *m.*
fear, to, mětuo, i, ūtum, 3; tĭmeo, ui, —,
feeble, dēbĭlis, e, *adj.* [2; věreor, ĭtus, 2.
feed on, vescor, —, i, 3.
feel, sentio, si, sum, 4.
feign, sĭmŭlo, avi, atum, 1.
fellow-citizen, cīvis, is, *c.*
fellow-soldier, commīlĭto, ōnis, *m.*
few, paucus, a, um, *adj.*
fidelity, fĭdes, ěi, *f.*
field, ăger, gri, *m.*
fierce, fěrox, ōcis, *adj.*
fiery, made of fire, igneus, a, um, *adj.*
fig, fig-tree, fĭcus, i, *f.*
fight, pugno, avi, atum, 1.
fight (a battle), committo, mīsi, missum, 3.
find, rěpěrio, pěri, pertum, 4; invěnio,
 vēni, ventum, 4.
find fault with, culpo, vĭtŭpěro, avi,
 atum, 1.
finish, confĭcio, fēci, fectum, 3.
finished, perfectus, a, um, *adj.*
fire, ignis, is, *m.*
—— *= conflagration*, incendium, i, *n.*
fire, be on, ardeo, si, sum, 2.
first (adv.), prīmo, prīmum, *adv.*
first-rate, prīmārius, a, um, *adj.*
fish, piscis, is, *m.*
fix, fīgo, xi, xum, 3.
flatter, ădūlor, atus, 1.
flattery, ădūlātio, ōnis, *f.*
flee, fŭgio, fūgi, fŭgĭtum, 3.
flee to, confŭgio, etc.
fleet, classis, is, *f.*

M 2

FLESH.

flesh, căro, carnis, *f.*
flower, flos, ōris, *m.*
follow, sĕquor, secūtus, 3.
follow up, subsĕquor, etc.
folly, stultĭtia, ae, *f.*
foolish, stultus, a, um, *adj.*
foot-soldier, pĕdĕs, ĭtis, *m.*
for (*prep.*), pro, *prep.* with *abl.*
——— (*conj.*), nam, ĕnim, *conj.*
forage, pābŭlor, atus, 1.
forced marches, maxĭma ĭtĭnĕra (ĭter).
forces, cōpiae, arum, *pl. f.*
forehead, frons, tis, *f.*
foresee, prōvĭdeo, vīdi, vīsum, 2.
forget, oblīviscor, lītus, 3, with *gen.*
form (*a plan*), ĭneo, p. 83.
former, pristĭnus, a, um ; prior, us, *adj.*
formerly, ōlim, quondam, *adv.*
fortification,   munīmentum,   i,   *n.* ;
    moenia, um, *pl. n.*
fortify, mūnio, ĭvi, ĭtum, 4.
fortune, fortūna, ae, *f.*
fortunate, fēlix, īcis, *adj.*
fountain, fons, ntis, *m.*
frame, to, fabrĭco, avi, atum, 1.
free, līber, ĕra, ĕrum, *adj.*
freedom, lībertas, ātis, *f.*
freely, lībĕrē, *adv.*
friend, ămīcus, i, *m.*
friendship, ămīcĭtia, ae, *f.*
frighten, terreo, ui, ĭtum, 2.
from, ā (ăb), dē, *prep.* with *abl.*
fruit, fructus, us, *m.*
full, plēnus, a, um, *adj.*
function, mūnus, ĕris, *n.*
funeral, fūnus, ĕris, *n.*
furnish = *supply,* praebeo, ui, ĭtum, 2.

gain = *get, obtain,* păro, avi, atum, 1.
game, lūdus, i, *m.*
garden, hortus, i, *m.*
garment, vestis, is, *f.* ; vestīmentum, i, *n.*
gate, porta, ae, *f.*
gather, lĕgo, lēgi, lectum, 3.
——— *together,* contrăho, xi, ctum, 3.
Gaul, Gallia, ae, *f.*
gaze, tueor, ĭtus and tūtus, 2.
general, impĕrātor, ōris, *m.*   [eptus, 3.
get, gain, păro, avi, atum, 1 ; ădĭpiscor,
get back, rĕcŭpĕro, avi, atum, 1.
get together, cōgo, cŏēgi, cŏactum, 3.

HAVE.

gift, dōnum, i, *n.*
girl, pŭella, ae, *f.*
give, do, dĕdi, dătum, dăre, 1.
glide, lābor, lapsus, 3.
glory, glōria, ae, *f.*
go, eo, *see* p. 82.
——— *in, out, &c.,* see comps. of eo, p. 83.
——— *to see,* vīso, i, um, 3.
God, Deus, i, *m.,* p. 22.
goddess, dea, ae, *f.*
gods, of the, dīvīnus, a, um, *adj.*
gold, aurum, i, *n.*
golden, aureus, a, um, *adj.*
good, bŏnus, prŏbus, a, um, *adj.*
good, subs., bŏnum, i, *n.*
good, do, prōsum, p. 7.
goods, bŏna, ōrum, *pl. n.*
govern, gŭberno, avi, atum, 1.
grandfather, ăvus, i, *m.*
grass, grāmen, ĭnis, *n.*
great, magnus, a, um, *adj.*
great, how, quantus, a, um, *rel. adj.*
greatly, magnŏpĕrĕ, *adv.*
Greece, Graecia, ae, *f.*
Greek, Grecian, Graecus, a, um, *adj.*
grief, dŏlor, ōris, *m.*
grieves, it, pĭget, p. 86.
grievously, grăvĭtĕr, *adv.*
ground, hŭmus, i, *f.*
guard, to, custōdio, īvi, ītum, 4 ; tŭeor.
guardian, custos, ōdis, *m.*   [ĭtus, 2
guilt, scĕlus, ĕris, *n.*
guilty, noxius, a, um, *adj.*

Habit, consuētūdo, ĭnis, *f.*
hails, it, grandĭnat, p. 87.
hand, mănus, us, *f.*
hand down, trādo, prōdo, dĭdi, dĭtum, 3.
handle, tracto, avi, atum, 1.
happen, fīo, p. 84.
happy, bĕātus, a, um, *adj.*
happily, bĕātē, *adv.*
harass, vexo, avi, atum, 1.
harbour, portus, us, *m.*
hard, durus, a, um, *adj.*
hardship, lăbor, ōris, *m.*
hare, lĕpus, ōris, *m.*
hasten, contendo, di, sum & tum, 3.
hatred, ŏdium, ii, *n.*
have, hăbeo, ui, ĭtum, 2.
———, *rather, prefer,* mălo, p. 77.

HEAD.

head, căpŭt, ĭtis, *n.*

——, *be at the*, praesum, p. 31.

health, vălētūdo, ĭnis, *f.*

health, be in, văleo, ui, itum, 2.

heap up, extruo, xi, ctum, 3.

hear, audio, ivi, itum, 4.

hearing, audītus, us, *m.*

heart, cŏr, dis, *n.*

heat, călor, ōris, *m.*

heaven, coelum, ĭ, *n.*

heavenly, belonging to the heavens, coe-

heavily, grăvĭter, *adv.*   [lestis, e, *adj.*

heavy, grăvis, e, *adj.*

help, adjŭvo, jūvi, jūtum, 1.

helpless, ĭners, ertis, *adj*

high, altus, a, um, *adj.*

——, *very*, praealtus, a, um, *adj.*

highest, summus, a, um, *adj. sup.*

his, hers, gen. of is, ea : when referring

   to subj., sŭus, a, um, *adj. pron.*

hold a levy, dēlectum hăbeo, ui, itum, 2.

hold together, contĭneo, ui, entum, 2.

honesty, prŏbĭtas, ātis, *f.*

honour, hŏnŏr, ōris, *m.*

hope, spēro, avĭ, atum, 1.

——, *subs.*, spes, ēi, *f.*

hoped for, sperātus, a, um, *adj*

horn, cornu, us, *n.*

horse, ĕquus, i, *m.*

horse-soldier, ĕquĕs, ĭtis, *m.*

hostage, obsĕs, ĭdis, *c.*

hour, hōra, ae, *f.*

house, dŏmus, *see* p. 22.

how great, quantus, a, um, *rel. adj.*

how many, quŏt, *indecl. rel. adj.*

human, hūmānus, a, um, *adj.*

hunger, fămes, is, *f.*

hunt, vēnor, atus, 1.

hurt, harm, nŏceo, ui, itum, 2, with *dat.*;

   obsum, 2, with *dat.*

hurtful, noxius, a, um, *adj.*

hurtful, to be, obsum, p. 31.

husbandman, agrĭcŏla, ae, *m.*

If, sī, *conj.*

if, as, quăsĭ, *conj.*

ignorance, ignōrātio, ōnis, *f.*

ignorant of (be), ignōro, avi, atum, 1.

ill, adj., mălus, a, um, *adj.*

——, *adv.*, mălĕ, *adv.*

illness, morbus, i, *m.*

JUDGMENT.

ill-will, invĭdia, ae, *f.*

ill-wishing, malĕvŏlus, a, um, *adj.*

image, ĭmāgo, ĭnis, *f.*; sĭmŭlăcrum, i, *n.*

imitate, ĭmĭtor, atus, 1.

immediately, stătim, *adv.*

immense, ingens, tis, *adj.*

immortal, immortālis, e, *adj.*

immortality, immortālĭtas, ātis, *f.*

impair, infringo, frēgi, fractum, 3.

impiety, impious, nĕfas, *indec. subs.*

improve, ēmendo, avi, atum, 1.

imprudence, imprūdentia, ae, *f.*

in, into, ĭn, *prep.* with *acc.* and *abl.*

indeed, quĭdem, *conj.*

indolence, ignāvia, ae; segnĭties, ĕi, *f.*

indolently, ignāvĕ, *adv.*

indulge, indulgeo, si, sum, 2, with *dat.*

industrious, industrius, a, um, *adj.*

infamous, infāmis, e, *adj.*

infamy, infāmia, ae, *f.*

infantry, pĕdĭtātus, us, *m.*

inferior, infĕrior, us, *adj. comp*

infinite, infinītus, a, um, *adj.*

infirm, dēbĭlis, e, *adj.*

inhabitant, incŏla, ae, *c.*   [2, with *dat.*

injure, obsum, p. 31 ; nŏceo, ui, itum,

injurious, noxius, a, um, *adj.*

innumerable, innŭmĕrus, a, um, *adj.*

inquire, rŏgo, avi, atum, 1 ; quaero,

   quaesīvi, quaesītum, 3.

insect, bestiŏla, ae, *f.*

institute, instĭtuo, ui, ūtum, 3.

instrument, instrūmentum, i, *n.*

integrity, prŏbĭtas, ātis, *f.*

intellect, mens, tis, *f.*

intercept, interclūdo, si, sum, 3.

invent, rĕpĕrio, pĕri, pertum, 4.

iron, ferrum, i, *n.*

island, insŭla, ae, *f.*

Italy, Itălia, ae, *f.*

its, sŭus, a, um, *adj. pron.*

Join, jungo, xi, ctum, 3.

join (battle), proelium committo, misi,

   missum, 3.

journey, ĭter, ĭtĭnĕris, *n.*

joy, gaudium, ii, *n.*

joyful, laetus, a, um, *adj.*

judge, judex, ĭcis, *m.*

——, *verb*, jūdĭco, avi, atum, 1.

judgment, jŭdĭcium, ii, *n.*

M 3

just, justus, a, um, *adj.*
justly, justō, *adv.*

Keen, ācer, cris, cre, *adj.*
keep off, prŏhĭbeo, ui, ĭtum, 2.
keep guard, vĭgĭlo, avi, atum, 1.
kill, interfĭcio, fēci, fectum, 3.
kind, bĕnignus, a, um, *adj.*
kindly, bĕnignĕ, *adv.*
king, rex, rēgis, m.
——, *be*, regno, avi, atum, 1.
kingdom, regnum, i, n.
knee, gĕnu, us, m.
know, scio, īvi and ĭi, ĭtum, 4.
—— *not*, nescio, etc.
knowledge, scientia, prūdentia, ae, f.
——, *without*, clam, *prep.* with acc. and
known, nŏtus, a, um, *adj.*   [abl.

Labour, lăbor, ōris, m.
lake, lăcus, us, m.
lament over, dēplōro, avi, atum, 1.
land, terra, ae, f.; ăger, gri, m.
language, lingua, ae, f.
large, magnus, a, um, *adj.*
last day, suprēmus dies, m.
last, at, dēmum, *adv.*
Latin, Lătīnus, a, um, *adj.*
law, lex, lēgis, f.
lay waste, vasto, avi, atum, 1.
lay siege to, obsĭdeo, ēdi, essum, 2.
lead, dŭco, xi, ctum, 3.
lead across, transdūco. xi, ctum, 3.
lead out, ēdūco.
leader, dux, dŭcis, c.
learn, disco, dĭdĭci, —, 3.
learn in addition, addisco, etc.
—— = *ascertain*, cognosco, ōvi, ĭtum, 3.
learned, doctus, a, um, *adj.*
leave, rĕlinquo, īqui, ictum, 3.
leg, crūs, ūris, n.
legion, lĕgio, ōnis, f.
length, longĭtūdo, ĭnis, f.
lest, nĕ, p. 97.
lest, and, nēvĕ.
letter of the alphabet, lĭtĕra, ae, f.
letter (an epistle), lĭtĕrae, ārum; ĕpistŏla, ae, f.
letters, literature, lĭtĕrae, ārum, f.
levy, dēlectus, us, m.
liar, lying, mendax, ācis, *adj.*

lictor, lictor, ōris, m.
lie (on the ground), jăceo, ui, —, 2.
lie (to speak falsely), mentior, ītus, 4.
lieutenant, lēgātus, i, m.
life, vīta, ae, f.
light (adj.), lēvis, e, *adj.*
light (subs.), lux, lūcis, f.
light, it becomes, lūcescit, p. 87.
lightning, fulmen, ĭnis, n.
like, sĭmĭlis, e, *adj.*
likely, vērĭsĭmĭlis, e, *adj.*
likeness, ĭmāgo, ĭnis, f.
limit, fīnis, m.
limit, to, fīnio, īvi, ĭtum, 4.
line of battle, ăcies, ēi, f.
lion, leo, ōnis, m.
little, parvus, a, um, *adj.*
live, vīvo, vixi, victum, 3.
live on, vescor, i, 3.
live in exile, exĭlium ago, ēgi, actum, 3.
Livy, Līvius, ii, m.
load, ŏnus, ĕris, n.
lofty, celsus, a, um, *adj.*
long (adj.), longus, a, um, *adj.*
long (adv.), dĭū, *adv.*
look at, specto, avi, atum, 1.
look upon or into, intueor, tuĭtus and
looks, vultus, us, m.   [tūtus, 2.
loosen, solvo, solvi, sŏlūtum, 3.
lord, dŏmĭnus, i, m.
lot, sors, rtis, f.   [lectum, 3.
love, ămo, avi, atum, 1; dĭlĭgo, lexi,
love in return, rĕdămo, avi, atum, 1.
lovely, ămābĭlis, e, *adj*
low, hŭmĭlis, e, *adj.*
lower, infĕrior, us, *adj. comp.*
luckily, fēlīcĭtĕr, *adv.*
lucky, fēlix, īcis, *adj.*

Macedonian, Măcĕdo, ŏnis, m.
made, factus, affectus, a, um, *part.* and
madness, fŭror, ōris, m.   [adj.
magistrate, măgistrātus, us, m.
magnificent, magnĭfĭcus, a, um, *adj*
maiden, virgo, ĭnis, f.
maintain, servo, avi, atum, 1.
make, făcio, fēci, factum, 3.
man, hŏmo, c.; vir, vĭri, m.
manage, gĕro, gessi, gestum, 3.
manifest, mănĭfestus, a, um, *adj.*
maniple, mănĭpŭlus, i, m.

MANNER.

manner, mos, mōris, *m.*
many, multus, a, um, *adj.*
many, how, quŏt, *indec. rel. adj.*
many, very, permulti, ae, a, *adj.*
marble, marmor, ŏris, *n.*
market-place, fŏrum, i, *n.*
master, dŏmĭnus, i, *m.*; măgister, tri, *m.*
measure, to, mētior, mensus, 4.
meditate, mĕdĭtor, atus, 1.
meet, ŏbeo, īvi and ĭi, ĭtum, 4.
mellow, mollia, e, *adj.*
membrane, membrāna, ae, *f.*
memorable, mĕmŏrābĭlis, e, *adj.*
memory, mĕmŏria, ae, *f.*
metal, mĕtallum, i, *n.*
migrate, migro, avi, atum, 1
mild, mītis, e, *adj.*
milk, lac, lactis, *n.*
mind, mens, ntis, *f.*
mindful, mĕmor, ŏris, *adj.*
miserable, mĭser, a, um, *adj.*
mistake, error, ōris, *m.*
——, *make a*, erro, avi, atum, 1.
mistress, dŏmĭna, ae, *f.*
money, pĕcūnia, ae, *f.*
month, mensis, is, *m.*
monument, mŏnŭmentum, i, *n.*
moon, lūna, ae, *f.*
more, plus, plūris, *neut. adj.; in pl.*
mortal, mortālis, e, *adj.* [plūres, a.
mother, māter, tris, *f.*
mound, agger, ĕris, *m.*
mount, to, conscendo, di, sum, 3.
mountain, mons, ntis, *m.*
mouth, ōs, ōris, *n.*
move, mŏveo, mŏvi, mōtum, 2.
much, multus, a, um, *adj.*
multitude, multĭtūdo, ĭnis, *f.*
my (mine), meus, a, um *adj. pron.*

Name, nōmen, ĭnis, *n.*
narrow, angustus, a, um, *adj.*
native-land, patria, ae, *f.*
nature, nātūra, ae, *f.*
naval, nāvālis, e, *adj.*
near to (prep.), prŏpĕ, *adv.*
near (adj.), prŏpinquus, a, um, *adj.*
necessary, nĕcessārius, a, um, *adj.*
necessity, nĕcessĭtas, ātis, *f.*
need, ŏpus, *indec. subs.*, with *abl.* and
needful, nĕcessārius, a, um, *adj.* [adj.

OWE.

needle, ăcus, us, *f.*
neither, neuter, tra, trum, *indef. pron.*
neither, nor, nĕquĕ, nec, *conj.*
nest, nīdus, i, *m.*
net, rēte, is, *n.*
never, nunquam, *adv.*
new, nŏvus, a, um, *adj.*
next, proxĭmus, a, um, *adj. sup.*
night, nox, ctis, *f.*
nightingale, lŭscĭnia, ae, *f.*
no, none, nullus, a, um, *indef. pron.*
noble, nōbĭlis, e, *adj.*
nobody, no one, nēmo, ĭnis, *c.*
not, nōn, haud, *adv.*
nothing, nĭhil, *indec. subs.*
nourish, nūtrio, īvi, ītum, 4.
now, nunc, jam, *adv.*
number, nŭmĕrus, i, *m.*
nurture, nutrio, īvi, ītum, 4.

Oak, quercus, us, *f.*
oath, jusjūrandum, *see p.* 22.
obey, păreo, ui, itum, 2; ŏbēdio, īvi,
  ītum, 4, with *dat.*
object, rĕcūso, avi, atum, 1.
obscure, obscūrus, a, um, *adj.*
observe (carefully), contemplor, atus, 1.
obtain, păro, avi, atum, 1; ădĭpiscor,
  eptus, 3.
—— *possession of*, pŏtior, ītus, 4.
ocean, ōcĕănus, i, *m.*
often, saepĕ, *adv.*
often, very, saepissĭmĕ, *adv.*
oftentimes, saepĕnŭmĕro, *adv.*
old, sĕnex, sĕnis (of persons only);
old age, sĕnectūs, ūtis, *f.* [vĕtus, ĕris, adj
olden, antīquus, a, um, *adj.*
one, ūnus, a, um, *adj.*
one of the two, alter, a, um, *indef. pron.*
only, sōlum, *adv.*
onset, impĕtus, us, *m.*
oppose, resisto, stĭti, stĭtum, 3; oppugno,
  avi, atum, 1, with *dat.*
oracle, ōrācŭlum, i, *n.*
oration, ōrātio, ōnis, *f.*
orator, ōrātor, ōris, *m.*
order, jŭbeo, jussi, jussum, 2. [ōris, n.
ornament, ornāmentum, i, n.; dĕcus,
other, of two, alter, a, um, *indef. pron.*
overcome, sŭpĕro, āvi, ātum, 1.
owe, ought, dēbeo, ui, itum, 2.

RAPACIOUS.

rapacious, răpax, ācis, *adj.*
rapid, răpĭdus, a, um, *adj.*
rare, rārus, a, um, *adj.*
rashness, tĕmĕrĭtas, ātis, *f.*
rather, have, mālo, p. 77.
read, lĕgo, lēgi, lectum, 3.
read aloud, rĕcĭto, avi, atum, 1.
read through, perlĕgo, lēgi, lectum, 3.
ready, părātus, a, um, *part.* and *adj.*
reason, rătio, ōnis, *f.*
receive, accĭpio, cēpi, ceptum, 3.
recklessness, tĕmĕrĭtas, ātis, *f.*
recover, rĕcŭpĕro, avi, atum, 1.
refresh, recreo, avi, atum, 1.
refuse, recūso, avi, atum, 1.
reign, regno, avi, atum, 1.
reject, aspernor, atus, 1.
rejoice, gaudeo, *see* p. 85.
relate, narro, avi, atum, 1.
remain, măneo, mansi, mansum, 2.
remain over, sŭpersum, p. 31.
remember, rĕmĭniscor, —, 3.
remembered, to be, mĕmŏrābĭlis, e, *adj.*
render assistance, auxĭlium fero, tŭli, lātum, ferre, 3, *irr.*
renowned, clārus, a, um, *adj.*
repents, it, poenĭtet, p. 86.
resist, resisto, stĭti, stĭtum, 3, with *dat.*
resolve, constĭtuo, ŭi, ūtum, 3.
respect, to, observo, avi, atum, 1.
rest, the, cēter, ĕra, ĕrum, *adj.*: usu. *pl.*
restrain, cŏerceo, ui, ĭtum, 2.
retire, cēdo, concēdo, cessi, cessum, 3.
return, rĕdeo, p. 83; rĕverto, ti, sum; rĕvertor, sus, 3.
reverence, to, vĕnĕror, atus, 1.
reward, praemium, ii, *n.*
Rhine, Rhēnus, i, *m.*
Rhodes, Rhŏdus, i, *f.*
Rhone, Rhŏdănus, i, *m.*
rich, dīves, ĭtis, *adj.*
riches, dīvĭtiae, arum, *pl. f.*
ride, to, vĕhor, vectus, 3.
right, rectus, a, um, *adj.*
rightly, prŏbē, rectē, *adv.*
rise, to, ŏrior, ortus, ŏrīri, 3.
river, flŭvius, i, *m.*; flūmen, ĭnis, *n.*
robber, lātro, ōnis, *m*
rock, rūpes, is, *f.*
Roman, Rōmānus, a, um, *adj.*
Rome, Rōma, ae, *f.*

SET OUT.

root, rădix, īcis, *f.*
rose, rŏsa, ae, *f.*
rough, rugged, asper, a, um, *adj.*
round, circum, *prep.* with *acc.*
rule, rĕgo, xi, ctum, 3.
run, curro, cŭcurri, cursum, 3.
rush together, cŏnvŏlo, avi, atum, 1.

Sacred, săcer, cra, crum, *adj.*
sacrifice, to, immŏlo, avi, atum, 1.
sad, tristis, e, *adj.*
safe, tūtus, a, um, *adj.*
safety, sălus, ūtis, *f.*
sagacious, prūdens, tis, *adj.*
sailor, nauta, ae, *m.*
sake of, for the, grātiā, causā, *abl.* with *gen.*
Sallust, Sallustius, ii, *m.*
same, īdem, ĕădem, ĭdem, *adj. pron.*
sanguinary, ătrox, ōcis, *adj.*
save, servo, conservo, avi, atum, 1.
savour of, săpio, ŭi, 3.
say, dīco, xi, ctum, 3.
scarcely, vix, *adv.*
scent, ŏdor, ōris, *m.*
scholar, discĭpŭlus, i, *m.*
school, schŏla, ae, *f.*
Scythian, Scȳtha, ae, *m.*
sea, măre, is, *n.*
———, *of the*, mărīnus, a, um, *adj.*
seat, sēdes, is, *f.*
second, sĕcundus, a, um; alter, a, um, *adj.*
secretly, clam, *adv.*
see, vĭdeo, īdi, īsum, 2; cerno, crēvi, crētum, 3.
see, go to, vīso, i, um, 3.
seeing, vīsus, us, *m.*
seek, quaero, quaesīvi, quaesītum, 3.
seem, vĭdeor, vīsus, 2.
seize, comprĕhendo, di, sum, 3; răpio, ŭi, tum, 3.
seize on, arrĭpio, ui, eptum, 3.
seldom, rāro, *adv.*
senate, sĕnātus, us, *m.*
send, mitto, mīsi, missum, 3.
—— *on before*, praemitto, etc
—— *together*, committo, etc.
sense, sensus, us, *m.* [vīsi, vīsum, 3.
separate, sēpăro, avi, atum, 1; dīvĭdo,
servant, mĭnister, tri, *m.*
serviceable, ūtĭlis, e, *adj.*
———, *to be*, prōsum, p. 31.
set out, prŏfĭciscor, fectus, 3.
—— *(an example)*, praebeo, ui, ĭtum, 2.

SEVERE

severe, sĕvĕrus, a, um ; grăvis, e, adj.
severely, grăvĭtĕr, adv.
shake, quătio, quassi, quassum, 3
shames, it, pŭdet, p. 86.
share, to, partior, ītus, 4.
sharp, ăcūtus, a, um, adj.
sharpen, ăcuo, ŭi, ūtum, 3.
shield, scūtum, i, n.
shine, fulgeo, si, sum, 2.
ship, nāvis, is, f.
shore, lītus, ŏris, n.
short, brĕvis, e, adj.
shortly, mox, adv.
shout, to, clāmo, avi, atum, 1.
shut off, interclūdo, si, sum, 3.
Sicily, Sĭcĭlia, ae, f.
sick, aeger, gra, grum, adj.
side with, adsum, p. 31.
side, on this, cis, cĭtrā, prep. with acc.
siege, obsĭdĭo, ōnis, f.
sign, signum, i, n.
silence, sĭlentium, ĭi, n.
silent, be, tăceo, ui, ĭtum, 2.
silver, argentum, i, n.
sing, canto, avi, atum, 1 ; căno, cĕcĭni,
sister, sŏror, ōris, f.   [cantum, 3.
sit, sĕdeo, ēdi, essum, 2.
skilful, skilled in, perītus, a, um ; sōlers,
skin (of animal), pellis, is, f. [rtis, adj.
slaughter, caedes, is, f.
slave, servus, i, m.
slavery, servĭtūs, ūtis, f.
slay, interfĭcio, fēci, fectum ; occīdo,
    cīdi, cīsum, 3.
sleep (subs.), somnus, i, m.
——, to, dormio, īvi and ĭi, ītum, 4.
slender, tenuis, e, adj.
slothfulness, segnĭties, ēi, f.
sluggish, segnis, e ; ignāvus, a, um, adj.
small, parvus, a, um, adj
smell, ŏdor, ōris, m.
snow, nix, nĭvis, f.
snows, it, ningit, p. 87.
so, ĭtă, tam, adv.
soft, mollis, e, adj.
soften, mollio, īvi, ĭtum, 4.
soldier, mīles, ĭtis, c.
some, nonnullus, a, um, adj.
some one, some thing, ălĭquis, ălĭquĭd,
sometime, quondam, adv. [indef. pron.
sometimes, nonnunquam, adv.

SUP.

son, fīlius, ii, m. ; voc. fĭlī.
son-in-law, gĕner, ĕri, m.
song, carmen, ĭnis, n. ; cantus, us, m.
soon, mox, adv.
soon as, sĭmŭl atquĕ (ac), conj.
sorrow, dŏlor, ōris, m.
soul, ănĭmus, i, m.
sound, sŏnĭtus, us, m.
sovereignty, dŏmĭnātus, us, m.
sow, sĕro, sēvi, sătum, 3.
speak, lŏquor, lŏcūtus, 3.
—— to, allŏquor, etc.
speech, a, ōrātio, ōnis, f.
spend life, aetātem ago, ēgi, actum, 3.
spirited, fĕrox, ōcis, adj.
splendid, splendĭdus, a, um, adj.
spring, vēr, vēris, n.
sprout, planta, ae, f.
spur, calcar, āris, n.
spy out, spĕcŭlor, atus, 1.
stag, cervus, i, m.
stand, sto, stĕti, statum, 1.
star, stella, ae, f.
state, cīvĭtas, ātis, f.
station, stătio, ōnis, f.

statue, ĭmāgo, ĭnis, f.
steep, arduus, a, um, adj.
stern, atrox, ōcis, adj.
stone, lăpis, ĭdis, m.
stone, of, lăpĭdeus, a, um, adj.
storm, tempestas, ātis, f.
storm, take by, expugno, avi, atum, 1.
story, făbŭla, ae, f.
straight, rectus, a, um, adj.
strength, vis, f.: see p. 22.
strengthen, firmo, avi, atum, 1.
strive, nītor, xus, 3.
—— hard, ēnītor, etc.
strong, vălĭdus, a, um, adj.
——, make, firmo, avi, atum, 1.
study, stŭdium, ĭi, n.
study, to, stŭdeo, ui, ——, 2, with dat.
successful, fēlix, īcis, adj.
sudden, sŭbĭtus, a, um, adj
suddenly, sŭbĭto, adv.
suffer, pătior, passus, 3.
sufficiently, sătis, adv.
summer, aestas, ātis, f.
sun, sol, sōlis, m.
sup, coeno, avi, atum, 1 : see p. 85.

SUPPLIES.

supplies, commeātūs, ūum, *m.*
surround, cingo, xi, ctum, 3.
survive, sŭpersum, p. 31.
swear, jūro, avi, atum, 1 : *see* p. 85.
sweet, dulcis, suāvis, e, *adj.*
swell, intŭmesco, tŭmui, 3.
swift, cĕlĕr, ĕris, re, *adj.*
sword, glădĭus, i, *m.*
Syracuse, Sўrăcūsae, arum, *f.*

Table, mensa, ae, *f.*
take, căpio, cēpi, captum, 3.
—— *by storm*, expugno, avi, atum, 1.
tall, celsus, a, um, *adj.*
taste, to, gusto, avi, atum, 1.
tax, vectīgal, ālis, *n.*
teach, dŏceo, ui, ctum, 2.
teacher, măgister, tri, *m.*
tell, dico, xi, ctum, 3.
tempest, tempestas, ātis, *f.*
temple, templum, i, *n.*
tender, tĕnĕr, a, um, *adj.*
tent, tăbernācŭlum, i, *n.*
terrify, terreo, ui, ĭtum, 2.
territories, fīnes, ium, *m.*
terror, terror, ōris, *m.*
that (*pron.*), iste, ille, is, p. 34.
—— (*conj.*), ŭt, p. 97.
—— *not*, nē, quīn, p. 97.
their own, gen. pl. of is, ea, id ; when
 referring to subject, sŭus, a, um, *adj.*
then, tum, *adv.* [*pron.*
then indeed, tum dēmum.
there, ĭbi, *adv.*
thin, tĕnuis, e, *adj.*
thing, res, ĕi, *f.*
think, pŭto, cōgĭto, avi, atum, 1.
thither, ĕō, *adv.*
through, pĕr, *prep.* with *acc.* [jectum, 3.
throw, jăcio, jēci, jactum ; conjicio, jēci,
—— *a bridge over a river*, flūmen
 ponte jungo, junxi, nctum, 3.
thunderbolt, fulmen, ĭnis, *n*
thunders, it, tŏnăt, p. 87.
thus, ĭtĭ, *adv.*
tiger, tigris, is and ĭdis, *c.*
time, tempus, ōris, *n.*
timid, tĭmĭdūs, a, um, *adj.*
to, ăd, *prep.* with *acc.*
too, too much, nĭmis, *adv.*
tongue, lingua, ae, *f.*

VICTORY.

torture, crŭcĭātus, us, *m.*
towards, versus, adversus, *prep.* with·
tower, turris, is, *f.* [*acc.*
town, oppĭdum, i, *n.*
train up, ērŭdio, īvi, ĭtum, 4.
trained, ērŭdītus, a, um, *part.* and *adj.*
tree, arbor, ŏris, *f.*
triumph, triumpho, avi, atum, 1.
trouble, to, mŏveo, mōvi, mōtum, 2.
—— (*subs.*), aerumna, ae, *f.*
troublesome, mŏlestus, a, um, *adj.*
Troy, Trōja, ae, *f.*
true, vērus, a, um, *adj.*
trust, fīdo, p. 85.
try, expĕrior, rtus, 4.
turn back, rĕverto, ti, sum, and tor, sus,
tyrant, tўrannus, i, *m.* [3.

Unable, am, nĕqueo, īvi and ĭi, ĭtum, 4.
unbecoming, it is, dĕdĕcĕt, p. 86.
unbounded, infīnītus, a, um, *adj.*
unbreakfasted, impransus, a, um, *adj.*
uncertain, incertus, a, um, *adj.* [*abl.*
under, sŭb, subtĕr, *prep.* with *acc.* and
undergo, sŭbeo, īvi and ĭi, ĭtum, 4.
understand, intellĭgo, lexi, lectum, 3.
undertake, suscĭpio, cēpi, ceptum, 3.
undone, infectus, a, um, *adj.*
unfriendly, inĭmīcus, a, um, *adj*
unjust, injustus, a, um, *adj.*
unjustly, injustē, *adv.*
unlearned, indoctus, a, um, *adj.*
unless, nĭsi, *conj.*
unlike, dissĭmĭlis, e, *adj.*
unskilful, impĕrītus, a, um, *adj.*
unwilling, to be, nōlo, p. 77.
upper, sŭpĕrior, us, *adj. comp.*
upright, prŏbus, a, um, *adj.*
use, to, ūtor, ūsus, 3, with *abl.*
useful, ūtĭlis, e, *adj.*
utmost, summus, a, um, *adj. sup.*

Valley, vallis, is, *f.*
valour, virtūs, ūtis, *f.*
various, vărius, a, um, *adj.*
vehemently, vĕhĕmentĕr, *adv.*
verse, versus, us, *m.*
vex, vexo, avi, atum, 1.
vexes, it, pĭget, p. 86.
victim, hostia, victĭma, ae, *f.*
victory, victōria, ae, *f.*

LONDON: PRINTED BY WILLIAM CLOWES AND SONS, STAMFORD STREET
AND CHARING CROSS.